Images of
Kingship in
Paradise Lost

Images of
Kingship in
Paradise Lost

Milton's Politics and
Christian Liberty

Stevie Davies

University of Missouri Press

Columbia

1983

Copyright © 1983 by
The Curators of the University of Missouri
University of Missouri Press, Columbia, Missouri 65211
Library of Congress Catalog Card Number 82–17485
Printed and bound in the United States of America
All rights reserved

Library of Congress Cataloging in Publication Data

Davies, Stephanie, 1946–
  Images of kingship in Milton's Paradise Lost.

  Bibliography: p.
  Includes Index.
    1. Milton, John, 1608–1674. Paradise lost.
  2. Milton, John, 1608–1674—Allegory and
  symbolism. 3. Milton, John, 1608–1674—
  Political and social views. 4. Kings and
  rulers in literature. I. Title.

  PR3562.D36   1983   821'.4   82–17485
  ISBN 0–8262–0392–2

to Douglas
who made hell grant what love did seek

Contents

Acknowledgments, *1*
Note on Texts and Abbreviations, *2*
Introduction, *3*
1. Kings of This World, *9*
2. Sultan and Barbarian, *51*
3. Imperial Caesar, *89*
4. Feudal Lord, *127*
5. The Father-King, *164*
6. Naked Majesty, *195*
Notes, *217*
Bibliography, *228*
Index, *242*

Acknowledgments

My primary debt in the shaping of this book must be to Douglas Brooks-Davies, Senior Lecturer in English Literature at the University of Manchester, with whom over a period of years I have enjoyed the benefits of quiet, continuous, and absorbing debate about Milton, Spenser, and the Renaissance period, exchanging and clarifying ideas and information, and receiving the fruits of a richly learned and also brilliantly intuitive mind. Without this uninterrupted stream of mutual thought, I do not think this book would have been written.

I should like to acknowledge here the debt I owe to the late Francis Noel Lees, Reader in English at the University of Manchester, who during my earlier years inspired in me the love of and veneration for classical literature of which he was such a scholarly exponent.

I should like to express my gratitude to several generations of undergraduate students at Manchester University who chose to study Milton as a special author in their final year, especially Katherine Spearman, Gary Holden, Andrew Howdle, David Batki-Braun, Penny Cannon, and Mark Farrell. Discussions with them have been constantly stimulating and thought-provoking. Of Katherine Spearman it may authentically be said that she has gone out from her studies to raise "Eden . . . in the waste wilderness."

My thanks are due to Penny Evans for her immaculate and patient typing and retyping of the manuscript in its various stages.

My loving thanks must go to my closest friend, Rosalie Wilkins, for her unfailing support; to my daughters, Emily and Grace, and my son, Robin, for the special quality of the joy and hope they have brought into my life while I have been preparing this book; to my late father, Harry Davies, for nurturing me to love knowledge and providing me with the means to seek it; and finally to my dear mother, Monica Davies, who has tenderly supported and encouraged me throughout the writing of this book.

S. D.
University of Manchester, England   1 February 1983

1

Note on Texts and Abbreviations

I have used Alastair Fowler's edition of *Paradise Lost* (London: Longman, 1968) in citing references to and quotations from the poem. For Milton's prose works I have largely referred to the Yale edition, *Complete Prose Works of John Milton*, general editor A. S. P. Woodhouse, 7 out of 8 volumes (New Haven: Yale University Press, 1953–), cited as Yale. On occasions where a work is not yet available in this edition, I refer to the Columbia edition of *The Works of John Milton*, general editor F. A. Patterson, 18 volumes (New York: Columbia University Press, 1931–1938).

Frequent reference has been made to volumes 4, 5, and 6 of Lord Somers's *Collection of Scarce and Valuable Tracts . . .* , edited by Sir Walter Scott (London, 1811), abbreviated in the present work to *SCT*. The Bible alluded to is the King James version, unless otherwise specified.

Introduction

Political study of the figures and themes of *Paradise Lost*, and a desire to equate them with the events of English political history in which Milton took such a powerful part, both before and during the writing of the epic, is a very old preoccupation among readers of the poem, though in recent years it has grown more intense and exciting through the works of critics like S. P. Revard, Joan Bennett, Joan Webber, Andrew Milner, and Christopher Hill. In a sense, the civil wars are eternally and recurrently fought out in the consciousness of each generation. Anachronistic personal loyalties, Royalist or Roundhead, are universally cherished and difficult to renounce when we come to read and interpret a poem written by a passionate exponent of republicanism and civil and spiritual liberty—England's defender of the regicide, whose epic concerns a rebellion against the monarchy of Heaven together with a defense of that monarchy. The apparent gap between Milton's prose theories and his poetic practice seems to invite critical participation, in order to close it. During the Second World War, critics wishing to use *Paradise Lost* as a weapon of the embattled British monarchy against *Mein Kampf* resorted to denying that Milton was genuinely antiroyalist at all.[1] *Paradise Lost* could then be used as a tract for the times, the Messiah of the English monarchy against the German fiend. In the 1970s, the controversy still had power to provoke fury in critics disliking Milton's political stance but loving his poetry. A. L. Rowse was vehement in *Milton the Puritan* about those "liars" the Puritans and their "nasty" ideas.[2] It was also astonishingly suggested that revolutionary idealism "almost destroyed Milton, not to mention its dislocation of his mind."[3] But perhaps the zeitgeist has been more exactly expressed during the 1970s by those Marxist analyses of *Paradise Lost* that emphasize Milton's radical commitment and propose a Leveler God and a counterrevolutionary Satan. The greatest of these is Christopher Hill, who in *Milton and the English Revolution* opened out to modern students a way of thinking about the poetry that is contemporary in both seventeenth-century and twentieth-century terms.[4]

Deeply personal political commitments in many cases dominate and inform literary judgments. Critics used to feel that the image of Satan in *Paradise Lost* was a disguised version of Oliver Cromwell:

> In the war on the plains of Heaven Satan ranges
> up and down the fighting line, like Cromwell;
> he fortifies his comrades to endurance, and
> encourages them to attack.[5]

Wilson Knight saw Satan as "a Cromwell casting an 'experienced eye' over his ironside warriors," his mode of government being parliamentary.[6] William Empson, in *Milton's God*, prodigal of insights, offered a succession of satanic prototypes: a Norman baron, a republican, or "a rippingly grand aristocrat; when he withdraws his troops to the northern fortresses . . . he is not so much a Scotsman . . . as a Yorkshireman."[7] J. B. Broadbent circled back to the original candidate when he said, "Satan is the devils' Cromwell," but he also recognized the monarchical allusions attached to Milton's Satan, which during the 1970s critics tended to emphasize more fully.[8] In later analyses, attributions tend to be reversed: Cromwell is considered as candidate for God or the Son and his New Model Army for Christ's army of saints in Book 6 of *Paradise Lost*. Hill compares the first battle in Heaven to Edgehill.[9] Under this interpretation, Milton's Satan is seen as corresponding to the figure of Charles I, the tyrant of the regicide tracts and the enemy of human liberty. The advantage of this point of view is that it allows coherency between the message of Milton's prose works and that of his poetry. His political writings may be brought directly to bear upon analysis of the poetry. A unity may be demonstrated between Milton's life and poetry that alleviates the distress felt by a reader who sees the polemicist writing with his left hand (Milton's term for his prose writing) against human kingship, contradicted by the right hand of poetry in favor of divine kingship of the most absolute kind. This reading also seems truer to some of the facts of the poem in acknowledging the monarchical images, allusions, and occasional allegories by which the poet of *Paradise Lost* characterized, defined, and poetically denounced the satanic principle.

Any such method, however, is instinct with dangers for the reader of *Paradise Lost* as a poem about God and man rather than as a versified treatise. I became more aware of these dangers as I observed myself readily and repeatedly falling into them when I undertook the present study. The primary danger seemed to involve a too rationalizing and therefore reductive approach to the poem, bred of a fanatical determination on one's own part to master the beautiful complexities of Milton's epic—the paradoxes at its core, the freedom of its poetic movement—until the poetry could be subdued into making a linear kind of sense. Allied with this problem was the difficulty of handling allegory in the context of a narrative and symbolism of such cosmic dimensions, without claiming an exclusive key to meaning, that would be fruitlessly reductive because it could not cope with the diversity of perspective, the many-faceted richness of *Paradise Lost.* "Irreconcilable hypotheses"[10] compose the very basis not only of Milton's poetry but of his political thinking itself. A critic wishing to stress Milton's radicalism will tend to select some hypotheses at the expense of others, so that there must always be within a mind committed to ideological assertions but also candid enough to realize that the greatness of *Paradise Lost* utterly transcends dogma, an awareness such as Christopher Hill generously shows when he admits, "It is possible that I have imagined interpretations which were not in Milton's mind at all."[11] This possibility is always present for any reader, of course, but it is all the more open when the application of political material to a work of art consistently yields nearly allegorical readings that might be considered naive or reductive in a literary sense. I found that this was an especially pressing danger if the political material chosen was exclusively contemporary and Milton's eclecticism was rejected. Milton's political thinking comprises ancient and modern elements. Overton and Lilburne meet Aristotle and Cicero in his mind, and humanism and Puritanism, classical and contemporary, contend or marry there. This is true both in his political prose and in his poetry. The surface of *Paradise Lost* is alive with glimpses of apparently contradictory associations: a clear image may elusively imply its opposite.

The present study is neither sociological nor political in aim, not only for the sensible reason that I am not an expert in political theory but also because my primary interest lies in the images of *Paradise Lost* as distinct from the concepts they embody. This is a work of literary criticism that has as its main aim a desire to understand how Milton's poetry absorbs and re-creates the political material on which it draws. It stresses the metamorphosing power of poetry, the gap between a theory and a symbol, and the way that in *Paradise Lost* allegory blends into symbol; exemplum becomes allusion; bare statement of a theory becomes charged with new life and meaning when it reveals itself in an image. My book has as its premise an idea of Milton's epic as a great, fluid structure of symbolism into which images, allegories, or concepts melt or blend with other areas of allusion—theological, mystical, pastoral—to yield rich clusters of meaning that transcend any specifically political constituent. In other words, I assume not that we can use political material to define *Paradise Lost* but that *Paradise Lost* assimilates and transforms political structures, with the visionary and liberating power of its poetry. The structures of meaning born of this poetic metamorphosis are clear in themselves, but I have not thought it possible to interpret them as one would a polemic, rationalistically, believing rather that its images need to be seen, felt, "proved on the pulses" in order to be comprehended.

Another premise of this book is the almost shamefully simple perception that every major character in *Paradise Lost* is alluded to by Milton as a king, and the more minor ones are all in the service of a monarchy, whether they belong to the good or evil parties. While God is King of Heaven, Satan is monarch of the underworld; Moloch is a king, but so is Adam; Death, Chaos, and Christ are all represented as kings. Eve before her fall is a queen but falls partly out of desire to become an empress. This is one reason that it is so tantalizingly difficult to assimilate the image of the good in *Paradise Lost* to the image of republican liberty, and evil to the corrupted monarchy, defined in Milton's tracts. The central problem for me as a reader of the poetry became how to distinguish one kind of kingship from another in *Paradise Lost,* so as to remain true to the spirit of the poetry while simultaneously equating the types of kingship with the conceptions expressed by the self-styled defender of the people of England on behalf of the good old cause. This book offers a partial solution based on assessment of Milton's distribution of images drawn from certain kinds of monarchy among the characters of his epic. Historical archetypes—such as the English warrior king, Charles Stuart, whose career had been studied to such deadly purpose in the prose writings of the late 1640s and 1650s—seemed to be attached solely to Satan and the fallen kingship that stretches through the evil king-gods of *Paradise Lost* like Moloch and Baal-peor, to human rebels against the law of nature like Nimrod and the Stuart kings. Likewise, a recurrent emblem of the oriental tyrant is attached solely to Satan in Milton's poem, and the dark, corrosive cruelty traditionally associated with this figure, together with its malignance not only to enemies but to its own followers, deeply informs Milton's presentation of Satan as the leader of the forces of Hell. In both the Stuart and the oriental images, there is an accompanying providential framework, each prototype enacting the role of the scourge of God, self-punishing political engines. The occurrence of such structures in both Milton's narrative and his vastly allusive epic similes gives aesthetic structure to the theological concept so central to *Paradise Lost,* of God's bringing forth good from evil. Repetition of these images throughout the poem, either explicitly or implicitly, combined with development of their providential significance as the epic unfolds, suggests the way in which the poet used political material to unify his symbolism. A great chain of vitiated kingship is shown across all time and all space, as Satan's family—from Moloch to Pharaoh, from Turkish sultan to Charles I—engenders new forms of evil in history. Fittingly, this account covers the whole poem.

A third image, associated largely with the satanic kingship, but this time having a converse side of radiant goodness identified with the victorious King of Heaven, is that of the Roman emperor. Milton used both the historical pattern of the Caesars' destruction of the Roman republic and the political and literary form of the triumph to unveil the sham egalitarian and libertarian rhetoric of Satan. This is one of the most deeply buried and subtle of the images covered by this book, but is is also one of the most morally telling. Its inclusion here demonstrates the extraordinary richness of Milton's allusive poetry, for it reveals that the relation between one image (the oriental) and another (the Roman) may be one of partial antagonism rather than pure parallelism. The Roman stands for reason in the service of despotism, the sultan for barbarous savagery; the Romans quelled in order to civilize the barbarians, but the barbarians overwhelmed the empire. I suggest this fundamental antagonism in the monarchical allusions attached to Satan by studying the building of the triumphal bridge (or arch) across Chaos. The triumph celebrated by Satan in Book 10 is related to historical triumphs that fell flat for the Caesars. The providential structure overshadowing this imperial image of Satan and promising his fall is nothing less than the entire architecture of *Paradise Lost* itself, which stands like a colossal triumphal arch with Christ as its central point purging Heaven of rebellion. It is here that a single image is used for two opposite purposes, as the fraudulent emperors of history are set against the one true Emperor, God.

From the presentation of God and Christ as kings in *Paradise Lost*, a massive and central image, biblical in origin but bewildering or upsetting to many readers, I extract two images. The first is a study of the feudal terms in which the poet chose to establish God's rule and the symbolic structure of the circle in which he embodied this feudal conception, together with suggestions as to how a conception of a pure and pristine feudal structure may not essentially contradict Puritan beliefs in human liberty. His feudal God is seen as liberty guaranteeing; his anointed Son, the founder of a unique kingship based on mediatorial self-reduction and a feudal image of Christ as *primus inter pares*. The focus for study here is what I see as a coronation in Book 5. The final attribute of the divine kingship is God's fathering creativity: he is *pater patriae* politically in a literal way (as Creator), a status to which no human king could have pretensions. Book 7, Milton's exquisite account of the creation of the world, with a twofold structure based on Psalm 24, is central to my analysis of the love that informs and redefines the divine kingship and the lyric poetry by which Milton justified God's kingship to man. Finally, there is Adam, king over Eden, an image until his fall of naked truth and simplicity, and in his fall a Solomon who loses himself in concupiscence and gains a world in which power is coercion and nakedness shame. This is the most poignant image of kingship analyzed in the book.

I cannot pretend to have covered all the images that give color and form to the politics of kingship in Milton's poem, though I have tried in my account to emulate his own eclecticism, linking each phase of my study to his statements in the prose works, when he urgently confronted the immediate political issues of his day. I believe that there are many images and interactions of images of monarchy still to be explored.

1

Kings of This World

Milton after the Restoration turned away from the turned backs of his contemporaries. He viewed the new government with an inflexible scorn based on political convictions evolved in the late 1640s and only changed in emphasis to fit the altered circumstances of the 1660s. He is often identified with the isolated Abdiel, mocked by Satan's friends at the end of Book 5 of *Paradise Lost:*[1]

> So spake the seraph Abdiel faithful found,
> Among the faithless, faithful only he;
> Among innumerable false, unmoved,
> Unshaken, unseduced, unterrified
> His loyalty he kept, his love, his zeal;
> Nor number nor example with him wrought
> To swerve from truth, or change his constant mind
> Though single. From amidst them forth he passed,
> Long way through hostile scorn, which he sustained
> Superior, nor of violence feared aught;
> And with retorted scorn his back he turned
> On those proud towers to swift destruction doomed.
>
> (5.896–907)

Abdiel in the rebellion in Heaven, Milton in the revolutionary return of Charles II, is the remnant reduced to a community of a single person. Like Abdiel, Milton withdrew not just with bitterness, but with that more positive "retorted scorn" into his solitude. This scorn is expressed in *Paradise Lost* in many forms of contempt: either in moments of direct or implied satire on the court, in veiled regicide allegories, or (much more massively) in recurrent images of kingship attached to evil or falling characters in the poem. Milton purged some ire in *Paradise Lost* by attributing the characteristics of the monarchy for whose destruction he had labored to mythical kings—Satan, Death, and Moloch—and to the savage human kings who preyed on their brothers from Nimrod's time into Milton's, all within a providential and punitive framework. Kings, *Paradise Lost* assures the reader, in appearing to reign are only experiencing a pause on the route to execution. All belong to a recognizable single family, whose shared traits Milton had elucidated in *Eikonoklastes* (1649).

Eikonoklastes yields a vision of Charles I as a usurper stemming from a long line of Norman conquerors, an egoist opposed to the good of the nation and claiming to be above the law. Milton had conceived him less as a person than as an embodied force in history, working satanically against Reformation, "usurping over spiritual things, as *Lucifer* beyond his sphere" (Yale 3:502). An idol (*eikon*), a false god who in *Eikon Basilike* had in many a glowing fit of imagery identified himself with the sun and the divine monarchy, and a protean liar, Charles was seen as a politician who was also God's archenemy in the terrestrial sphere and must like the whole lawless tradition of kings be purged from the body politic, as Satan had to be expelled from Heaven, and no tears shed. Charles was self-tempted, contaminated by belonging to a family famous for sexual license (as though one were to blame for one's grandmother [Yale 3:600–601]), and hypocritical in his nature, and Milton affects to marvel over his adversary's ability to coexist with himself: "Which of him shall we believe? For hee seemes not one, but double" (371). He was a satanic rhetorician who required prompt eradication in order to hasten the day of the Second Coming. He was also covered with blood. In other words, Milton in this punitive, deadly tract has transferred to the image of the earthly monarch associations traditionally attached to Satan and made him into a human incarnation. When Milton came to write *Paradise Lost*, the poet was able to draw upon the work he had done as a politician and reintroduce into the poem this composite image made of the face of a man and the face of a devil, where it appears in many metamorphoses.[2] He was able to locate this face and its concomitant associations in many persons in the poem; wherever it appears, as Satan, as Moloch, as Nimrod, it brings a certain recognizable expression and a train of images, as well as a sense of revulsion on the part of the reader.

The nature of a family is traditionally modeled on its father, and in *Paradise Lost*, Satan, the father of kings as well as of Sin and Death, is the archetype upon which his royal line varies.

Each descendant may specialize in one feature of false kingship
or be a miniature of the whole: Satan includes all, as pride
includes all the vices but monopolizes none. Each petty or brutal tyrant may copy. Satan is identified first by his rebellion at
the opening of Book 1 and by his kingship at the opening of
Book 2. The organic connection between rebellion and monarchy that had preoccupied Milton in the regicide tracts is therefore dramatized within the very structure of the first two books
as being fundamental to the satanic principle. By emphasizing
the "royal" nature of Satan, Milton thus provided himself with
a body of images and a complex of ideas with which to make
Satan conceivable to his reader. Once he alluded to one image
or idea, the rest (as with all allusive poetry) were implied, so
that the monarchical image by which he characterized Satan is
an extremely rich one, both in visual and in conceptual terms.
Everyone remembers the spectacular picture of Satan enthroned that unfolds at the opening of Book 2:

> High on a throne of royal state, which far
> Outshone the wealth of Ormus and of Ind,
> Or where the gorgeous East with richest hand
> Showers on her kings barbaric pearl and gold,
> Satan exalted sat, by merit raised
> To that bad eminence; and from despair
> Thus high uplifted beyond hope, aspires
> Beyond thus high, insatiate to pursue
> Vain war with heaven, and by success untaught,
> His proud imaginations thus displayed.
>
> (2.1–10)

Nobody with the least feeling for the magnificence of the poetry
that presents the enthronement, of course, would suggest that
for the unseen face of the protagonist we should substitute our
own image of the delicate features of Charles I, with his dapper
mustache and beard and the Olympian grave expression upon
his small face. Any suggestion of a one-to-one ratio between
Milton's creation of the king of Hell and the bygone king of
England is not only fruitlessly reductive but ridiculous. Though
Satan is king of this world, he is not comparable to a human
king save by a scale of comparatives at a successive and increasing number of removes: "High on a throne . . . which far /
Outshone . . . Thus high . . . Beyond thus high."

If Charles I were to be placed in his throne beside Satan's towering throne in Pandemonium, the difference in dimension would be so colossal that the Lilliputian human king would diminish to the point of virtual disappearance. The massive and baroque outbursts of scale in *Paradise Lost,* in which relative sizes seem to square rather than multiply and the imagination—however far it bounds after the poet from one dimension to a greater one—cannot regulate its impressions into manageable scope, utterly reject any attempt to allegorize the poem. Prose and poetry, human history and the cosmic vision, only relate according to the doctrine of accommodation, explained by Raphael to Adam in Book 5, whereby we are able to glimpse and recognize supernatural events and persons because they bear some slight relation to those on earth, despite outdoing them in every way. The likenesses are so remote that they are almost distortions: almost, but not quite.

The image of the human king, his manifestation and nature, has supplied to Milton the square root, as it were, of the image of Satan, so that we would not dream of endowing the Arch-enemy with the Stuart dimensions; but because we have contemplated what Milton thought of Stuarts, the qualities of Satan are momentarily focused and given body for us. The hatred Milton brought to the gorgeous affluence of the monarchy addicted to a majesty that was outward and material rather than inner and spiritual informs Milton's account of Satan's enthronement and is caught in the final verb, *displayed,* which links Satan's words (a form of rhetorical display, meant to hide the corrosively impure heart from which it comes) with the dazzling magnificence of his throne. But because we stare upward at Satan elevated, as if he mounted higher and higher in our vision with every clause of the description, we are left with an impression distinct from that produced in us by Milton's prose onslaughts on the unholy glitter of Stuart finery and the people's adulation of it.[3] His contempt in *Eikonoklastes* for the popular habit of groveling to "the gaudy name of Majesty" (Yale 3:338) was generated by the folly of the indecorum involved in venerating an individual so demonstrably life-size as if he were the wonder he impersonated; in the *First Defence* Milton laughed at Salmasius's regard for the "king in Parliament seated on his throne under that canopy of silk and gold" and mocked those "whose minds are so dazzled by the very

idea of gazing on the royal splendor that they can see no brilliance or magnificence in honest virtue and freedom" (Yale 4,
pt. 1:506, 507).

Milton's mockery is of the easy, uncomplicated sort, which
can hardly imagine that anyone could seriously confuse a tawdry masquerade with a living reality. His contempt satirizes an
object that is only life-size or a bit smaller, and he shows absolutely no temptation to complicity with that vulgar show. The
satanic display, however, is rendered by the metamorphosing
power of poetry into an experience of a different order. The
moral nausea felt for human kings is still there, informing the
passage. But as the reader's neck cranes further and further
back mentally, to try to encompass Milton's soaring image of
Satan in majesty, there is a dizzying sense of both poet and
reader being "Outshone" by the astonishing scale of Satan's
opulence, which transports the mind to the very sources of this
world's wealth, Ormus and India, where the raw gold pours in
eternal freakish showers upon inhuman Eastern despots, only
to eclipse the image in the blinding "Outshone." Whereas in the
prose literature the reader is not inclined to participate in the
idolatry of Kings, because no one would wish to be associated
with "this mob of ours"—barbarous as the demon- and king-
worshiping Indians (*Second Defence,* Yale 4, pt. 1:551)—in *Paradise Lost* there is an initial awe and admiration elicited from the
most intransigently republican of readers by the very fact that
rebellion could be so colossal, usurping a monarchy as gorgeous
as this. We may conclude, therefore, that the fundamental attribute of earthly kingship as analyzed by Milton has been
adopted into the poetry only to be transformed by the new
medium and context.

Nevertheless, the undercutting that we would expect of the
poet who had also been a regicide is plainly there, in the characterization of Satan as a king. The image of Satan surveying his
troops in Book 1 is instructive, for through a complex logic
Milton offers a simile that explicitly links the demonic to the
human kingship, leading the mind from contemplation of the
foundation of Satan's rule into memories of recent history close
to the lives of his contemporaries:

> he above the rest
> In shape and gesture proudly eminent
> Stood like a tower; his form had yet not lost

All her original brightness, nor appeared
Less than archangel ruined, and the excess
Of glory obscured: as when the sun new risen
Looks through the horizontal misty air
Shorn of his beams, or from behind the moon
In dim eclipse disastrous twilight sheds
On half the nations, and with fear of change
Perplexes monarchs.

(1.589–99)

Babel is in him ("like a tower"), but so is his earlier nature as Lucifer, remembered in the waning light he continues to bear. The poetry is elegiac, with the prophet's lament, "How art thou fallen from heaven, O Lucifer, son of the morning."[4] In contrast to the prodigious and rather tactile glory of the satanic throne in the golden palace of Pandemonium, to which Satan will descend in the next book, the "glory" recorded here as being "obscured" is the real sort, pure light, which cannot be touched, which Milton in the Invocation to Book 3 will wonder if he may without blasphemy include in his song. But with the introduction of the symbol of the sun in the twofold epic simile, the reader's attention is diverted from Satan's archangelic status and focused down through a series of shifts of logic and allusion to the earthly political structures he foreshadows. At least three traditions of sun symbolism are here alluded to in an ironic complex of meanings: the Platonic sun of the *Republic*, representing the reality that is the guiding principle in the universe, but which human beings going about their business in the care of the senses fail to perceive; the Christian sun that is Christ the Son, arising with healing in his wings for those in a state of grace, but bringing harsh justice to the reprobate in his role as *sol iustitiae* (sun of justice); the sun-king, miming God in the political hierarchy, an act crucial to the paraphernalia of royalist thinking about the divine right of monarchs.

In the first part of the simile, Satan is the sun at dawn. He

new risen
Looks through the horizontal misty air
Shorn of his beams.

The visual effect is powerful; it represents a moment of stasis, a pause implying expectation of a day to come, and because "horizontal . . . air" is an impossible phenomenon to view except by extension, the mind of the reader also pauses, stretching to see the image, finding repose in the layered mist absorbing the sun's rays or filtering some through. Because the symbol of the rising sun inevitably recalls the tradition of Christ arising, we question the attribution of the image with all its pristine qualities to Satan. Aware that moral blindness is implied; that mist will later be a manifestation of Satan about to film over man's vision as he silently penetrates the hushed world of Paradise "involved in rising mist" (9.75); that Satan is an impotent sun if he cannot shoot his rays through a few clouds; that "Shorn" implies Samson in his humiliation—still the image taunts the reader with its innately harmonious qualities. In its concurrence with the natural cycle of the day, it seems to be assimilable to the pastoral in which purity is embodied in *Paradise Lost*. Yet the reader of Milton's prose works may be drawn back to that moment in *Eikonoklastes* when the regicide apologist mingled imagery of mist and sun in reply to the dead king's claim to be the sun of the political sphere:

> He bodes *much horror and bad influence after his ecclips*. He speakes his wishes: But they who by weighing prudently things past, foresee things to come, the best Divination, may hope rather all good success and happiness by removing that darkness which the mistie cloud of his prerogative made between us and a peacefull Reformation, which is our true Sun light, and not he, though he would be tak'n for our sun it self. (Yale 3:455)

The method pursued by Milton in *Eikonoklastes* is to incorporate units of his adversary's argument and then to contradict them fragment by fragment, accepting the image initiated by the adversary but reversing it with accompanying ridicule or sarcastic asides.[5] The impression given is of a talking voice, engaged in dialectic. In the above example, Charles had presented him with an identification of himself as a sun eclipsed by murder, portending ruin to the sublunary world. Milton reversed and transformed the image and its application. The sun is not Charles but reformed religion; there is no eclipse at all, only an obscuring of the constant light by the autocrat's exercise of a nonexistent right, a "mistie cloud" because its use automatically affects all souls until it is cleared. There is an implication that superstition is the prerogative of kings, standing against the true spirit of prophecy. In the pamphlet, then, the mist represents an aspect of the king; in the poem we are not at first aware that it does so, but on rereading this seems clearly implied. Satan is self-blinded by his own egoism: he is not the sun-king he would wish to appear, for like Charles he sheds no real light, "though he would be tak'n for our sun it self."

This image is exquisitely connected by Milton to the variant (of eclipse behind the moon) that follows:

> or from behind the moon
> In dim eclipse disastrous twilight sheds
> On half the nations, and with fear of change
> Perplexes monarchs.

The court censor's anxiety about this passage when he came to examine *Paradise Lost* for publication is understandable, though we can conceive that he may have spent many fruitless hours perplexed over its logic and actual application. If he suspected that the sun "Shorn of his beams" was a disguised allusion to Charles shorn of his head, he was surely right to hear the old thunder of revolutionary Puritanism threatening again in the final clause, which brings the whole image down to earth in the present day. He might have pondered upon which monarch and which changes were implied, and, with the sleepless vigilance of the Restoration scouring England and its literature for signs of renewed unrest, he might reasonably have felt distrustful.

Human kings look very small here, in the context of the cosmic image for Satan: the expression on their faces (Milton has reduced them still further by collecting them up into a group of monarchs) is finely implied by the crucial verb *Perplexes*, suggesting their discomfort and an insecure sensation of being ignorant of the great forces that govern history—forces the kings of this earth claim to control. The verb also suggests their unquiet discussions as to what the present portents might mean and their sensible conviction that they are bound to be hostile. But the logical curiosity of the simile is that the satanic principle, conceiving of itself as a sun-king identical in kind to the dark kings of earth, is in fact fundamentally inimical to them. Satan lodging behind the moon (reversing the natural order and

foreshadowing the fall of man through Eve, whose lunar associations are frequent) is the enemy of all mankind, including the
evil members of humanity who are his disciples and bear his
likeness. This is the brilliant logical twist in the development of
the image, brilliant because it introduces the theme of Satan as a
scourge of God, acting against his own interest even when he
most surely appears to be fulfilling it.

In the dawning of the satanic sun, Christ as *sol iustitiae* is
understood to rise, denounced by Satan in his shriek of hatred
as he lands on Niphates Top:

> to thee I call,
> But with no friendly voice, and add thy name
> O sun, to tell thee how I hate thy beams

> (4.35–37)

By this time, Satan has journeyed far both physically and mentally from his initial arising in Book 1 and can tell how different
he is from "our true sun light," but in Book 1 his consciousness
is reflected in an impersonated image, an *eikon* rather than a
living symbol. We may compare the claims made by Charles I in
Eikon Basiliké for his own cosmic status and Milton's comments
upon them in *Eikonoklastes* in order to comprehend Milton's
attribution of an image to an agent whose nature contradicts it
and to explain the gap between the beauty of the sun image by
which Satan is poetically displayed here and the nature of the
wearer. Charles had announced that after his execution he
would rise again as the sun, terrifying owls, bats, and miscellaneous night creatures with the blaze of his resurrected
glory, congratulating himself on being personally elected by

> that supreme and adorable Majesty, in comparison of whom all the
> glory of men and angels is but obscurity; yet hath He given such
> characters of divine authority and sacred power upon kings, as none
> may without sin seek to blot them out. Nor shall their black veils be
> able to hide the shining of my face while God gives me a heart
> frequently and humbly to converse with Him, from whom alone are
> all the irradiations of true glory and majesty.[6]

Milton's reply (speaking no doubt in the character of one of the
slandered owls or bats of his generation) is a dismissive gesture
to all Charles's soaring Platonisms and lyrical fits. He simply

indicated that the royal author committed a violation of decorum by deviating into fiction:

> Poets indeed use to vapor much after this manner. But to bad Kings, who without cause expect future glory from their actions, it happ'ns as to bad Poets; who sit and starve themselves with a delusive hope to win immortality by thir bad lines. . . . And those *black vailes* of his own misdeeds he might be sure would ever keep *his face from shining,* til he could *refute evil speaking with wel doing.* (Yale 3:502)

Attention is drawn here to the relationship between words and things, which should be justly proportioned, and by using the word *poet* in its old abusive meaning, Milton emphasized a conviction from which he never departed, that egoism and rhetorical fantasy are always to be found in one another's arms. Satan, thus, is known by his lies—he speaks "Semblance of worth, not substance" (1.529); Charles is known by his fraudulent imagery, violating the just relation between reality and symbol: "with Scolastic flourishes beneath the decencie of a King, [he] compares [Strafford] to *the Sun,* which in all figurative use, and significance beares allusion to a King, not to a Subject: No marvel though he knit contradictions as close as words can lye together" (Yale 3:372–73). The fruitful pun on "lie," in the double sense of telling untruths and sexual coupling to convey distaste at Charles's image mongering, reflects Milton's humanistic reverence for the value of words as the index of mankind's noble spirit, inspired by the divinity, and his concern for the appropriate use of those words, which, once separated from the reality they utter, defile human life and are sources of moral pollution. Most specifically, the poetry shows Milton's concern that symbolism should be justly used according to time-honored traditions, so that "*the Sun* . . . beares allusion to a King," but the king may not legitimately apotheosize himself by describing himself as gifted with a "shining face," as though he were not a merely human king but translated overnight by pure poetic force into an angel.

This profound concern for the purity of linguistic and symbolic decorum in relation to the pronouncements of the kings of this world is everywhere obvious in *Paradise Lost,* transferred to the characterization of Satan. Prolific of words and shifty in grammar and logic, his speeches throughout the poem dazzle with exotic grandeur that impresses the reader while it often seriously confuses him. It violates decorum. Symbolically, and even within the narrative voice (which we learn to trust but which can often turn without one's being aware of transition to a rehearsal of a character's interior monologue), such violations may also be recorded. The identification of Satan with the sun, like Charles's self-identification with the sun, is finally spurious, the product of a corrupted imagination. The portent that perplexes monarchs in Book 1 appears to be produced by an eclipse of the satanic "sun," but there can be no such sun, and Satan is ultimately at one with the earthly kings whom he opposes in being subject to the dominating Son, seen in his ascension at the center of the poem.[7]

Though the vestigial beauty bestowed by heavenly birth and his incomparably more massive eternal scale set Satan opposite to the little kings of temporal history agitating within their reigning hour, the image of his kingship contains apocalyptic hints that swell as *Paradise Lost* unfolds and indicate a complete equation at the penultimate point of history of Satan and earthly kings. Milton quoted from Rev. 17:13–14 in *Eikonoklastes:* "at last, *joyning thir Armies with the Beast,* whose power first rais'd them, they shall perish with him by the *King of Kings* against whom they have rebell'd; and *the Foules shall eat thir flesh"*(Yale 3:599). The mighty scale of Satan initially dwarfs the image of the human kings of this world; but latterly the infinitely more mighty scale of Christ the King reduces the figure of Satan to microscopic stature by presenting him in the context of one who shall be "all in all" (3.341). In Milton's extraordinary and powerful simile, Satan enacts his future role as Enemy to all his friends—both the armies on whom he rests his eyes (1.604–6), whom he has already led into perdition, and the future kings whom as his viceroys he betrays. It is Satan's special property automatically to oppose any being whom he confronts and looks upon. This role is determined by the providential pattern under which in *Paradise Lost* our experience of him is structured and poetically by the system of epic similes embedded in the narrative voice. That is why these similes will often be illuminating in the present study, miming as they so marvelously do the complex mathematical relationships and ratios that structure the figures within *Paradise Lost.*

In the regicide tracts Milton had shown that the human tyrant was the worst that can be imagined of a human being, because he is the one example possible in the state of the unlimited, rampant human ego, which, because it is opposed to all order and sensitive only to self, is infinitely dangerous to humanity. In *Paradise Lost* he was able to show this principle given full rein on a universal scale, ascending "Self-raised" (1.634), with its inbred royal family, coiling downward into creation only to reveal the nemesis that belongs to unlimited egoism from its very inception: the curdling of consciousness in the tasting only of "Bane" (9.123) in all its actions; the loneliness of carrying such animus that chews "bitter ashes" (10.566) to eternity. The providential hand that had reached into English history to remove the Stuarts is held out lightly and mockingly over all the events in *Paradise Lost* so that Satan's unlimited adventure is seen proverbially as limited in its very nature,

> Who aspires must down as low
> As high he soared,
>
> (9.169–70)

and by the controlling power of omniscience linked with omnipotence. In his analysis of Satan's psyche, Milton was able to explore more deeply in *Paradise Lost* the private agony of the tyrant. To have done so in the tracts, when he was tied to the demands of political propaganda, might have invited undesirable sympathy for a figure he wished to present more as an embodied force than as a recognizably human being with whom we might identify. Conversely, Satan, in order to be recognizable, might be humanized to a remarkable degree, and we often pursue at length his inward meditations—which coincide with mental states universally known among the human race—habitual, circular traps of the mind in which all of us have been caught and none voluntarily reenters:

> Me miserable! which way shall I fly
> Infinite wrath, and infinite despair?
> Which way I fly is hell; myself am hell;
> And in the lowest deep a lower deep
> Still threatening to devour me opens wide,
> To which the hell I suffer seems a heaven.
>
> (4.73–78)

We may look in vain through the regicide literature to find any precedent for this reading of the consciousness of the tyrant from within. The Stuart kings are deliberately depersonalized by Milton, as fit objects not for our understanding but for "Truth the avenger" (*Second Defence,* Yale 4, pt. 1:558) and "the unsparing Sword of Justice" (*Eikonoklastes,* Yale 3:346). He went so far as to say of Charles I that "the chief of his adherents never lov'd him, never honour'd either him or his cause, but as they took him to set a face upon thir own malignant designes; nor bemoan his loss at all, but the loss of thir own aspiring hopes" (ibid., 345). In presenting the king, Milton offers a kind of behavioral reading, as if it were open to doubt whether Charles had an inner self at all; if it must be allowed that he did, then we are safe to attribute only the worst motives, the most unscrupulous and cynical thoughts to it. This erasing of personality in the royal adversary contrasts with the willingness of Milton as a poet to investigate the inner processes of the king Satan, a rebel against "heaven's matchless king" (4.41) as Charles was to be, and with his lack of reluctance to allow Satan to define himself as "miserable" and trapped by his own self-defeating choice, static between opposing calamities: "wrath" on the outside, "despair" within. This experience is recognizable by all human beings who have been afflicted by self-pity, which surely means all human beings.

We have seen that the relativistic opening out of scale in Milton's descriptions of Satan's external glory allowed him to soar beyond the astonished onlooker's mental and visual range. The same technique, employed in relation to inner states of the spirit, takes us down into the self, where self-consciousness reveals itself as a condition of darkness and void—"in the lowest deep a lower deep / . . . opens wide"—where superlatives metamorphose into further comparatives that (the reader feels) might in turn give birth to new superlatives. Thus, the technique reveals an image of an archetypal experience in which all have participated in nightmare, if not in reality. In this passage, Milton has opened the inward experience of Satan for the reader to share, and there is a fascination in the way he has removed at one sweep the bedrock of common experience from our minds, so that we too stand with Satan in the claustrophobic interior of the self where there is no ground for standing, only a chilled perception of there being a night within plunging away to infinity. The infinity of God's wrath in the outside world is equaled by the probably more horrific sensation of an infinity within, down which consciousness may infinitely fall and never find bottom. For us, it is a brief sensation, of unspeakable dizziness above the abyss, a moment extracted from Satan's experience in which it is possible to be absorbed in his self-terror: the real horror is the one we perceive when we are released and allowed to move on in the speech, and we can see that this sensation is a continuous experience for Satan, not as for us a momentary, nauseating glimpse into a dream-state. In sharing the criminal's psychological anguish, Milton dramatized "the unsparing Sword of Justice" to which Satan, or anyone, who has broken the sacred taboo of murderous rebellion against his own source must remorselessly submit in his mind. It is a perception that Milton did not explore in his regicide literature when he analyzed the mind of the human king, so that although he was willing to attribute to the source of all evil a conscience that accurately distinguishes right from wrong, he allowed his human king no such conscience, a tyrant being "by nature the lowest of all men" (*Defence,* Yale 4, pt. 1:466) and scarcely to be credited with a more than animal moral understanding. In these respects, then, Milton has moved away from the acid condemnation of kingship in the regicide prose toward a poetic recognition of the sumptuousness of the glory in which satanic monarchy invests itself and combined with that recognition an exploration of the corroding loneliness of the tyrant. Satan's royalty, spurious as it is, soars into a more than earthly glory, while inwardly his mind descends to experience universal human pains and fears. King Charles's image had descended to the ridiculous and smaller-than-life in Milton's representation of his outward show, while the polemicist had disdained to enter imaginatively into any supposed pain endured by a fallen individual with whom he engaged at arm's length and to whom he ruthlessly refused any human claim upon our sympathies.

In *Paradise Lost,* no "king of this world" save Satan can move us in this way, for we never overhear them in soliloquy nor impute understandable motives or feelings to them. As the false kings within human history become part of the poem's fabric, we are not brought to study any sense of alienation in their own awareness but to an awareness within ourselves of how to repudiate them and cast their images away as alien from what is proper to human nature. Milton so treated them in his poetry that we feel not only an obligation to reject them but also a repugnance that makes us need to do so. This "regicide" treatment may fruitfully be studied in Milton's first sustained vision of human history in the catalog of devils in Book 1 of *Paradise Lost,* for it is here that royal tyranny is first seen moving down the ladder of being from Satan through the false gods who represent the transition between Satan's tyranny and man's.[8]

As the fallen angels rise and assemble, our attention is drawn immediately to the noble origins of the future false gods:

> godlike shapes and forms
> Excelling human, princely dignities,
> And powers that erst in heaven sat on thrones;
> Though of their names in heavenly records now
> Be no memorial blotted out and razed
> By their rebellion, from the books of life.

> (1.358–63)

In Milton's usage, the word *princely* has no necessary connotation of evil (not even the word *king,* he repeatedly insisted in the prose works, had any such connotation of itself[9]): used with the austere simplicity of these lines, it expresses an exact relationship between essence and appearance, spiritual goodness and external honor. We have here a glimpse of these fallen angels then as they were in heaven, "erst," in a quiet and stately sentence, with the subtle yet terrible violence of Milton's concluding statement that their names have been obliterated from the "books of life." They have no names and (because of Milton's belief in the proper relationship of name to thing) no true existence "now." We know Satan to have been Lucifer, the light-bearer, but we have no names by which to know Mammon, Moloch, or Belial in their unfallen state. It is as if, through denying their origins, they are purged of their origins, have never been born at all. The reader is disquieted by the terror of anonymity. Falling so far from the safety of innocence, the fallen angels are in a limbo of namelessness that we may compare with Satan's experience of inner void and contrast with Adam's joyous account of his giving of names to the animals, a sign, as the verse makes explicit, of his innate, effective (and feudal) royalty.[10] Naming is here seen as integral to the creation of individual happiness within a coherent structure; unnaming threatens existence itself. Unhinged and unbalanced, the angels who so cavalierly rescinded their allegiance in Heaven become the mad gods of the Philistines, in animal images "adorned / With gay religions full of pomp and gold" (1.371–72).

In Milton's exploration of Satan, we are aware of a developing evolutionary fall that the poet follows through ten books of narrative, and even in Book 10 he has not finished falling. But in the case of the angels included within the catalog in Book 1, the fall is telescoped and foreshortened. The natures that were princely in heaven blacken precipitately as they career down from grace; their names are abolished and new ones conceived as they set themselves up in human history to disseminate their own depravity in ugly and irrational forms. Milton's angels fall quickly, then, out of Heaven into Hell, from eternity into time, from the "books of life" to the dubious histories compiled by ignorant men. With the reference to their "gay religions full of pomp and gold," they almost fall into the poet's time, for Milton's harsh and vivid attacks on the prelacy in the earlier prose dwelt upon "the luxurious and ribald feasts of *Baal-peor*" to which the Popish Anglican Church had degenerated, not to mention "the Idolatrous erection of Temples beautified exquisitely to out-vie the Papists, the costly and deare-bought Scandals, and snares of Images, Pictures, rich Coaps, gorgeous Altar-cloths" (*Of Reformation in England*, Yale 1:589–90). This is the first of several semi-allegorical allusions in the catalog of devils, allusions that in due course become explicit. We are led to perceive the devils, in their emergence as king-gods, as occupying a place of intersection between hell and earth: they bring to our human borders an infernal perversion of heavenly order, just as Nimrod in Book 12, the incarnation of human rebellion, predatory, and a pretender to monarchy, takes human deviation from the fraternal norm of a proper social structure to the very borders of the devilish. The chiasmus of Books 1 and 12 may be seen as embodying this relationship of fallen angel to fallen man, mirroring one another across the borders of the natural.[11]

Before the catalog, Satan is significantly styled as "their great emperor," calling the leaders into order, and it would be useful to see them as standing in the relation of tributary kings to their leader, a notion endorsed by the description of the first of their number:

> First Moloch, horrid king besmeared with blood
> Of human sacrifice, and parents' tears,
> Though for the noise of drums and timbrels loud
> Their children's cries unheard, that passed through fire
> To his grim idol.
>
> (1.392–96)

The blood-stained appearance of Moloch and Milton's insistence on an allegorical translation of his name as "king" links him symbolically, and according to chiasmus, with the Nimrod of Book 12, hunter of his fellowmen (12.30), who breaks the political blood tie by forsaking fraternal rule in favor of kingship. By extension (because there are powerfully allegorical allusions within the Nimrod passage), blood-smeared Moloch relates directly to the Stuart monarchy and its bloody condition after all the "human sacrifice, and parents' tears" of the English civil war. The false gods in piercing down into the material world engender institutions (king-gods, god-kings) that blight human history until history ends. The poet has thus begun to forge an infernal chain of being, from metaphorical father of crime through all his ancestry into the present and—most nightmarishly of all—the far future:

> so shall the world go on,
> To good malignant, to bad men benign,
> Under her own weight groaning.
>
> (12.537–39)

There will always be Satan, Moloch, Nimrod, Charles, until time itself is replaced and we are all dead and gone. Nevertheless, Milton's treatment of the false gods presents them as if static in a frieze surrounded by details representing both their power and their destruction. The nemesis implied by the references to the royal city of Rabba, captured by David, as well as Argob and Basan, conquered by the Israelites in a tremendous victory,[12] points forward to the destruction of every civilization that is erected on the Moloch principle of children's blood and parents' tears. The overwhelming weight of allusion here is to the two Books of Kings, which largely concern the struggle by the Israelites to eradicate idolatrous practices from their people, internecine struggles paralleled by assaults from neighboring countries, the conflict of good kings against bad kings, and the pollution of fundamentally pious kings (like Solomon by Astoreth) by alien rituals and gods. Milton has thus crossed the transitional point at which demonic royalty meets human royalty, and then either mixes with it or is repelled by it.

It is fitting that the first human king to be mentioned should be David's son, Solomon, whose "wisest heart" was turned away from the male Hebrew deity to the female lunar deity, Astarte (Astoreth), through the women to whom he so liberally gave himself:

> But king Solomon loved many strange women, together with the daughter of Pharaoh, women of the Moabites, Ammonites, Edomites, Zidonians, and Hittites. . . .
> . . . Solomon clave unto these in love.
>
> (1 Kings: 11:1–2)

Solomon, a figure so important to the unfolding of the story of Adam and Eve that I consider him at length in Chapter 6, is a kind of test case for human kingship. He stands on the border of pure and vitiated kingship, at that vulnerable point where the most excellent of men is open to contagion from the satanic principle, and because he occupies such a dangerously exposed and dominant position at the apex of society, he is the door by which the principles of Moloch and Baal-peor (Chemos) can enter history and possess it.

During that literary ordeal of Milton's pilgrimage down the ages through the catalog of kings and tyrants that forms the structure of his first *Defence of the People of England*, Solomon's name recurs like a refrain. At the end of chapter 2, because 'iis opponent Salmasius had slandered Solomon by comparing him with Charles I, Milton evolved a lengthy and sarcastic comparison of his own, in an effort to prove that Old Testament monarchies were limited under God and the Law, as well as subject to the people, and that Solomon was less corrupt than Charles (by this time dead and buried);

I still do not see how it could have occurred to you to compare Charles with Solomon. It is that same Charles you praise so highly whose obstinacy, greed, and cruelty, whose fierce tyranny over all good and god-fearing men whose wars, arsons, and countless killings of his wretched subjects his own son Charles is at this very moment confessing. . . .

. . . Solomon "oppressed the people with heavy taxes": at least he spent them on God's temple and public buildings, while Charles spent his on debauchery. Solomon was lured to idolatry by many wives; Charles by one. Solomon was lured to crime, but it is not said that he lured others: Charles not only lured others by the richest rewards of a corrupt church, but also compelled them by edicts and ecclesiastical regulations to erect those altars which are abhorred by all Protestants, and to worship crucifixes painted on the walls hanging over these altars. (Yale 4, pt. 1:372–73)

Here, Charles is clearly assimilated to the pattern of satanic kingship and Solomon to another model: that of the fundamentally virtuous but deeply fallen man (though Milton did remark that he may well have deserved death from the people to whom he was accountable). Charles appears as the tempter, Solomon the tempted, so that the first kind of king would correspond with Milton's Satan in *Paradise Lost,* the second with falling Adam (3.129–31). In both cases, the stigma of sensual weakness attaches, but Milton has adroitly reversed the normal standard of judgment to suggest that it is worse to fall through the love of one wife than by the use of many women. When he came to write his poem, Milton wanted to include both sides of Solomon's dual image, its nobility and its sensual fallenness. Given the former, how powerful must the vice embodied in Moloch be, to incline with his blood-drenched obscenity "the wisest heart" of David's son to taint the worship of God with rituals of inhuman sacrifice. Given the latter, how fallible man must be, both as individual soul and as social being, to the temptation of idolatry, savage, bizarre, and unlovely as this is, seen from a proper distance. In introducing Solomon, then, Milton brought Moloch across the boundary of nature into the human world; implied the terrible struggle of humanity to resist its influence and the wise man's liability to capitulate; and related kingly power with luxurious appetite, so that two distinct kinds of evil are set in juxtaposition, Baal-peor and Moloch:

Yet thence his lustful orgies he enlarged
Even to that hill of scandal, by the grove
Of Moloch homicide, lust hard by hate;
Till good Josiah drove them thence to hell.

(1.415–18)

The final line is simple, single, and refreshes, like a short breath of fresh air in the general dark, unholy, and Dionysian atmosphere of the catalog. In defiling the idolatrous altars, "good Josiah" prefigures Christ's conquest in Book 6, when he "Drove them before him thunderstruck" (858), as well as the regicide cleansing of the body politic in 1649. Josiah needs only the one adjective, *good,* proverbial as he had become. He acted as a king in the right sense, one not of this world, just as Christ purges Heaven in the role of its King[13] and as the English nation executed Charles Stuart by virtue of the sovereign power vested in freeborn men by their Creator.[14] Amid the welter and tumult of persons spilling over one another in chaotic succession through this passage in Book 1 (the reader scarcely knows who or what he is seeing in the hordes of brutal worshipers running about after their bestial gods) the line describing Josiah stands out by its quietness. The good king gains stature in Milton's poem by the simple directness of his action. The biblical account records his iconoclasm in detail, and we see him laying waste about him on all sides with relish. Indeed, Josiah is *Eikonoklastes* in person:

And he brake in pieces the images, and cut down the groves, and filled their places with the bones of men. (2 Kings 23:14)

Abominations fall about him thick and fast, but Milton in his poem, because he could assume that the reader would call to mind Josiah's well-known activities, could afford to dispense with detail altogether. To the violent pounding of four evil monosyllables in which he expresses the union of Moloch and Baal-peor—"lust hard by hate"—the poet offers the answering monosyllables that express Josiah's efficient retribution. "Moloch homicide," its syntax reversed and rendered natural, is replaced by "good Josiah": evil kingship answered by a good king. The phrase is without ire, and the action looks easy, as if a

good man could see right through wickedness to the charlatanism it really is. For a moment it seems a very long time ago that
the pandemonium of Moloch-worship reigned.

. But with the introduction of Solomon and then Baal-peor, the
theme of lust and wantonness enters the catalog, and the feminine principle in the false religions begins to emerge. An-
drogynous angels give way to

> Astoreth, whom the Phoenicians called
> Astarte, queen of heaven, with crescent horns;
> To whose bright image nightly by the moon
> Sidonian virgins paid their vows and songs,
> In Sion also not unsung, where stood
> Her temple on the offensive mountain, built
> By that uxorious king, whose heart though large,
> Beguiled by fair idolatresses, fell
> To idols foul.

(1.438–46)

The deceptively lyrical beauty of these lines, with the appearance of a sort of purity in the description of "Sidonian
virgins," is itself a warning, for "the queen of heaven, with
crescent horns," in distracting attention from the true pa-
triarchal sun, is performing an eclipse that leads our minds to
Satan in lunar eclipse and prefigures both the fall of Eve, "Empress of this fair world" (9.568), to the tree that is the "Mother of
Science" (9.680), and Adam's fall to Eve. Elevation of the feminine principle above the male was for Milton axiomatically ob-
noxious to right reason and essential decorum, just as for the
prophet Jeremiah when he promised God's curse on Israel for
the worship of Astarte, whom he too called "queen of heaven"
(Jeremiah 44:17). Indeed, domination of a king by a queen
(Charles by Henrietta Maria with all her papal superstitions;
Solomon by his wives) leads to inevitable destruction. The unnatural implications of the catalog are emphasized by the yielding of male to female, as well as man to animal (1.481–82) in the
Egyptian gods. No more Josiahs emerge to reassert order, and
of human kings only the wicked Ahaz and "the rebel king"
(Jeroboam) are recorded as being instinct with the evil princi-
ple, as though, with the unfolding of history, human nature

both individually and collectively had become progressively more impotent to resist the sordid and fanatical worship of the malignant deities.

Of these two, Jeroboam presents a curious problem to the reader of the earlier pamphlet literature, wishing to emphasize the parallels between prose and poem. It has not been noticed by critics and annotators that Milton's presentation of this king in *Paradise Lost* contradicts his treatment of the same king in the first *Defence of the People of England*. The case of Rehoboam and Jeroboam, recorded in 1 Kings, chapters 12–14, was a bitterly contested issue during the civil war and interregnum period (on the principle that the Bible could and should be read as a system of divine legal precedents for the edification of later societies). In that story, the natural heir Rehoboam presents himself to his people in an arrogant bid for their acknowledgment, is rejected by them, and is replaced by Jeroboam on the elective principle, God having forbidden Rehoboam's army to make war upon their "brethren the children of Israel" (12:24). Rehoboam, the wicked fratricidal monarch, could be taken by Puritans as a model for Charles I, rightfully rejected by his own people. Milton accordingly used him thus in *The Tenure of Kings and Magistrates*, to prove that the kingship is a human, not a divine, ordinance and that the revolutionary party opposing Rehoboam and now Charles I were "Brethren, not Rebels" (Yale 3:209). So far, the story is a convenient one for republican apologists, but the problem lies with the fact that Jeroboam (the elective king) turns out to be a worthless and idolatrous leader and is succeeded by the "rightful heir," Rehoboam. This highly unsatisfactory denouement caused antimonarchist writers to avoid discussion of Jeroboam in favor of more rewarding candidates, including the iniquitous King Ahab, who "did more to provoke the LORD God of Israel to anger than all the kings of Israel that were before him" (1 Kings 16:33).[15] When Milton replied to Salmasius's *Defensio Regia*, however, he had necessarily to encounter the Jeroboam conundrum, advanced by his adversary.

> You say that "Jeroboam's deed was always disapproved, his defection abominated, his followers considered rebels." I have often read of the censure of his defection, not from Rehoboam but from the true worship of God, and I recall that his followers were indeed often termed wicked, but never rebels. (Yale 4, pt. 1:406)

Yet in *Paradise Lost* Milton clearly altered his apparent opinion:

> the rebel king
> Doubled that sin in Bethel and in Dan,
> Likening his maker to the grazed ox.

(1.484–86)

This apparent contradiction between prose and poetry may serve as a warning to the reader to modify his expectations of the manner in which the former will elucidate the latter. In the prose, we see Milton enthralled by the demands of history and the mode of argument chosen by his opponent, a rhetorical servitude against which he frequently and irascibly protested. In the poetry, we see him free to create his own terms within a self-chosen and inwardly coherent structure. Fighting in the dark place selected by Salmasius on the grindingly dreary topic of whether Jeroboam by replacing the rightful heir was or was not a rebel, Milton had little choice but to separate the king's assumption of power from his use of it and deny his rebellion at all. But standing in the light of his own chosen vision, Milton's conviction that Jeroboam impiously rebelled against God and in this coincided with all the other "rebel" kings of history dominates his account. The poet's aim was to show the puny stature of this misguided monarch, the final impotence of his rebellion, in the mighty retribution effected by Jehovah striking the first-born of Egypt dead as he passes. Jeroboam's little farce of rebellion is emphasized by Milton's gesture of not even bothering to name him; in being "that rebel king" he could be anyone of his tribe, nameless as the tribe of gods he served.

The final biblical false god, Belial, both circles back to Moloch in uniting lust and hatred—his followers filled "With lust and violence the house of God" ("lust hard by hate")—and points explicitly forward into the present day. It is as if the whole catalog has been pointing forward to this moment, when the obscenities of false religion permitted by or institutionalized in the state shall be seen flooding into present-day experience:

> In courts and palaces he also reigns
> And in luxurious cities, where the noise
> Of riot ascends above their loftiest towers,
> And injury and outrage: and when night
> Darkens the streets, then wander forth the sons

Of Belial, flown with insolence and wine.
Witness the streets of Sodom.

(1.497–503)

Belial, if he "reigns" in "courts and palaces," must be a king: in
his intemperance he represents the same Dionysian principle as
"Bacchus and his revellers" by whom the art of sacred poetry is
threatened in these latter days, as Milton explicitly showed in
the Invocation to Book 7 (33). Like Bacchus, Belial had been
commonly used as an emblem of the Cavalier King and his
court during the civil wars and interregnum, and (with the
Restoration) he was reattached to the luxury and disorder of the
new court of Charles II.[16] Like Bacchus-Charles II, whose "barbarous dissonance" (7.32) echoes the vile noise of the "drums
and timbrels" concealing Moloch's cruelties (1.394) from the
ears of bereaved parents, Belial's creatures utter "noise / Of
riot" (1.498–99).

The monarchical principle is thus seen as an undoing of
order, breaking reason by flooding it with wine, breaking harmony by turning measured language to mere noise, breaking
social cohesion by overflowing from its source (the court) into
the streets to persecute the citizens. Unmistakably, this image,
so vividly presented by the poet—to be seen as if from a distance by the reader who looks back from beyond the darkened
cities under the misrule of the young abroad—looks forward to
the vicious rule of Nimrod and the confusion of tongues in Book
12, for the "noise / Of riot ascends above their loftiest towers." It
is a Babel image of ambition bred in man's childishly literal
brain, arguing that one can climb up on matter into heaven:

Of brick, and of that stuff they cast to build
A city and tower, whose top may reach to heaven;
And get themselves a name, lest far dispersed
In foreign lands their memory be lost
Regardless whether good or evil fame.

(12.43–47)

In Milton's Belial image, noise is sent insolently "above their
. . . towers" from the carousers below, and in the biblical account, both Eli and his house are punished "for ever" because
of their lack of restraint (1 Sam. 3:14). The nameless Babylonians
of Milton's Babel image (echoing the nameless false gods) in

throwing up their tower are answered from above by the confusion of tongues that is visited upon them by a mocking Heaven
in "a jangling noise," "a hideous gabble," "hubbub strange,"
"din" (12.55–61). This structural symbolism reveals not solely
parallelism of dark king against dark king but development as
well, for whereas Moloch, Belial, Bacchus, and their followers
had apparently been free to "wander" (1.501) in enjoyment of
their barbarous noise, in the final and crucial case of Nimrod,
this noise is the punishment itself. It is one thing to generate
confusion, so as to confound others—the quiet citizenry of
1.500, the mediatating poet of 7.32–33—another to be confusion's involuntary victim. Michael, whose major message to
Adam is the necessity of temperance in a fallen world and the
difficult but always possible sustaining of order in soul and
state, demonstrates in his vision that it is profoundly fitting for
the Dionysian principle that Milton's poem has been striving to
include and transcend to be visited with a Dionysian punishment, the Nimrod workmanship being labeled "Ridiculous" in
an exquisitely bathetic and derisive polysyllable (12.62).

The Nimrod allusion is paramount and crucial in Milton's
unfolding of his analysis of the descent of the satanic kingship
into human history in *Paradise Lost.* It is here that, in a supreme
moment of allegory, the poet has swept his experience of Stuart
tyranny into the poem, offering to us a type of vitiated rule that
can include all those supernatural and human kings glimpsed
in the poem into one easily recognizable family. Tyranny has
been characterized by violence, lust, disorder, and inhumanity.
It is in violation of the law of God, the law of nature, and the law
of nations. With the story of Nimrod at this crucial moment at
the beginning of Book 12 (the beginning of the end), the poet
offers a final definition of the hell in the human heart that
characterizes the king of this earth; he is a warrior, blood-
stained and fratricidal, in his rise inhuman, in his fall
unpitiable.

Such an image could scarcely help but pick up, given the
special circumstances of the times in which Milton was writing,
reverberations from contemporary history. In *The Tenure of
Kings and Magistrates,* Milton had demanded execution of justice
upon a man who is "lad'n with all the innocent blood spilt in
three Kingdoms," "by whose Commission, whole massachers

have been committed on his faithful subjects" (Yale 3:197). Charles's "blood-guiltiness" was a commonplace image in antimonarchist literature and the chief justification for the regicide.[17] Milton had used it in combination with the Nimrod allusion when he wrote the savage last chapter of *Eikonoklastes* with all its biting laughter, a chapter in which he completed the smashing of the image of the dead king, presenting Charles

> dipt from head to foot and staind over with the blood of thousands that were his faithfull subjects, forc'd to thir own defence against a civil Warr by him first rais'd upon them, and to receive him thus, in this goarie pickle, to all his dignities and honours, covering the ignominious and horrid purple-robe of innocent blood that sate so close about him, with the glorious purple of Royaltie and Supreme Rule, the reward of highest excellence and vertue here on earth, were not only to sweare and covnant the performance of an unjust Vow, the strangest and most impious to the face of God, but were the most unwise and unprudential act as to civil government. (Yale 3:595)

Shortly afterward, he concluded:

> Therfore *To bind thir Kings in Chaines, and thir Nobles with links of Iron*, is an honour belonging to his Saints; not to build *Babel* (which was *Nimrods* work the first King, *and the beginning of his Kingdom was Babel*) but to destroy it, especially that spiritual *Babel*. (Ibid., 598)

Charles, imagined as wearing his two contradictory coats, the under coat fashioned of sticky, still-fresh human blood not long shed ("in this goarie pickle") and the upper coat of purple state to hide it, has preyed upon his people in just the same way as Nimrod built his rule upon conquest. Nimrod was commonly taken by republicans as offering a disgraceful precedent for Charles's activities in his kingdom. The lawyer John Cook, piqued by the king's tactics at his trial, which prevented Cook's delivery of the voluble prosecution speech he had prepared, shortly published it as a pamphlet, *King Charles His Case*. He too identified the careers of Charles and Nimrod, "the first tyrant and conqueror that had no title" (*SCT* 5:217), adding, "I mean that great Nimrod that would have made all England a forrest, and the people, which the bishops call his sheep, to be his venison, to be hunted at his pleasure" (ibid., 220). These bishops were properly to be thought of as "bitesheeps" (ibid., 226), hunters after the manner of their monarch.

Critics have always been aware of the importance of Milton's treatment of Nimrod in Book 12 of *Paradise Lost*.[18] Joseph H. Summers in *The Muse's Method* said that Nimrod had "central significance" as being "the human type of Satan, the destroyer, the Antichrist."[19] However, the subtlety of Milton's use of contemporary allusion in the Nimrod episode (partly due, surely, to his awareness of censorship) may be illustrated by Burden's assumption in *The Logical Epic* that the political material in Book 12 is "uncontroversial and unquarrelsome."[20] Though this is the reverse of the truth, it is an understandable supposition. Milton's account of Nimrod is both allusive and allegorical: through it the reader may pass from art to life and back again, if he sees the door. But the reader will need to be in some sense an initiate, for the allegorical moments in *Paradise Lost* are both fairly rare and well camouflaged, doors consciously but silently left open by the poet, who is terse in allegorical assertions and does not normally gesture explicitly toward the political referent.[21] Milton's work allows but does not coerce modern experience to illumine universal truth.

Michael tells Adam that men for some time after the Covenant

> Shall spend their days in joy unblamed, and dwell
> Long time in peace by families and tribes
> Under paternal rule; till one shall rise
> Of proud ambitious heart, who not content
> With fair equality, fraternal state,
> Will arrogate dominion undeserved
> Over his brethren, and quite dispossess
> Concord and law of nature from the earth,
> Hunting (and men not beasts shall be his game)
> With war and hostile snare such as refuse
> Subjection to his empire tyrannous:
> A mighty hunter thence he shall be styled
> Before the Lord, as in despite of heaven,
> Or from heaven claiming second sovereignty;
> And from rebellion shall derive his name,
> Though of rebellion others he accuse.

(12.22–37)

Delicate threads of irony and allusion lead into the heart of the poem, to the warrior-king Satan hunting down mankind to be

Sin's "prey" (2.844) and giving him over to Death, who wears in Book 2 "The likeness of a kingly crown" (673), with the terse injunction, "lastly kill" (10.402). Child-consuming Moloch and man-eating Death are aped by the ruthlessly predatory, and again unnamed, mighty hunter. Simultaneously, allusions wander out into the immediate past, evoking the fresh memory of a king who set his hounds upon his brothers. "Know you not," called out the self-styled "distressed and almost destroyed subjects of England" in *England's Petition*, "how our bloud is spilt" by the king's men hunting down the common people in their homes.[22] Hunting, traditionally the favorite pastime of English kings, was notoriously dear to both King James and King Charles.[23] An assimilation of the Stuart way of life to the satanic is therefore effectively implied, even endorsed by the use of the word *game* at the end of line 30. *Prey* would have scanned and provided the basic meaning intended, but *game* links the aristocratic leisure activity with the human victims of the civil wars and dramatizes the frivolous cruelty with which the tyrant amuses himself. Milton had made this pun explicit in *Eikonoklastes* when he observed caustically, "the Bishops could have told him, that *Nimrod*, the first that hunted after Faction is reputed, by ancient Tradition, the first that founded Monarchy; whence it appears that to hunt after Faction is more properly the Kings Game" (Yale 3:466). Like Satan, who was "enamoured" with Sin (2.765) and who deeply relished his rebellion and the impression of himself as swaggering conqueror of Heaven—"with vast and haughty strides [he] advanced / . . . towering" (6.109–10)—Nimrod here breaks the law of nature with a casual flourish. It is "lust hard by hate" all over again.

There had been a permanent sense of affront among antimonarchist writers that Charles I could remain so serene in the face of the massacre of his subjects. His repudiation of personal responsibility for the war, endowing him in his public appearances with quietude and disdain for his accusers,[24] was interpreted by his enemies as callousness toward his subjects' miseries, which made him comparable with Richard III, the type of sardonic tyranny.[25] Milton showed kings of this world as cherishing their own viciousness, playing with it or manifesting it with jaunty indifference. The Nimrod episode depicts a fall from a society organized along paternalistic, meritocratic, and broadly republican lines, into a condition of reciprocal tyranny and slavery. In the primary society, joy unblamed is stressed, and the reader (decorously, as Milton is presenting a cyclical theory of history with recurrent falls and ascents) may recall Adam and Eve sharing "all these joys" in Paradise (4.411), inviolate from "sin or blame" (4.758). Allusion to joy of sexual love may at first seem curious in so austerely political a context, but it is an important association, for by the doctrine of increase Milton had shown that sexual joy was a civilizing power. Engaging male and female initially, it led to the framework of patriarchy that he everywhere agreed was the foundation of just order. By "wedded love,"

> adulterous lust was driven from men
> Among the bestial herds to range, by thee
> Founded in reason, loyal, just, and pure,
> Relations dear, and all the charities
> Of father, son, and brother first were known.
>
> (4.753–57)

The prose works prove that Milton was by no means happy about the theory that the origins of royal power lie in the rights of the paterfamilias. In *The Tenure,* he preferred a theory of social contract; in the first *Defence,* he claimed the authority of Aristotle, Diodorus, and Justinus as tending to the view that paternal authority is historically superseded at an early date by meritocracy and then democracy (Yale 3:199–200; 4, pt. 1:472). Politically, the problem about patriarchy is that it entails hereditary power, anathema to Milton. In showing the pacific government violated by Nimrod in the poem, however, Milton avoided the problem by stressing not rule by the one father but rule by "families and tribes," implying a network of relationships indicative of a sort of fraternal rule—the "charities / Of father, son, and brother," men in reciprocal union, enjoying rights proper to each within a family, with society as a whole organized upon the same principle. The experience of joy unblamed in such a structure looks back past the male network to its paradisal origins, the natural tie of man and woman free from "God-forbidd'n loneliness" or "unkindly solitariness."[26] By representing married love as the foundation of social order in Book 4 and recalling its nativity in that most emotive word *joy* in Book 12,

Milton tried to make his reader feel the loss of right rule in society as a personal loss, with poignancy of the other losses the poem discloses—to make his reader feel it as well as understand it. For the fall whose catalyst is Nimrod is a collapse from joy into savage mockery.

Paradise Lost provides nothing for man to laugh at after the Fall. The only valid mirth, as in the Babel incident, is cosmic and ironic, so that the amusement Nimrod finds in his "game" is answered by the "laughter" in Heaven (12.59), while the sarcastic utterance of Satan in the act of rebellion on preparing "Fit entertainment to receive our king" (6.690) is met by God's broader smile (based on omniscience) as the Omnipotent prepares to meet a minor challenge.

The fall from man's joy into God's satire is announced by the phrase "one shall rise." Superficially innocous, this description looks darkly back to the twin dreams of Eve and Adam reported in Books 5 and 8. In each, an anonymous figure approaches under cover of sleep and, through an intricate pattern of verbal parallelism, leads the human dreamers to a discovery of their individual inner nature, figuring in miniature the moral structure of the part that each shall play in the whole poem. In Eve's dream, she explains to Adam,

> methought
> Close at mine ear one called me forth to walk
> With gentle voice.
>
> (5.35–37)

And in response to that voice, "I rose as at thy call" (5.48). In Adam's dream, "one came, methought, of shape divine," spoke, and "by the hand he took me raised" (8.295–300). Both dreams show the advent of an anonymous "one" who claims the trust of the protagonist, a being of obscure identity, drawing his chosen creature into a significant event that predicts the personal future of each. In Adam's case, the movement is through humility into exaltation, being "raised"; his "one" is Christ, the true One, and his dream is "all real" (8.310). Eve's visitor is the nameless Satan, whose proximity to her seems to violate a taboo; she actively follows him, and a humiliation comes after the exaltation of her flight (5.90–92). The episode leads into the fall of Eve itself, the tragic "hour of noon" at which Eve will rise, stretching out her hand to become Empress, Queen, Goddess (9.568, 684, 732), with the nameless figure at her side, teaching her from his own experience how to break the law of nature. This "one" parodying of the *one* just man celebrated by the poet in Books 11 and 12 in the redemptive figures of Abraham, Enoch, and Noah who typify Christ, emerges in different disguises throughout human history in Milton's account. He is the "some one intent on mischief" (6.503) whom Raphael prophesies as inventing gunpowder "In future days" (6.502). Again, the equivocal "one" has brought the satanic and human into anonymous, sinister union, breaking "Concord and law of nature" (12.29). Milton denies him a name or personality, for the dreamer cannot define him accurately, and the prophesying angel only names the "one" who is Nimrod allegorically (12.36–37). In a sense, names do not matter where these rebellious evil figures are concerned: they are denied individuality because evil, properly speaking, has none. Moloch, Dagon ("one / Who mourned in earnest" [1.457–58]), the inventor of gunpowder, Nimrod, and Charles I are literally one and the same person. This is a reason for Milton's referring to unsavory individual kings, whose identity he wants recognized but from whom he wishes to remain scornfully detached, by circumlocutions or generic titles such as "that uxorious king" and "the rebel king"; it is, moreover, the reason for his tendency to define them rather by actions than by character. Seen from the right perspective, the cosmic, there is nothing more to say about them. All tyrants are one. Personality is the prerogative of the innocent, the redeemable, or the still falling.

For this reason, the allegorical moments in *Paradise Lost*, when events contemporary to Milton come to bear on the poem, are especially decorous. Readers will have a special awareness of "some one intent on mischief" who diabolically invented gunpowder as operating in history if they remember what it felt like when "that hellish invention of powder . . . thundered in every corner."[27] If we link Nimrod with the Stuart monarch, we will understand the demonic more clearly by recognizing its general nature from a specific manifestation. Milton made a great point of emphasizing the generally agreed derivation of Nimrod's name from the Hebrew for *rebellious*.[28] He also made Nimrod claim "second sovereignty" from God

(12.35), a clear reference to the royalist theory of divine right, sanctioning the earthly monarch's precedence over and immunity to the law (*rex* over *lex*). This is a belief that Milton had spent many years resisting: "to say Kings are accountable to none but God, is the overturning of all Law and government" (*Tenure*, Yale 3:204). The attack on divine right, only slightly veiled in application, signals the reader to be alert for any development of the allegorical meaning. It comes immediately in a most subtle play upon words. Nimrod

> from rebellion shall derive his name,
> Though of rebellion others he accuse.

(12.36–37)

Here is an oblique allusion to the ancient theory (patronized by contemporary antiroyalists) that the only right to govern held by the line of English kings since William the Conqueror was the right of conquest—judged to be no right at all when it was considered that the Anglo-Saxons were still enduring slavery under the Normans, a foreign ruling class, who did not hold native title to the English crown.[29] According to this theory, English law, pristine and liberty guaranteeing, lay lost in the past, while the people had been alienated from their just freedoms by generations of Norman usurpers—rebels against both divine and civil law.

But the body of law, from the time of Alfred—who "'turn'd the old laws into english' . . . I would he liv'd now to rid us of this norman gibbrish"[30]—and of Edward the Confessor— whose "Laws held good and just, and [were] long after desir'd by the English of thir Norman Kings, are yet extant"[31]—might one day be reintroduced. The Norman conquerors would be legally expelled and a truly English constitution would be enacted. Indeed, Milton's rage and disgust at England's taking "the Yoke of an out-landish Conqueror," expressed at the end of his *History of Britain* (Yale 5, pt. 1:402) is squarely in the tradition of Anglo-Saxon repudiation of what was still regarded, after six hundred years of intermarriage and cultural assimilation, as an alien society. Charles I in a literal way had derived his name— that is, the name of king—from rebellion, for the titles of the reigning houses of Britain were seen as rested, as the republican author of *The true Portraiture of the Kings of England* put

it, on "force, so the succession hath been continued by usurpation," William the Conqueror having "laid the foundation of his
right in the blood of the English" (*SCT* 6:85). The same author
then asked, "Is not five or six hundred years enough for England to be under the succession of a Norman bastard (pardon
the expression, its true though plain) and to be sold, with all its
liberties, from usurpation to usurpation, as well as from generation to generation?" (ibid., 87). Charles, disgraced and condemned by the laws of nature, nations, and God for his bad
pedigree and void title to the throne, is also the authentic heir of
the blood guiltiness of his line, for he accused others of rebellion. Nimrod, then, prefigures Charles as a foreigner impiously claiming soil he does not own and monstrously killing
those he fraudulently calls his own people. The law of conquest
invests the rebellious Satan, Moloch, Nimrod, and Charles with
an identical coat of blood, the "horrid purple-robe of innocent
blood" by which each heir to the line of kings of this world may
be known.

The origin of this line is found in *Paradise Lost* in the "royal
family" of Satan, Sin, and Death. In discussion with his nearest
and dearest, Satan is intimate and truthful, especially so in
Book 10, their final encounter. The image here is massively monarchical in its emphasis, and it is the king conceived as Nimrod
will be, as the mighty hunter claiming his title in a welter of
human blood: "here thou shalt monarch reign," says Sin fondly
to her incestuous parent (10.375); henceforth God must "monarchy with thee divide" (379). Satan's answering speech is one
of blustering pride in both himself and his family, accepting the
kingship and sharing the spoils among his own. There is a
particular sense of terror in the reader at this point, for man has
only just been left behind, hurt to death and frightened by a
guilty future of which he understands hardly anything. The
sudden violence of the irruption of Sin and Death into the poem
at this point, with Sin feeling "new strength . . . / Wings growing" (243–44) and Death scenting "carnage, prey innumerable"
(268), reduces the figures of Adam and Eve past the homely
smallness to which they had shrunk after the Fall to a scale on
which they are immeasurably tiny in the context of the ferocity
they have let loose. We become aware that *they* are, after all, the
empire about which Satan has prophesied. They and all their

unborn children until the end of the world have become mere food for Death the vulture, who waits ravenously for them to be converted into his meat (273–78). We look back at them from the end of their story, with all the grief of hindsight.

Satan's speech of welcome to his royal family seems to answer that with which he left Hell in Book 2 (430–66), when he announced his future royalty, "not refus[ing] to reign":

> Fair daughter, and thou son and grandchild both,
> High proof ye now have given to be the race
> Of Satan (for I glory in the name,
> Antagonist of heaven's almighty king)
> Amply have merited of me, of all
> The infernal empire, that so near heaven's door
> Triumphal with triumphal act have met,
> Mine with this glorious work, and made one realm
> Hell and this world, one realm, one continent
> Of easy thorough-fare. . . .
> . . . .
> You two this way, among these numerous orbs
> All yours, right down to Paradise descend;
> There dwell and reign in bliss, thence on the earth
> Dominion exercise and in the air,
> Chiefly on man, sole lord of all declared,
> Him first make sure your thrall, and lastly kill.
> My substitutes I send ye, and create
> Plenipotent on earth.
>
> (10.384–93, 397–404)

With his victory apparently won, Satan reveals to his admiring daughter the true nature of his kingship. His claims parallel Nimrod's, for in each there is self-conscious attention to the allegorical meaning of the name, Satan glorying in being the "Antagonist of heaven's almighty king," in both name and deed, as Nimrod will be rebel in both senses. Satan's encomium on Sin and Death's enterprise in building the bridge to Hell may bear a faint but bizarre likeness to John of Gaunt's meditation in Shakespeare's *Richard II*:

> This blessed plot, this earth, this realm, this England,
> This nurse, this teeming womb of royal kings,
> Fear'd by their breed and famous by their birth.
>
> (2.1.50–52)

> one realm
> Hell and this world, one realm, one continent
> Of easy thorough-fare.
>
> (10.391–93)

This echo of *Richard II* involves political irony in a directly applicable way, as Satan sends his children to "reign in bliss" in Paradise itself and dying John of Gaunt sees paradisal England, "this other Eden," fall from grace under tyranny. Sin and Death are the viceroys who will hold Earth for Satan: in their service all future kings will be contributory, mighty hunters in their own image.

The conversation between Satan and Sin in Book 10 sounds very like a discussion between the Whore of Babylon and Antichrist. *Eikonoklastes* demonstrates that Milton had made his own assessment of how to identify the Antichrist in "these latter days" (Yale 3:599). It had been easy for those of a millenarian disposition in the late 1640s to regard Charles I as the Antichrist and to see his execution as hastening the rule of the saints: Colonel Harrison, telling the imprisoned Charles his baleful opinion that "Justice had no respect to persons,"[32] undoubtedly saw the worldly king in this light, and so did Milton. The monarch as the blood-stained embodiment of the satanic principle in history, who will be purged as if "at one sling / Of thy victorious arm, well-pleasing Son" (10.633–34), is a powerful image that may have entered the poem to help characterize the Satan of Book 10 as he poises himself for triumph in his empire that will end all empires. There seems a distinct parody of the *regnum Christi* in Satan's crowings of delight over his "one realm . . . one realm, one continent" (10.391–92). He does not yet know that his empire can only be penultimate. It remains for God to show a justice that is comforting to us precisely *because* it is so rigidly absolute in relation to the lurid and inhuman forms that have appalled the imaginations of artists ever since, of Sin and Death whose prey we are. Satan's viceroys, "Plenipotent on earth," turn out to have only the status of "My hellhounds," says God,

> to lick up the draff and filth
> Which man's polluting sin with taint hath shed
> On what was pure, till crammed and gorged, nigh burst

With sucked and glutted offal, at one sling
Of thy victorious arm, well-pleasing Son,
Both Sin and Death, and yawning grave at last
Through chaos hurled, obstruct the mouth of hell
For ever, and seal up his ravenous jaws.

(10.630–37)

It seems strange to call this obscenely ugly speech an example of divine mercy, yet it is supremely so. Its mercy is that which *Eikonoklastes* had labored to define—a charity appearing so like violence that we are apt to mistake its character. As against the "un-warranted Revelation" of King Charles's *Eikon Basiliké,* prophesying "with the spirit of Enmity, not of St. *John,*" it proposes Revelation itself and our deliverance from the unnatural kings who feed upon us. The imagery is full of mouths: the open mouths of God's hell-hounds with licking tongues (reminiscent of Sin's odious offspring, characterized as "A cry of hell hounds" [2:654] tormenting her womb); the "yawning mouth of the grave" that at the apocalyptic moment will fill the "mouth of hell" for good. In this image, it becomes clear that neither a fallen angel nor a fallen man can take upon himself the role of a hunter, though each may fall upon prey. God is the hunter, Sin and Death the hounds, who are used by their master, called off, and disposed of at will. When we come to the Nimrod episode and read of that "mighty hunter against the Lord," we are therefore aware that he merely feigns a role he cannot sustain.

Milton's theme of inherent justice in events whereby the unnatural inevitably thwarts its own will, action by action, is demonstrated supremely here. These evil principles in nature, in a manner reminiscent of the offspring of Spenser's Errour in *The Faerie Queene* (1.1.25–26), have a nearly suicidal tendency; they are unnatural to such an extreme degree that they are already "nigh burst / With sucked and glutted offal," so subject to appetite as to be nearly impotent when the Son dispatches them. This final act of justice, scourging the instruments of scourging, is the fulfillment of the prophesies of Revelation and the condition of man's release from God's just curse. The harsh demeanor of Father and Son here is seen, as many Puritans saw justice, as the rigorous condition of love. As the Huguenot author of the *Vindiciae Contra Tyrannos* put it, there is such a thing as "cruel pity," releasing "plagues of mankind" among the people, and "that shepherd is much more pitiful who kills the wolf, than he who lets him escape."[33] In this tradition, Milton had challenged Charles's appeal to the mercy of the people and of God as being a covert way of liberating a predator to feed upon society: "Whatever mercy one man might have expected, tis too well known, the whole Nation found none" (*Eikonoklastes*, Yale 3:431). Milton only cooperated with a just and merciful providence in turning his pen so violently against the king.

But by the time the latter parts of *Paradise Lost* came to be written, the revolution had failed and the new tyrant, Charles II, had been restored. In that most passionate of his tracts, *The Readie and Easie Way to Establish a Free Commonwealth*, published in 1660 on the eve of the Restoration, Milton had prophetically foreseen that when the nation had once more enslaved itself to the "once abjur'd and detested thraldom of Kingship" (Yale 7:422), surrendering to the debauchery of kings and to the idolatry of adoring them (ibid., 426), history would turn against the British and accuse them. The Tower of Babel, which had seemed to one generation to have been erected by the Stuarts and brought down by the saints, would shift in the consciousness of history to be reidentified as the work of the Commonwealth:

> Where is this goodly tower of a Commonwealth which the English boasted they would build to overshaddow kings, and be another *Rome* in the west? The foundation indeed they laid gallantly; but fell into a wors confusion, not of tongues, but of factions, then those at the tower of *Babel*; and have left no memorial of thir work behinde them remaining, but in the common laughter of *Europ*. (Ibid., 423)

On the Continent, tyrants would gloat:

> Thir song will then be, to others, how sped the rebellious *English*? to our posteritie, how sped the rebells your fathers? (Ibid., 449)

Almost no reaction can pain the idealist more acutely than the response of laughter. It makes light of engrossingly serious affairs, makes nothing of past exploits. Milton's prediction of belittling laughter that is "common" in both senses (universal and vulgar) at the high hopes invested in the Commonwealth (*Common* as shared, mutual, and inclusive) is like the warning voice at the beginning of Book 4 of *Paradise Lost*, summoned under the willed delusion that time might double back and the Fall be prevented. It is as if Milton longed to insert the Book of Revelation (the last things) into the Book of Genesis (the first) and, arresting time, abolish history. In *The Readie and Easie Way* he looked forward and impersonated the leering voices of debased future generations mocking the Babel workmanship of the republic, in an effort to deprive such voices of their chance to speak: "how sped the rebells your fathers?" and "Where is this goodly tower?" If the prophet could impersonate their scorn realistically enough, the English might draw back from the imminent Restoration in time. The fact, however, that there was no time, and thus no ready and easy way, was perfectly clear to Milton. In Milton's vision of the Commonwealth Babel, the real anguish lies in the way he envisaged no memorial but laughter—the namelessness that *Paradise Lost* shows to be the condition of damnation. In both the poetry and the prose, Milton defied the inevitable and tried to undo time, with such austerity and conviction that the reader almost believes it can be done.

The fact that it cannot is testified to by the circles of history reiterated in Books 11 and 12 of *Paradise Lost,* in which tyranny succeeds tyranny, and society gets up only to fall again. As Adam is shown the giants of Genesis by Michael, he is told to learn the false virtue of those self-styled conquerors, "Destroyers rightlier called and plagues of men" (11.697). The roar of arms will punctuate human history in the succeeding account to such an extent that the silences between become always more brief, until, finally, in Book 12 tyranny is regarded as a nearly constant punishment for a race vitiated in nature. This book, balancing Book 1, also echoes much of its material. The story of Moses and the escape from Egypt is retold (12.163–214), but, remembering the first allusions (1.305–11, 338–43), we are disturbed by the knowledge that the "darksome cloud of locusts," which in line 185 swarms down upon the Egyptians in punishment from God, has been identified as the host of evil angels becoming active in history. Though we realize that God uses them to scourge the scourgers of his chosen people and that therefore we ought to be hopeful, we are also frightened, witnessing the original intrusion of the fiends into human life, seeing the eternal cycles of bondage and terror through which man must be hunted down until he reaches peace in eternity.

The view of history taken by Milton here is Augustinian and Orosian in its awareness of the relentless pursuit by historical events of their own tails, from bondage to liberty and back, with God repeating his familiar punishments at every turn. Milton wrote as one living under Church persecution and state tyranny just as consciously as did Tertullian, Lactantius, and Orosius when the Church was young and subject to the cruelties of "violent lords" (12.93). In the Restoration, Milton's "nation" had been delivered over into Egypt once again, and release in political terms was not to be expected. While Milton had been urging the "good old cause" in fighting the vision of his countrymen "chusing them a captain back for *Egypt,*"[34] General Monck, it appears, had been writing to Charles II to exhort him to free *his* countrymen "from their Egyptian bondage, as I may term it."[35] In the public mind, scriptural indexes were being detached from those they had labeled in the Commonwealth period and passed across to identify the other side. By 1660, Cromwell had been Nimrod breeding his predatory bloodhounds for years, and Charles II was transformed into Moses delivered from Pharaoh Cromwell's Egypt.[36] Cowley shows Charles II's royal family being miraculously led "through a *rough Red sea,*" and back to the Promised Land in 1660.[37] We need not multiply examples to glimpse the shock and alienation felt by one, like Milton, who knows himself to be in Egypt while official doctrine and public opinion alike declare that the place of occupation is certainly Israel.

The account of human history in *Paradise Lost* Book 12 is accordingly low-spirited and cursory. Like Orosius, Milton perceived that it was all over and to be done again, but in neither this world nor this incarnation:

> So alas a persecution by the Gentiles at some future time awaits us while we are journeying in freedom, until we cross the Red Sea, that is, the fire of the judgement, with our Lord Jesus Christ Himself as our leader and judge. Those, however, who assume the rôle of the Egyptians, the power having temporarily been given them by the permission of God, will show their fury and persecute the Christians with the most grievous tortures. But all those enemies of Christ,

together with their king, Antichrist, will be caught in the lake of eternal fire.[38]

Milton also prophesies in Book 12, as the world goes tumbling over itself, down toward the Last Judgment, the rise of a "heavy persecution" that nearly destroys Truth among mankind (531–37), a prophecy that comes so near to the end of Michael's account and so accurately expresses Milton's own perception of the period after the Restoration that we cannot doubt that it alludes to the established church under the second Charles.

Milton, who had resisted all views about tyranny by earthly monarchs save that of uncompromising refusal to bear it, in the end embraced an attitude that is ironically (or bitterly) close to what we might call the Romans 13 view—"the powers that be are ordained of God." Embodied in Calvin's *Commentaries*, this perspective says that the Christian, finding himself in Babylon or Egypt, must simply endure it, because he cannot have been put there without good reason, by a providential God who orders everything;[39] man is to accept patiently God's indignation until sin has been purged. It is a view that relies heavily on a doctrine of necessity, so that in *Paradise Lost* we are aware of an emphasis on the word *must*:

> tyranny *must* be,
> Though to the tyrant thereby no excuse.
>
> (95–96)
>
> But first the lawless tyrant, who denies
> To know their God, or message to regard,
> *Must* be compelled by signs and judgments dire;
> To blood unshed the rivers *must* be turned.
>
> (173–76; italics mine)

Servitude within the soul *must* logically issue in servitude institutionalized in society itself. The unnamed king who is the "lawless tyrant" of Egypt,[40] visited by plagues that evoke the wasteland of the civil wars, with icy hardness in his heart to equal in Milton's vision the fratricidal obduracy of Charles I (12.193–94), is seen as necessary in fallen history just as his drowning in the Red Sea is necessary. God through Moses "overwhelm[s] their war" (12.214). But war is just as inevitably renewed in a graceless humanity of whom Michael has to conclude:

so shall the world go on,
To good malignant, to bad men benign,
Under her own weight groaning.

(12.537–39)

Whereas in 1649 Milton perceived the earth as comparatively innocent, encumbered only by the weight of an evil not germane to itself, and humanity as informed by natural law and the spirit of grace, having only to purge itself to be free, after 1660 he saw the earth itself as too hopelessly infected to be purged except from without.

It is through the reiterated image of the king of this world that Milton embodied in *Paradise Lost* this cyclical pattern of corruption in human life. Once Satan has been established as the archetype of vitiated kingship, which displays itself in overpowering but tawdry magnificence while it feeds on unnatural, predatory cruelty, the image is extended through a kind of family or chain of subsidiary kings invading all time and all space, from Moloch to Pharaoh to Charles I. These figures recur from the beginning of the poem to its end and provide a unifying symbol of the nature and behavior of evil in the cosmos of *Paradise Lost.* In a sense, theirs is a chain of nonbeing, travestying the chain of reflections that Milton attaches to the image of God's creativity, a nihilism at the core of evil that unmakes (by divine providence) even itself. This is expressed both explicitly and with great poetic subtlety through Milton's insistence on the namelessness and anonymity of demonic kingship. The image of the king as presented in *Paradise Lost* is therefore a species of graven image, and Satan as spurious sun-king of his empire has a similar status to that which Milton believed Charles I presented in his *Eikon Basiliké.* The *Eikon* of evil must be answered, undermined by poetry, and repudiated in the total structure of the narrative by an effective *Eikonoklastes.* Milton in *Paradise Lost,* like that good Josiah who purged Israel, smashed with the power of the sacred muse the idolatrous images that obscure truth—uncovering the blood that is the true coat of King Moloch, King Death, King Satan, and in another manifestation King Charles, and demonstrating how ugly and offensive its presence is beneath the purple robes of state. Similarly, the poetry reveals the barbarous noise and disharmony of courts and palaces and breaks before our eyes the Babel workmanship of King Nimrod, showing simultaneously an image of the usurping injustice of evil and its due and appropriate punishment in a fundamentally just universe. Within this great chain of symbolism embodying the theme of evil within an image of false kingship in *Paradise Lost*, the moments of political allegory elucidated in this chapter serve to clarify the theme for modern man. They are not the most important aspects of the poem, nor does the poem exist as a cloak for them. Rather, the Stuart image embedded within *Paradise Lost* represents a channeling of the mighty tides of the poem's ideas into the immediate present, authenticating and dramatizing the action in an image that presses urgently upon the memory of the reader.

2

Sultan and Barbarian

During the period of the civil wars and the interregnum, the air was alive with insults delivered from one side to the other involving epithets like *Turkish* or *barbarian*. Royalists saw the revolutionaries as the forces of chaos, who, like visitations of Huns or Saracens, were treading down the ancient civilization and traditions of England into the same pulp as generations of their forerunners had done in Europe over the centuries. Roundheads regarded the king as no better than the great Turk, enslaving the noble English people until they had no more identity than the poor Eastern populations, famished and abject. The Turks were cruel, but the Royalists were worse: "From my very soul I doe believe that the barbariousnes inflicted upon the poore gally-slaves in Turky cannot parrallell those inhumane cruelties which abundance of poore men have undergone from the hands of Smith himselfe."[1] The Turkish monarchs were suffered by God's permissive will to be a scourge to their people, like the English king, said John Cook, but ought like him to be resisted.[2] Even by comparison with Turks, Russians, and the Moors, the British may "yet call Englands kings tyrants, and their subjects slaves," one pamphleteer insisted.[3] Another cry of protest was uttered by Levelers, who, persecuted by Parliament and Protector, transferred the oriental formula accordingly. Richard Overton wrote in desolating terms of the cruel detention of his wife: "Most inhumanely and barbarously they dragged her away from that prison, with her tender infant of halfe a yeares of age in her armes headlong upon the stones, through the streets, in the dirt and mire . . . not allowing her so much humane compassion, as might have been justly expected even from Turks, Infidels and Pagans."[4] Royalists saw the furious Puritan armies of the poor as barbarians, near kin to "Plague and Famine."[5] The same poor later discovered their leaders, Cromwell and his officers, to be "Great Moguls of the war."[6] The Commonwealth government had "Turkish power,"[7] and Cromwell could only be defended (even by his admirers) in a way that characterized the evil Turks themselves as "God's rod for the sins of the nation."[8]

This preoccupation with the "barbarian" empires of history not only served as material for abuse but also formed part of the intellectual structure for debate about the nature of tyranny and the relationship between ruler and subjects. In these terms, the Turks and their spiritual forebears (autocratic monarchies, lawless, anti-Christian, imperialist, and inhumane) were conceived of as a model with which to compare contemporary events by representing an extreme of political behavior, in which absolute rule by the one begets servile acquiescence in the many. Thus, Harrington in *Oceana* paused to define Turkey's pure military autocracy on his way to the formulation of his desired ideal state.[9]

During the interregnum, Milton had been employed in composing letters of state, which often engaged him indirectly with Turkish affairs, through correspondence with the Venetian republic, the outpost of Christendom against the sultan, and through discourse with other states on the Turkish problem. In 1653, Parliament, via Milton's hand, assured the doge of Venice of England's support against Turkish aggression (*The Miltonic State Papers*, Yale 5, pt. 2:647–48); in 1655, Cromwell congratulated Venice on its naval successes "against an enemy of the Christian name" (ibid., 715); and in 1657, while asking a favor of the Venetians, Cromwell congratulated them on making possible the freedom of "all Christians enslaved by the Turks" (ibid., 808). The fullest available statement of the Protectorate's view of the Turkish threat to Christendom and how it might be handled, ascribed to Milton's composition, lies in the "Instructions for the Agent to Russia" of 1657. This politic document suggested the use of one despot to scourge another, the Great Turk being a more absolute enemy than a Grand Duke, so that the agent was advised to address the Russian leader with "all his titles," for fear of giving offense, as happened to the Elizabethan ambassadors who neglected to grovel obsequiously enough (ibid., 786). The Grand Duke was to be congratulated on frightening "the greak Turk, the common foe of Christendome" (ibid.); encouraged to promote Christian unity against the enslaving infidel; and informed that if he attempted "a glorious expedition against the Turk, and thereby . . . win himselfe honor throughout Europe as the chief defender of Christendome" (ibid., 787), he could not do better than to leave the Protestant Swedish king to protect Russia's liberty (Protestantism being tolerant of individual conscience and in itself closer to Russian orthodoxy than the Catholic Polish alternative). In these Machiavellian proposals, Milton framed a plan to scourge the scourgers of Christianity, using an instrument not notably pure and holy but wielded on the excellent and unquestionable authority of Scripture:

> O Assyrian, the rod of mine anger, and the staff in their hand is mine indignation.
> I will send him against an hypocritical nation, and against the people of my wrath will I give him charge, to take the spoil, and to take the prey, and to tread them down like the mire of the streets.
> . . . .
> Wherefore it shall come to pass, that when the Lord hath performed his whole work upon mount Zion and on Jerusalem, I will punish the fruit of the stout heart of the king of Assyria, and the glory of his high looks. (Isa. 10:5–6, 12)

Under this divinely providential plan, God was seen by Renaissance historians as providing scourges for sinning Jewish and Christian civilizations. Pharaoh and Nebuchadnezzar in Old Testament times, followed by generations of khans, kings, moguls, shahs, czars, sultans, and emperors, were God's rod for his chosen that He then broke at will. The English infatuation for Marlowe's *Tamburlaine* is based in part on delight at seeing a succession of scourges scourged: the Turkish sultan in a cage; Egyptians routed; Babylonians hung in chains; and finally the scourge, Timur, discarded until a collection of "Assyrian" corpses is achieved to the satisfaction of a Europe that had shared neither the Turks' internal unity nor freedom from the threat of invasion from Ottoman military power perpetually battering at the door of Christianity, Venice. Commonwealth support for Venice and Russia expressed by Milton in his *State Papers* is an extension of the desire to cooperate with divine providence against the infernal anti-Christian armies in the east (the Sultan being proverbially the Devil and the Turks fiends, in contemporary parlance).[10]

Additionally, Milton during the regicide dispute had on frequent occasions maintained that "Turks" were not necessarily to be looked for in Turkey: they might be seen less as a geographical phenomenon than as a moral and political incarnation, capable of occurring in any time, in any place. In *The Tenure of Kings and Magistrates*, he formulated a just and memorable axiom, "Nor is it distance of place that makes enmitie, but enmity that makes distance"; Charles Stuart, though an Englishman, was no "neighbor" and, because he had assaulted English life and liberty, was no better then a Turk, a Sarasin, a Heathen" (Yale 3:215). Indeed, Milton called Charles an "unbridl'd Potentate" (ibid., 238). In *Eikonoklastes*, Milton poured scorn upon Charles's definition of liberty of property as conferring no privilege "above what the *Turks, Jewes,* and *Moores* enjoy under the Turkish Monarchy"; one might as well inhabit the pirateering port of Algiers as live content with a law so elementary (Yale 3:574). In response to Charles's brazen political claims, Milton argued that "Turkish Vassals enjoy as much liberty under *Mahomet* and the Grand Signor" (ibid., 575), meaning of course, no liberty at all. It is interesting that he mentions at once the prophet of Islam, Mahomet, the byword since the Crusades of anti-Christian infidelity, and the sultan who upheld him: Charles is to be seen not only as the Turk in England but as the Antichrist as well, turning both body and soul into vassals to an absolute dictatorship.

It is Milton's double faith, shown in the regicide literature, that a barbarous society begets its own servitude to an absolute ruler and, equally, that God, with his children coming to self-awareness and recognizing the ignominy of their slavery, will break tyrannical rule with the rod of justice. Justice for Milton is deeply embedded in affairs of state, so that just as God had punished the brutal Assyrian, so also he had punished Pharaoh, toppled Babel, and (though this had not yet come to pass) he would break the Turkish empire with Christian cooperation. The irony in which Milton took the deepest delight lay in the idea that God and man scarcely have to move a muscle to destroy Babylonian, Egyptian, or Turkish tyrannies. When the time is ripe, they give the appearance of committing involuntary suicide:

> And those Kings and Potentates who have strove most to ridd themselves of this feare, by cutting off or suppressing the true Church, have drawn upon themselves the occasion of thir own ruin, while they thought with most policy to prevent it. Thus *Pharaoh,* when

once he began to feare and wax jealous of the Israelites, least they should multiply and fight against him, and that his feare stirr'd him up to afflict and keep them under, as the onely remedy of what he feard, soon found that evil which before slept, came suddenly upon him, by the preposterous way he took to shun it. Passing by examples between, & not shutting wilfully our eyes, we may see the like story brought to pass in our own Land. (*Eikonoklastes,* Yale 3:509–10)

The pharaoh alluded to is that Busiris evoked in *Paradise Lost* when Milton came to describe the rebel angels, seen from the safe shore by the chosen people released from bondage into spiritual and political liberty only as "floating carcasses" (1.310), devoid of soul, and "broken chariot wheels" (1.311), void of power. In *Eikonoklastes* and in *Paradise Lost,* Milton regarded all kings and potentates as "preposterously" ordering their own downfall and as already (at whatever moment in their personal history one chooses to describe them) going down the same flood that took Pharaoh—already a "floating carcass" that even at the time of greatest splendor and success can be recognized through the purple robe of kingship. Once the tyrant is located, so is his bad end.

The image of the oriental potentate is, then, the most chilling, corrupt, sensual, and worldly that Milton could have invoked in *Paradise Lost,* carrying with it its own hidden message of providential control. It was a continuum, stretching backward into the ancient world, into the present day, and undoubtedly forward into the future. Its use involved both a reassurance (since nemesis had always been involved) and a challenge to the civilized reader, as well as the presentation of a contemporary threat, because only a great leap of faith could allow someone in politically fragmented seventeenth-century Europe, with the besieged Venetians at the tip, to conceive of ever overwhelming the wealth and power of the barbarian East. The poet, by including Pharaoh, may subdue fear in his contemporary reader, but by moving on to the sultan, he may freshly arouse it, suggesting a query as to how comforting is the providential historical structure provided to allay that fear. In a sense, the inclusion of the combined images of oriental tyranny and barbarian servitude in *Paradise Lost* is a test of the state of grace in which readers find themselves. If the West cannot stand against the sultan, how far can the Christian soul resist Satan?

Some of the best prose on *Paradise Lost* has been written out of fascination for these sensual, frightening images of orientalism that critics have always noted and admired in the poem.[11] One of the richest accounts is Rajan's. He speaks of Satan's heroic qualities as

> corroded and eaten out by the nemesis behind them. . . . Words like Memphis and Alcairo may be nothing more than brilliant names to us. To Milton's contemporaries they were darkened with contempt. When Satan was described to them as a "great Sultan" the phrase would have reminded them of tyranny rather than splendour. When the fallen angels were likened to the cavalry of Egypt, a plague of locusts and a barbarian invasion, they would have given full weight to the mounting disapproval which lies behind the simile.[12]

Rajan's evocation of a heroism "corroded and eaten out" by nemesis is horribly accurate, and decorous, because it draws our attention to the deathward tendency of barbarian culture, in which individuality is blackened into anonymity through the low value set on human life; in which the drive toward meaninglessness is manifested in the elevation of flesh above spirit. (Milton noted in the first *Defence* the sacramental qualities attached by the Egyptians to a human corpse [Yale 4, pt. 1:433].) Again, Rajan exactly identifies a contemporary response to the cities of Memphis and Cairo as being "darkened with contempt": the mind in hostility pulls away from and repudiates the now dead centers of absolute power. But Rajan's claim that Milton's allusion to a great sultan would have evoked ideas of tyranny rather than images of splendor carries a false emphasis. Both would have been involved, in the same measure and equally contending, so that rather than a pair of alternatives, the poem offers a paradox identical to that reptilian beauty displayed by Satan to Eve as he beguiled her toward the tree of knowledge: "So glistered the dire Snake" (9.643). Milton's oriental images both attract and repel, and do so with simultaneous violence, so that the initial reaction is fear and inner conflict, and only as a secondary reaction comes a calmly rational capacity to assign these violent areas of "delusive light" (9.639) in history to an acceptable place in the divine pattern.

This horrible beauty and potency in the imagery dramatize for the reader the final, most extreme image of evil in political terms, an image whose roots lie, in Milton's vision, at the very source of depravity. It therefore brings us closest of all to the innermost nature of Satan—his will to power—temptingly with the overwhelmingly golden imagery but distastefully: it lays quite bare the reality of unloosed egoism by defining the relation between sultan and his people, between Satan and man, as that of murderer and victim, owner and slave. Nothing in *Paradise Lost* analyzes in quite so deadly or displeasing a way the actual effects of unlimited egoism preying on the blood and soul of mankind. The simultaneous establishment by the poet of an intrinsic structure of providential control or nemesis redeems the reader's mind from the horror and splendor of the experience, allows transport of that mind into intellectual tranquillity at the final outcome of things, but never quite dissipates the force of the images that have so disturbed the reader. This is especially so when it is recognized that Milton created parallels and resonances of the oriental imagery throughout the poem (Books 6, 7, and 8 excepted, as pertaining to Raphael's heavenly discourse). They are most powerful in Books 1 and 2 and in Books 10 and 11, the fall of Satan, the fall of Adam and Eve, and the fall of society.

The first allusion to Turkish absolutism comes in combination with reference to Pharaoh and to the Scythian invaders of Europe who had slaughtered their way from behind the Caucasians from the fourth to the fourteenth centuries. It is at a crucial moment in *Paradise Lost,* when a political relationship between Satan and his subjects (literally, the fallen angels; metaphorically, our fallen selves) is initiated:

> They heard, and were abashed, and up they sprung
> Upon the wing, as when men wont to watch
> On duty, sleeping found by whom they dread,
> Rouse and bestir themselves ere well awake.
> Nor did they not perceive the evil plight
> In which they were, or the fierce pains not feel;
> Yet to their general's voice they soon obeyed
> Innumerable. As when the potent rod
> Of Amram's son in Egypt's evil day
> Waved round the coast, up called a pitchy cloud
> Of locusts, warping on the eastern wind,
> That o'er the realm of impious Pharaoh hung

> Like night, and darkened all the land of Nile:
> So numberless were those bad angels seen
> Hovering on wing under the cope of hell
> 'Twixt upper, nether, and surrounding fires;
> Till, as a signal given, the uplifted spear
> Of their great sultan waving to direct
> Their course, in even balance down they light
> On the firm brimstone, and fill all the plain;
> A multitude, like which the populous north
> Poured never from her frozen loins, to pass
> Rhene or the Danaw, when her barbarous sons
> Came like a deluge on the south, and spread
> Beneath Gibraltar to the Lybian sands.

(1.331–55)

Milton's description of the revival of the fallen angels, parodying the resurrection of the just at the end of time (for they are represented as sleepers startled into wakefulness) also relates them to recognizably human modern counterparts, "men wont to watch / On duty," military personnel who go in fear of their leadership, but who when left to their own devices on the night watch give evidence that their spirits are not very willing and their flesh is very weak. Politically, the important feature is the poet's assertion that the army was galvanized into action not by a beloved leader but in a state of shame, "abashed," caused by their being "sleeping found by whom they dread." The passage concerns an army's fear, not of its enemy, but of its own commander. Just as Satan is revealed as standing in relation to his tributary kings of this earth in an attitude of apparent intimacy, but really one of confrontation, so in his role as Pharaoh, sultan, barbarian leader, Satan is secretly felt by his own legions to be an enemy, inspiring their victory over sleep less by the idealism that seemed to ring in his invocation to them, "Awake, arise, or be for ever fallen" (1.330), than by simple, ominous dread. This experience in the minds of Satan's subjects is paralleled in Book 2, at that crucial moment when the grand patrician angels prudently refrain from offering themselves as hell's emissaries to the new world, for

> they
> Dreaded not more the adventure than his voice
> Forbidding; and at once with him they rose.

(2.473–75)

It is ironic that Eve, once fallen, refers to God as "Our great forbidder, safe with all his spies" (9.815) because it is Satan who has been proved by the poet at this early point in the poem to be the forbidder. We presume that his peers exercise care in their response because they have heard him practicing this mighty art of forbidding on previous occasions: like the rebel hosts they recognize the power and cruelty rising in his voice and sensibly forbear.

In this dread, instinctive because familiar, Satan's subjects are proved by Milton in exquisite touches of irony to be in a condition of hopeless slavery, great and small alike reduced to an identical abjectness that shows itself especially in their rising to a voice which, mere air as it is, has a terrible potency to them. This emotion of fear is one of the factors unifying the images of Pharaoh, sultan, and barbarians in Book 1. In likening Charles to Pharaoh and the sultan, operating his "Turkish tyranny" in the regicide literature, Milton had selected models of tyranny renowned for un-Christian cruelty on a global scale, able to violate every normal human tie. In linking these figures in the poem to the barbarian visitations into Europe, he only multiplied the same image. The Massagetae described by Herodotus were cannibals; Attila killed his brother Bleda in cold blood.[13] Travelers to Turkey reported in horror that it was the rule for a new sultan upon accession to murder all his brothers, to prevent any attempt at usurpation; Fynes Moryson said in his *Itinerary* that Turkish kings "begin their Tyrannicall government with the cruell strangling of all their brothers." These unpleasant domestic habits were the measure of the autocrat's contempt for human life and his property rights over subjects. Moryson shows the Turkish courtiers dancing attendance on the sultan's facial expression: "This Tyrant seldome speakes to any of his subjects, but wil be understood by his lookes." However, we may assume that ascertaining his meaning is rendered less easy to his petrified minions by the simultaneous prohibition against looking him full in the face.[14] He communicates his commands (like Satan through Beelzebub) through his Chief Vizier. It will be noticed too that when Satan meets his heir, Death, paternal feeling is singularly absent: they revile one another, and "Each at the head / Levelled his deadly aim" (2.711–12).

Milton had only needed to introduce one direct allusion to the sultan in Book 1 to clarify these relationships, full of dread and easily recognizable as they are, so proverbial had the idea of a Turkish tyranny become during the Renaissance. Having set forth the relation between Satan and his legions as that of sultan and slave (enemies ordered on the principle of terror), the enemy-relation of Satan and Death, as well as Satan's instrumental use of Beelzebub, logically follows. In *Observations on the Articles of Peace* (of 1649), Milton had been able to locate the persons of sultan, vizier, and mullah quite clearly in the English state, a perfect Turkish tyranny:

> which was so long modelling by the late King himself, with *Strafford,* and that arch Prelat of *Canterbury,* his chief Instruments; whose designes God hath dissipated. Neither is it any new project of the Monarchs, and their Courtiers in these dayes, though Christians they would be thought, to endeavour the introducing of a plain Turkish Tyranny. Witnesse that Consultation had in the Court of *France* under *Charles* the ninth at *Blois,* wherein *Poncet,* a certain Court projector, brought in secretly by the Chancellor *Biragha,* after many praises of the *Ottoman* Government; proposes . . . how with best expedition and least noyse the Turkish Tyranny might be set up in *France.* (Yale 3:313–14)

Pym had accused Strafford at his arraignment of bearing likeness to "the Minister of the Great Turke,"[15] and Milton's Strafford is also the vizier, the most hated, most feared, and most powerful officer in the Turkish court, famous for intrigue and for being the mouth, eyes, and hands of his master. To define Strafford so was to call him damned, and to say that the English monarchy had aspired to such corruption was to name it irredeemable. Conversely, when the regicide polemicist became the epic poet, he could characterize the demonic by linking its manners both to the Turkish model and to the English copy of that model, showing in the likenesses of Satan and Beelzebub a harmony of evil minds subversive of all order:

> Beelzebub . . . than whom,
> Satan except, none higher sat, with grave
> Aspect he rose, and in his rising seemed
> A pillar of state; deep on his front engraven
> Deliberation sat and public care;
> And princely council in his face yet shone,

Majestic though in ruin: sage he stood
With Atlantean shoulders fit to bear
The weight of mightiest monarchies; his look
Drew audience and attention still as night
Or summer's noontide air.

                                              (2.299–309)

                        Thus Beelzebub
Pleaded his devilish counsel, first devised
By Satan, and in part proposed.

                                              (2.378–80)

The monarchical allusions to Beelzebub come first, in a massive
cluster—"princely," "majestic," "mightiest monarchies"—and
we see him as a kind of Strafford, though infinitely grander (his
person magnified by the emblematic "Atlantean shoulders")
and more attractive, for the quiet image of hushed air at midday
in summer, with its hint of pastoralism, quite confuses the
reader's expectations. It is only later, when Milton reveals the
manner of conception of Beelzebub's scheme, by Satan, with a
poetic adroitness on Milton's part to match the secrecy of the
relationship between the two evil minds, that the upholder of
the state as mightiest monarchy is redefined as a projection of
the Strafford image in its Turkish denomination. The reader of
the prose works remembers Milton's definition of the Turkish
designs hatched between King Charles and his "Instruments,"
and perceives the rulers of hell working to place *rex* above *lex*,
and a sultan above them all, according to the pattern designated
in the *Observations on the Articles of Peace,* "with best expedition
and least noyse." Again, it is not that we substitute Strafford's
face for Beelzebub's; looking back to the *Observations* and
Eikonoklastes and finding there "a man whom all men look'd
upon as one of the boldest and most impetuous instruments
that the King had, to advance any violent or illegal designe"
(*Eikonoklastes,* Yale 3:369), we do not declare Strafford the
elected candidate for the role of Beelzebub. It is, rather, that
Milton with superb poetic and dramatic skill has held before
his readers' eyes the memories of English politics, superimposing upon them the specter of Ottoman barbarism, with all its
terror and corruption, and has used these kindled memories to
illuminate the inner rottenness and the outward splendors of
the infernal kingdom in *Paradise Lost.*

The allusion to Satan as a sultan in Book 1, then, opens the way for these details in analysis of satanic tyranny: it does much more than this, however, structurally and morally, within the total context both of the initiating simile and of the whole poem. Linking the Egyptian pharaoh with the Turkish sultan is not a Miltonic invention but an elaboration of a tradition according to which historians and theologians in the Christian tradition had traced a providential pattern of recurrences that simplified and explained the rise and fall of civilizations. The Babylonian and the Egyptian captivities of the Jewish nation had an obvious unity, and Münster described Cairo as *"Babylon Aegypti"* and as *"sedes Sultanorum Aegyptorum"* ("the capitol of the Egyptian sultans").[16] Richard Knolles, in his authoritative *Generall Historie of the Turkes*, reported that Baghdad was known as "new Babylon"[17] and explained that the reason for the Turks' emergence into modern history was nothing less than "the hand of the Almightie . . . as scourges wherewith to punish the world." The Almighty would then ruin them, "the course of their appointed time once run."[18] Milton recognized this traditional interlocking between the images of Egypt, Babylon, and Turkey by an explicit parallelism within the structure of his simile:

> As when the potent rod
> Of Amram's son in Egypt's evil day
> Waved round the coast, up called a pitchy cloud
> Of locusts

(1.338–41)

> Till, as a signal given, the uplifted spear
> Of their great sultan waving to direct
> Their course, in even balance down they light.

(1.347–49)

The balance of these two parts of the total simile is dramatized by complementary figures (Moses and the sultan) wielding instruments of power, by verbal repetition, and by the inclusion of the word "balance," quietly drawing attention to the poise and symmetry of the images. Yet this word alone persuades the reader that the parallelism is in part spurious, the symmetry violated, for the idea of balance leads the Christian mind to the Book of Daniel, in which the judgment against Babylon is recorded: "TEKEL; Thou art weighed in the balances, and art found wanting" (5:27).[19] Milton's reader also thinks forward to the creating and judging God who sets out the balance of Libra in the heavens to inform Satan of his impending destruction (4.995–1015). Within the apparent symmetry, there is imbalance, and Milton's poetry mimes both the illogic and the ignorance of the inhabitants of hell. Although "Amram's son" appears to be syntactically in balance with "their great sultan," he is in fact opposed and unequal. The sultan's counterpart in the first portion of the simile is really Pharaoh, the victim of the locusts called up by Moses, the figure for God's son. The object of the first simile therefore parallels the subject of the next. The apparent balance is actually an opposition, yet Milton's provocation of the reader to elicit structural harmony from the simile persists: and the question of how to reconcile this feeling of dichotomy is not fully reconciled, even by the knowledge that at the end of time Christ (personified here by Moses) will sweep up pharaohs, sultans, Huns, Vandals, Goths, and all into identical punishment. Indeed, Moses' potent rod recalls for us the rod lifted to scourge the scourging Assyrian in Isaiah 10:5: "O Assyrian, the rod of mine anger, and the staff in their hand is mine indignation." Egyptian, Assyrian, Turk are identified and condemned.

The irritating qualities sometimes discerned within the simile have been criticized by one scholar, Christopher Grose, who attacks what he sees as an unnecessary duplication: "The irony of providential control is clear enough without the additional homologous detail, gratuitously and self-consciously added after the fact, 'the uplifted Spear / of *thir* great Sultan.'"[20] It is, however, a mistake mentally to italicize "thir" as if Milton had intended that the reader distinguish one fiendish sultan exercising power from another just one: a sultan is never just. The poet was insisting that Satan and Moses (typologically, then, Christ) represent opposite types of rule. By presenting an apparent but unreal parallel between Moses and the great sultan, Milton was also implying that the sultan, functioning as God's scourge, however involuntarily, would fulfil God's will as potently as Moses: he too is a rod for the nations. But when the nations have been scourged—in Knolles's words, "the course of [the] appointed time once run"—the sultan will be discarded, exterminated by God. The great difference between Milton's Pharaoh, plagued by locusts, and his victorious sultan is that Pharaoh's criminality was enacted and punished aeons ago, whereas the great sultan (the Great Turk, the Grand Seigneur) was in Milton's time still lording it in the east. The analogy to Pharaoh provides a motive for believing in his and Satan's defeat, though in our own day, frankly, we see little. This is signaled in the preceding narrative by the word *dread*, and dramatized by the poet's implicit comparison of Satan's armies to the locusts who did Pharaoh no good at all in the biblical account: they scourged him. A relationship based on fear, as Milton had everywhere emphasized in the prose works, is no relationship at all. Fear is next to hatred, hatred close to violence. The sultan's own people will betray him; Satan's own armies will forsake their allegiance. This prediction is fulfilled in Book 10, on Satan's return to Hell. The oriental imagery again predominates, and the gate he enters is deserted; the applause he expects turns to revulsion.[21]

The final phase of the simile is even more bizarre and allusive than those of Pharaoh and sultan. Bentley's quaint and delightful puzzlings over the frozen loins that generated the barbarians are well known and need not be dwelt on here,[22] but his contention in 1732 that *"Frozen Loins are improper for Populousness"*[23] is a memorable perception that sheds light for us both on the abnormal, monstrous character of Milton's Satan and on the image of barbarian government upon which his vision of the evil perversion of our history is based. In moving from Pharaoh to sultan and finally to the barbarian invasions of Europe, the poet tried to include all times and places, all experiences and civilizations under the tyranny of Satan, whose angelic followers are

> A multitude, like which the populous north
> Poured never from her frozen loins, to pass
> Rhene or the Danaw, when her barbarous sons
> Came like a deluge on the south, and spread
> Beneath Gibraltar to the Lybian sands.

> (1.351–55)

These people are also, by extension, his followers. They are unnamed and anonymous: there is no discernible leader, like a pharaoh or a sultan, though they are clearly organized upon the same principle. Bush and Grose both suppose that only one invasion of barbarians is signified (Bush, "The barbarian invasions of the Middle Ages"; Grose, the horde that "overcame Rome in human history"),[24] but this is not so. The wording—"Poured *never*"—denies this. Nomadic invaders passed south across the Danube throughout European history, and the passage, with its chilling feeling of the unnatural power of the ice-bound north to reproduce inconceivable numbers of aliens, implies an organic rather than an organizing power. There is no way to stem this pouring, wave after wave, of fertile barbarism.

Inclusiveness is implied by the identical direction taken by the invaders in each phase of the total simile. The locusts that ravaged Egypt are borne on the eastern wind; that is, they move from east to west. The sultans directed the Turkish invasions of Europe from behind the Caucasus westward, then down into Mediterranean lands and North Africa, so that the Turkish part of the image includes the direction of the first and predicts the third. The Huns, as any map of their progress shows,[25] swept west across Sarmatia to the Carpathians and the Danube, then dropped north to south. The Goths also moved from north to south to destroy the Roman Empire. The westward movement linking all three images is a reminder of the mortality that hell brings to earth: traditionally, the place of sunset symbolizes our death. The movement from north to south represents the overwhelming of civilization (bred homeopathically in southern brains quickened by the sun's vital warmth) by the coarse, unsunned natures of the barren north. Milton recognized the uninspiring nature of the northern climate in *Paradise Lost* (9.44–45), *Mansus* (27–29), and *Reason of Church Government* (Yale 1:814). Christopher Hill notes that the Royalists raised their standard in the north of England.[26] Tacitus had agreed that the cold and dark upper reaches of Europe were near to the very borders of what can rightly be described as human. Images of these barbarians were of extreme cold; of water in flood; of multitude; of ferocity.[27] These images recur in the fascinated historians of the Huns, Goths, Alans, and Suebi, and even that most phlegmatic of the historians of the fourth and fifth centuries, Ammianus Marcellinus, still dazzles the reader with the powerful brevity of his description: "The people of the Huns,

but little known to ancient records, dwelling beyond the Maeotic Sea near the ice-bound ocean, exceed every degree of savagery."[28] Here in Ammianus's haunting, fearful vision of the
north is a parallel to Milton's populous north with its teeming
but frozen loins. The geography of his Hell in Book 2 also has its
basis in barbarous reality:

> many a frozen, many a fiery alp,
> Rocks, caves, lakes, fens, bogs, dens, and shades of death,
> A universe of death, which God by curse
> Created evil, for evil only good,
> Where all life dies, death lives, and nature breeds,
> Perverse, all monstrous, all prodigious things.

(2.620–25)

In "many a frozen" alp, he brings the north to "many a fiery
alp," the south. It is as if the pharaohs and sultans of the torrid
southern deserts inimical to civilized life join with the Attilas
and Alarics of the freezing north, to drive humanity out into its
west. The person of Satan and the landscape of Hell reflect this
monstrous government.

Two further parallels within the poem emphasize and endorse this tendency. Each is buried within the allusive texture of
the poem, so as to suggest how deeply the images of autocratic,
barbarian invasions penetrate into the poem's moral and spiritual center. When Satan in Book 9 scours the globe for a hiding
place, he is described thus:

> sea he had searched and land
> From Eden over Pontus, and the pool
> Maeotis, up beyond the river Ob;
> Downward as far antartic; and in length
> West from Orontes to the ocean barred
> At Darien, thence to the land where flows
> Ganges and Indus: thus the orb he roamed
> With narrow search.

(9.76–83)

The protean nature of Satan is following its own affinity when it
coincides in its movements with the waters that pour around
the globe. He belongs not to firm land but to the liquid element
Milton associated with the barbarian deluges, both in his *History of Britain* with its floods, deluges, and inundations of for-

eign barbarians and in his characterization of the fallen angels
in terms of those shoals of subhuman beings who broke the
barriers of the Rhine and Danube (described by Claudian as
mighty kings, set to guard the limits of the civilized Roman
world).[29] They "Came like a deluge on the south." Milton here
identified Satan's researches into our world with the barbarian
inundations that had engulfed even the Mediterranean Sea, as
though a sea could drown a sea, and by the reference to the
Maeotic Sea (the source of the barbarian invasions) our attention is drawn to this purpose: we travel first on a north–south
circle of the globe and are then led westward. With the miming
of directions described in the simile in Book 1, the poem here
looks forward to the breaking out of the winds in Book 10, the
anarchic product of man's fall:

> now from the north
> Of Norumbega, and the Samoed shore
> Bursting their brazen dungeon, armed with ice
> And snow and hail and stormy gust and flaw,
> Boreas.

> (10.695–99)

Here, however, the north–south, east–west direction of the
satanic movement into the human world violates even itself: no
ruling principle of any sort is discoverable, as the north wind is
"With adverse blast" (701) assaulted by the south; east and west
winds tear into one another, thus beginning "Outrage from life-
less things" (707). This lawlessness is represented as a condition
of misery for mankind, because it is an external representation
of his inward strife. Only the exercise of temperance in soul and
community may allay it.

This outrage is, then, the final product of the signal given by
the great sultan of Hell "waving to direct / Their course" to his
multitudinous army that somehow, fluid and inchoate as it is,
manages to achieve the formation of "squadron and . . . band"
(1.356). On a military level, the Turkish archetypes offered
Milton material both for spectacle in his poem and for structural
expression of some of his major themes. The East stood in a
permanently aggressive posture toward Christendom: together
with the Egyptians, Babylonians, and Persians of antiquity,
these races confronted the West intending only outrage, and,

being pure autocracies, they could claim to speak and act with one mind in a way that the fragmented European world, split between Catholic and Protestant, nation and nation, party and party, could never do. Milton's *State Papers*, especially those written under Cromwell, are urgent with the need for Protestant unity against the Catholic threat "when our enemies seem to rage most bitterly and everywhere to conspire upon our ruin" and with the more general need to show a decent and unified face to "the great Turk the common foe of Christendom."[30] In Books 1 and 2 of *Paradise Lost*, Milton builds a powerful image of Hell as a barbarous military culture, unified both by communal hatred of goodness and the tight hand of autocratic domination; this Hell is architecturally splendid beyond the manner of "Babel, and the works of Memphian kings" (1.694), beyond "Babilon" and "great Alcairo" (1.717–18). Just as barbarians seem to pour from the womb of the north and the fallen angels "fill all the plain" like a great sea, so also in Book 2 (in another water image linked with barbarism),

> the gorgeous East with richest hand
> Showers on her kings barbaric pearl and gold.

(2.3–4)

The showering is like Zeus pouring himself down in gold upon Danaë—the act that begot Perseus and, thus, the Persians; see below in this chapter—also an expression of European hunger and awe at the fabulous riches that gave the autocracies of the Orient from ancient times the appearance of having the key to a source of wealth that was not laboriously excavated but flowed with a largesse incomprehensible to the west. The protean barbarians flood the west, and liquid gold showers upon the east: the moral meaning, for the poet, was the same.

The first two books of *Paradise Lost* glitter and burn with golden images. Mammon, head bent even in Heaven, in a rare comic touch, went round admiring "The riches of heaven's pavement, trodden gold" (1.682); the devils find "ribs of gold" (1.690), build roofs of "fretted gold" (1.717), and hang lights like stars or suns (1.728). The very names of Cairo, Memphis, India, Babylon, and most especially Ormus would have brightened in the mind of the reader with tempting, golden implications, allied with a recoiling horror at the infernal origins of such splendor. The golden imagery gathers throughout the poem: from the image of Satan as the gold-guarding griffin (2.943–47) of Scythia; to his treading upon the gold and jewels of the sun (3.595); to his building of a northern seat in Heaven "with pyramids and towers / From diamond quarries hewn, and rocks of gold" (5.758–59)—a seat that reforges the link between Egyptian tyranny, northern barbarism, and raw gold; and to that final, magnificent but dreadful vision of the despots of the world "Down to the golden Chersonese" (11.392) and the secret location of Ophir. Across the poem, then, recurs the lure of gold, linked with violence and despotism. It is gold as matter— raw and unsanctified, the object of greed and the excuse for lawlessness—that is perceived through Satan's eyes and aggregated by him. The other, spiritual gold, opposes him in Heaven, refined beyond his mind's capacity to know it. Milton drew this image from both historical and geographical writings, all of which record the barbarian love and possession of gold. In *The Persians* by Aeschylus (the only surviving Greek historical tragedy),[31] the "loved Persian earth" is for its inhabitants "Haven of ample wealth" (250–51), and this wealth is the truest value known to the Persians; Aeschylus also referred to "Babylon the golden" (55), with her ravening hordes opposing chaste, austere Greece. Jerome described the Hun invaders of Christendom as murderers of children who smiled in their innocence, "wild beasts" who "poured forth from the distant Sea of Azov" (Milton's Maeotis) toward Jerusalem, to satiate "their excessive greed for gold."[32] Herodian of Antioch showed the barbarians at the Danube border "by nature fond of money" and willing to pay any human price to get it.[33] In modern European times, gold lust inspired many expeditions of navigation with a view to discovering Ophir, which Purchas located in India: "from Bengala to Menan is the Peguan Chersoneseus, which perhaps is the true Chryse and Aurea," because of all the mines there (Milton's Chersonese). In travelogues like those of Purchas, the oriental despots are depicted as blazing with pearls, rubies, diamonds, emeralds, silver, and gold, and they are shown to be cruel beyond our most lurid imaginings, like the great Mogul "ill beloved of the greater part of his Subjects, who stand greatly in feare of him."[34] This is the "Ind" of *Paradise Lost,* Book 2:

> High on a throne of royal state, which far
> Outshone the wealth of Ormus and of Ind,
> Or where the gorgeous East with richest hand
> Showers on her kings barbaric pearl and gold,
> Satan exalted sat.

$$(2.1-5)$$

The wealth of India, hoarded by the great Mogul, was the material base from which he practiced grandiose atrocities. Ormus had been a byword for wealth, a great island-market dealing in spices, drugs, silk, brocade, and pearls, and Chew reports the common aphoristic couplet:

> If all the world were but a Ring
> Ormuz the Diamond should bring.[35]

While these images raise the reader of *Paradise Lost* into dazzled awe, as though the poet were leading our minds (as the travel writers had tried to do) to the very source and origin of the world's glory, he has also undermined these images not just occasionally but on every single occasion, either by tone of voice, by explicit comment, or by the subtle art of his allusion, which, forcing us to supply explanatory material out of our own experience and information, also extracts by positive coercion information that vitiates the splendor of the image. Robert R. Cawley, in *Milton and the Literature of Travel*, expresses bewilderment at the poet's failure to recognize in the allusion to Ormus that the "most famous Mart towne of all East India" (Hakluyt) should have "lapsed into obscurity following the Persian-British capture in 1622."[36] But this is the very point that Milton, with his thorough knowledge of history and his experience of foreign affairs, would have wished his reader to appreciate and be reassured by. I have suggested that in the image of Satan's throne our perspective soars upward, in phases, and we are awed by a grandeur that dwarfs the world of human kingship. But now, recognizing that Ormus, the "diamond of the ring of the world," is perished and empty, we feel a contrary impulse. Ormus, ransacked, goes into the past: it is consigned to time, like the pyramids of the pharaohs, those mere mausoleums. Babylon is shattered; the Huns outlived; and Mammon, the barbarian of Heaven, looking downward rather than concentrating on his direction, has fallen. It is this movement toward death within the images themselves that distances the contemplating mind from the extravagant glimmer of false oriental gold in Milton's Hell.

The only barbarian civilization that had not yet been consigned to time in this manner was Turkey. And surely it is to the proverbial Christian complaint that internal conflicts opened Christianity up to Turkish militarism that we owe the at once tender, grotesque, and wistful image of the concord of the devils in Book 2, when pastoral symbolism briefly irradiates the unyielding surface of Hell before a contrasting image of earth in the future—scarred by evil wars,

> the fields revive,
> The birds their notes renew, and bleating herds
> Attest their joy, that hill and valley rings.
> O shame to men! Devil with devil damned
> Firm concord holds, men only disagree
> Of creatures rational, though under hope
> Of heavenly grace: and God proclaiming peace,
> Yet live in hatred, enmity, and strife
> Among themselves, and levy cruel wars,
> Wasting the earth, each other to destroy:
> As if (which might induce us to accord)
> Man had not hellish foes enow besides,
> That day and night for his destruction wait.
>
> (2.493–505)

Here is one of those doors into the present day, explicitly opened by the poet, through which readers are required (not silently invited) to pass. As we do so, we encounter memories of an England desecrated by recent civil war, for the passage is so bitter in ascribing Golden Age qualities to Hell, a virtual paradise compared to our own "Wasting" of our own world, that it is scarcely possible to read it without remembering that "Sea of innocent blood" in which England had been weltering in the 1640s (*Eikonoklastes,* Yale 3:376). Yet the passage seems larger than this: it blames us all for the shame of discord, involving conflict of persons, parties, churches, and nations. The pathos of the Cromwellian call to Protestant Europe for peace against the "hellish foes" on the borders of our vulnerable community is evoked; united peace or resolute aggression against the Ottoman threat was the watchword of Milton's State Pa-

pers. The vigilance of the enemy, almost a kind of unholy omniscience, is implied in the final line of this verse paragraph,
describing enemies that "day and night for his destruction
wait": a quietude travestying God's and an unsleeping eye
looking into the Christian brain incapable of concord (again, a
parody of God's unsleeping eye) are attributed to the enemy.
Widespread in all forms of Renaissance literature was the warning that unless the Christian nations could agree, the absolute
unity of the Ottoman Empire would destroy them. The Turks
were models of unity; they were incarnate devils. Fulke Greville's poem *A Treatie of Warres,* mingling Calvinistic Protestantism and worldly cynicism, ends:

> Thus wave we *Christians* still betwixt two aires;
> Nor leave the world for God, nor God for it;
> While these Turkes climing up united staires,
> Above the Superstitions double wit,
> Leave us as to the Jewish *Bondage* heires,
> A Saboth rest for selfe-confusion fit:
>> *Since States will then leave warre, when men begin*
>> *For Gods sake to abhorre this world of sinne.* [37]

This is wholly commonplace. It is why Milton was for sending
off the Grand Duke of Russia to eliminate the Great Turk, with
the king of Sweden guaranteeing his security in his absence on
the "glorious expedition against the Turk." It is why he presented the hall of Pandemonium as:

> like a covered field, where champions bold
> Wont ride in armed, and at the soldan's chair
> Defied the best of paynim chivalry
> To mortal combat or career with lance.

> (1.763–66)

The sultan lounges to survey the game, for this is all that the
crusader's fight against the infidel (and the Christians' against
Satan) had been, and "champions bold" has a sardonic edge to
it. Europe has fought Islam as if it were practicing a romantic
war game, so that the Sultan may negligently get the pleasure of
the fight from his vantage point, watching and waiting. Earlier,
this same sarcasm was applied to "all who . . . baptized or
infidel / Jousted in Aspramont" (1.582–83), where Milton as-
signed the crusades to the level of romance, confounding "bap-

tized or infidel" into identity where opposition would be expected. "Paynim chivalry" and "Memphian chivalry" are infernal, and, he implied, the European fancy for romantic tilting with the Antichrist is a fitting image of man's incapacity to face with any degree of realism the autocratic and murderous designs of Satan upon the human race. Thus, in the pastoral image for Hell, with a springtime growth and innocence, Milton bitterly blamed modern man, in his own voice: "O shame to men!" By a strange, ironic transformation, the sultan's despotic rule over his servile people (and Satan's ascendancy over the infidel angels) becomes a perfect haven of tranquillity, worthy to have the supreme blessing of a pastoral image bestowed upon it; whereas modern Christians, with whom God has made his peace, cannot keep it with one another. In each case, attributes proper only to one group attach themselves ironically to the other. The Christians are "cruel" (2.501), a condition suitable only to barbarians; the sultan-Satan, all power and activity as he is, has only to "wait" (2.505) peaceably for the Christians to deliver themselves into his hands. The poem thus threatens its reader with scourging in the present day by the vigilant sultan, for all time by Satan; in the conversational "which might induce us to accord," Milton expressed a world-weary awareness that we never will achieve accord.

This must be a moment of recoil for the contemporary Christian reader of *Paradise Lost,* for the poem in reaching into the present day challenges, accuses, and menaces a fallen civilization. Nevertheless, such a reader, having the faith of Isaiah that the scourge of God, having enacted vengeance, will itself be scourged, finds throughout the poem—and increasingly as the narrative develops—evidence that Satan in his sultan manifestation shall go the way of Babel and Egypt. By the mid-seventeenth century, Turkey had suffered several catastrophes, the most notable victories having been won by the popular Tamburlaine, others by the Persians and Venetians. Allusion to eastern tyrannies was therefore especially appropriate to a poet who wished to emphasize the justice of God as enacting punishment in the shape of the sin that occasioned it. In the *Commonplace Book,* Milton noted as a curiosity and as an exemplum the capture of the caliph of Baldac by the baptized emperor of the Tartars who, as fitting punishment for his avarice, imprisoned the caliph in a tower full of his own treasures and "starved him to death by saying that it would be fitting that he should live by his treasure, and 'feed upon it without getting any other food'" (Yale 1:366). Likewise, in the tenth book of *Paradise Lost*, Satan, who has tempted man in serpent form, is punished by God through the involuntary assumption of a serpent form: under this traditional and elementary system of justice, one's choice becomes one's bane, and evil behavior becomes personal misery. The caliph in his tower, who has fed his eyes upon gold in a life long orgy, dies famishing in his treasure house. On the same principle, Satan as sultan may be discerned in *Paradise Lost* as succumbing to a Turkish punishment enacted in the course of the poem and completed in Book 10.

The symbol of the Turkish nation is a crescent—the crescent moon—derived from the battle formation that characterized its armies, which, arraying in two flanks, closed in on their victims in a pincer movement. Although it is true that, as Fowler says, such battle formation was "classic in warfare" (4.978n), it was so closely associated with the Turkish tradition as to be emblematic. There are three major uses of the Turkish crescent in *Paradise Lost*, each reflecting indirectly or directly upon the satanic kingship. The first is a travesty usage at the end of Book 4, in which Satan, having been detected by Gabriel and his colleagues imparting false dreams to Eve, hurls defiance at the spies of "heaven's king" and is met with this response:

> While thus he spake, the angelic squadrons bright
> Turned fiery red, sharpening in mooned horns
> Their phalanx, and began to hem him round
> With posted spears, as thick as when a field
> Of Ceres ripe for harvest waving bends
> Her bearded grove of ears, which way the wind
> Sways them.

> (4.977–83)

While it may be true, as Fowler claims, that the choleric angels become red to express the facts that they are cherubim and that they are angry, the much more obvious connotation for the image of a *red* crescent formation is that this is the color of the Turkish crescent. The lunar implications, made in the reference to the "mooned horns" of the phalanx, echo the lunar deities like Astoreth into whose shapes and names the fallen angels will metamorphose in human history:

> Astoreth, whom the Phoenicians called
> Astarte, queen of heaven, with crescent horns.

(1.438–39)

The crescent horns of the queen of the night and her intemperate worshipers create a verbal resonance with the mooned horns of the angelic discoverers, for this too is nighttime, and the feminine associations of the allusion to Ceres in the simile and to Eve, her bad dream violating her sleeping innocence, look back to the lyrically beautiful Astarte, served by virgins, but a sham.

However, if God's angels take the form of the Turkish red crescent, with its power and infidelity, there is an obvious moral confusion implied. Can God turn Turk? The answer must be that he can (and this must be threatening to Satan, who responds in a grotesque dilation of size) but that he will not. It is a static moment. The angels form themselves into this potentially lethal military structure, the same formation that in Asian history massacred hosts both of Christians and of fellow infidels, but they refrain from action. There is no military encounter; to suspend their movement, God "Hung forth in heaven his golden scales" (4.997), predicting final judgment. It is an image of supreme irony, which calls up in the reader's mind Satan's posture toward his armies in Book 1, as "their great sultan waving to direct / Their course" (1.348–49), confident in his autocracy; it is now an image of Satan proud but solitary, confronted by enemies assuming an aggressive parody of his own traditions. In this brief vision the reader is aware of a movement in the narrative toward the fundamental recoil of Satan's policies and attitudes against himself: there is no self-image which his mind is able to breed that God cannot travesty and include under the heading of retributive justice. Satan, the Great Turk, here becomes the victim of a Turkish circle closing round him like a trap. It is an image of his growing forfeiture of power and freedom, directing the reader's eye onward, to the much more explicit but equally complex and dextrous use of the same type of allusion in Book 10.

Satan loose in the cosmos has fulfilled, or given himself credit for fulfilling, the sultan's role as empire builder, there being a sacred injunction in Islam to convert the world. In causing man's fall, he is introducing into the human race a degeneracy that works to consolidate his empire, for it was a commonplace upon which Milton in his prose works had frequently fallen back that despotism begets servitude and servitude despotism, reciprocally.[38] Once started, it is a circular process, gathering momentum and repeated through generations, in which barbarism is passed back and forth from despot to servile people who equally cooperate to establish and preserve tyranny. Satan's aim in establishing himself among mankind is to begin this reciprocity between barbaric leader and barbarous people, which, once initiated, can be trusted to continue almost of its own accord in a kind of perpetual motion, since the polluted minds of a quelled nation automatically renew their own servitude. During the Renaissance, the byword for this process was the condition of the modern Greeks under the tyranny of the Turks. As Bishop King put it, they were

> Once the Worlde's Lord, now the beslaved Greek:
> Made by a Turkish Yoake, and Fortune's hate
> In Language, as in Mind, degenerate.[39]

Milton alluded to this ugly reciprocity in *Eikonoklastes*, describing Charles I (and by implication identifying him as a sultan over the English) as milking Parliament of more money "then would have bought the *Turk* out of *Morea*, and set free all the Greeks"—an impossible sum (Yale 3:448). But the condition inevitably, in Milton's theory, moves toward breakdown and divine judgment. Politically, this optimism is most powerfully expressed in the regicide literature. Speaking in *The Tenure of Kings and Magistrates* of civil glory, he commented that it "heretofore, in the persuance of fame and forren dominion, spent it self vain-gloriously abroad; but henceforth may learn a better fortitude, to dare execute highest Justice on them that shall by force of Armes endeavour the oppressing and bereaving of Religion and thir liberty at home: that no unbridl'd Potentate or Tyrant, but to his sorrow for the future, may presume such high and irresponsible licence over mankinde, to havock and turn upside-down whole Kingdoms of men, as though they were no more in respect of his perverse will then a Nation of Pismires" (Yale 3:238). Civil glory is here defined not as the old vanity of imperialism but as the natural movement of human societies in the direction of inner liberty, involving the inevitable removal of "unbridl'd Potentate[s]." Such optimism, if it could not be retained after the Restoration in the political world, might yet be incorporated into a poem like *Paradise Lost;* in the scourging of the unbridled potentate whose empire is the human soul; in the symbolic unshackling of "Greek" hearts, minds, and language from the Turkish dominion.

This metaphorical redemption of Europe from Asia, Christendom from infidel, and Greek from Oriental is not achieved but predicted in Book 10 of *Paradise Lost,* in which Satan, having been able to "havock and turn upside-down whole Kingdoms of men," returns victoriously to Hell. Oriental symbolism, especially in the epic similes but also in the narrative, recurs massively here, as Satan approaches and reenters Hell and attempts to celebrate triumph over his new world. In Book 2, the image of Turkish concord had expressed the genuine threat Satan presents to humanity, even after the Fall and the saving crucifixion; in Book 4, God's justice impersonates the Turkish instrument of the crescent, turning momentarily like a retributive scythe upon Satan; in Book 10, new images of Persian, Turkish, Russian, and Tartar armies prelude the destruction of Satan as God's scourge, and a new emphasis in the poetry begins to reveal the underlying hatred of Satan's creatures to himself, compromising their obedience to him. The barbarian world of evil is now shown as having its own internal dissensions, and the multitudes that had massed in Book 1 under sole command of Satan are momentarily represented (in that subtle, penetrating irony that characterizes Milton's epic similes) as harboring essential shiftiness and antagonism to their commander. The oriental theme is announced during Milton's description of the building by Sin and Death of the bridge between Hell and Earth, down which the souls of the lost might travel and up which demonic adventurers shall pass. It is linked again with the image of the icy north, which, unnaturally fertile as Milton had demonstrated in Book 1, is inimical to human, or at least to humane, life and, driving against the south, is the source of the "Outrage" that Milton has presented as the lawless meeting of extremes of barbarism in the conjunction of barbarous north with barbarous south. In Book 10, where all this symbolism culminates and is rounded off in connection with Satan, an image of northern violence precedes one of southern violence within a pair of epic similes elucidating the building of the infernal bridge, and this pattern is mimed in the double epic simile that defines Satan's reentry into Hell (10.431– 36).

The first pair of similes involves Russia and Persia, north and south; they are linked by Death. With his unholy but energetic mother, let loose by the fall of man to join Earth and Hell, Death flies out toward his human prey:

> what they met
> Solid or slimy, as in raging sea
> Tossed up and down, together crowded drove
> From each side shoaling towards the mouth of hell.
> As when two polar winds blowing adverse
> Upon the Cronian sea, together drive
> Mountains of ice, that stop the imagined way
> Beyond Petsora eastward, to the rich
> Cathaian coast.

(10.285–93)

The sea of chaos raging predicts the violence of the outrage that will curse the human condition with its fall (10.659–707) and will characterize it throughout history. Again, Sin and Death as winds blowing "adverse" look forward to the uncreative conjunction of north and south winds "With adverse blast" (701) in that same passage. This parallel turns Paradise into a poignant terrestrial Chaos, ruled by tyrannical disorder. Politically, it is an image of that formless but vicious and highly effective government practiced by barbarians, and the vivid verb *shoaling*, used to describe the chaotic matter from which Sin and Death will create, with its fluidity and suggestion of innumerable masses, returns the reader's mind to the pouring mass of barbarians vigorously coercing one another downward from the north. The reference to the "imagined way" to Cathay across Russia is one of the most sorrowful of all the touches of realism with which Milton's account of the human species is increasingly darkened. He had contemplated the places mentioned here in the writing of his *Brief History of Moscovia*, in all the fascination of their strangeness: "The River *Pechora*," for example, "holding his course through *Siberia,* how far, the Russians thereabouts know not, runneth into the sea at 72. mouths, full of Ice: abounding with Swans."[40] Alongside his account of this white river with its white birds, Milton described the terrible sterility and cold of the country, as well as the despotic rule of the emperors, with their absolute power of life, death, and property (336–37). The Pechora, he noted, was at that time chiefly uncharted, and though the estuaries were counted and documented (seventy-two), its inner reaches were unknown. All that was certain was the ice. When the river reappears in *Paradise Lost,* the ice is still its main feature, though swollen now into "Mountains," and the river is not simply full as in the prose account, but stopped. All that European yearning for the northeastern passages to the riches of Cathay is there, but Milton showed it in the poem as forever destined to famish in the freezing, icebound experience of the survivors of the Fall. His *Moscovia* described Cathay with sober admiration as an imperial city "of White-stone four-square . . . corner'd with four White Towers, very high and great, and others very fair along the Wall, white intermingl'd with blew" (347–48), and in the middle stood a "sumptuous palace, the top whereof is overlaid with Gold" (348). A dazzling image emerges, the white river of Petzora, white birds, snowbound earth, and finally the symmetries of this white palace of the Cathaian khan, a fabulous account made suggestive by the very austerity of the telling. But it was the degrading greed for wealth, as the *Moscovia* tells us, that made the English expeditions into this land rather less than heroic (363), a fact indicated in the poem by the emphatic positioning of the equivocal adjective *rich* at the end of the line, stretching toward the "Cathaian coast" that can never now be reached. Milton in *Moscovia* rehearsed the history of the Russian autocracy in its icebound country, covered in "Orient Pearls and Stones" (354) amid an ignorant, starving, and frequently murderous people. The imagined way to the splendors of Cathay would be through this unyielding country, and besides, the poem suggests at this point, there is now no eastward for the human race since the accomplishment of the Fall, only a westward passage to the setting of the sun. The image of extreme cold and of violent tyranny, allegorized in Death, is also one of obstruction. In this arctic image, Milton showed the blocking of human hopes at the very origin of our enterprise.

This cold empire of the north is as if joined by means of Death's "petrific mace" to the southern empire of the Persians, so that the movement between similes is a downward one, structured like the bridge itself, "Smooth, easy, inoffensive down to hell" (10.305).

> So, if great things to small may be compared,
> Xerxes, the liberty of Greece to yoke,
> From Susa his Memnonian palace high
> Came to the sea, and over Hellespont
> Bridging his way, Europe with Asia joined,
> And scourged with many a stroke the indignant waves.
> Now had they brought the work by wondrous art
> Pontifical.
>
> (10.306–13)

Myth had it that Xerxes, the formidable son of the Asiatic tyrant Darius, was descended from Perseus (therefore etymologically *Persian*), the son of Danaë, whom Zeus impregnated by the unusual resort of appearing in a shower of gold. Aeschylus alluded to the Persians as a race "sown in gold" in his play recounting the battles of Salamis and Plataea to which Milton here referred his reader (*The Persians*, line 79). Xerxes' capital at Susa was a gold-encrusted marvel of the ancient world, the "palace high" of his pride: we are looking backward here to the demonic construction of Pandemonium in Book 1 and to the triumphal reentry that is to come. Unfortunately, Xerxes, whose intention Milton recorded but whose failure to fulfil it he left to the reader's memory, reentered Susa in a very sorry state, having violated the sacred injunction not to fight at sea; lost the battles and his armies to "masterless" Greeks (ibid., line 242); alienated his people; been blamed by his mother; and mocked by the aroused ghost of his conquering father, Darius:

> From east to west the Asian race
> No more will own our Persian sway,
> Nor on the king's compulsion pay
> Tribute, nor bow to earth their face
> In homage; for the kingly power
> Is lost and vanished from this hour.

Now fear no more shall bridle speech;
Uncurbed, the common tongue shall prate
Of freedom.

(Ibid., lines 583–91)

Here the Chorus laments the fact that the free people of Greece repulsed and decimated the armies and the technology of the Persian king; later, his father bitterly satirizes Xerxes' clever architecture by saying that not only is it ill-advised to build upon a foundation of water but to "turn sea into land" violates both nature and sanctity (ibid., 748–53). Xerxes is a vain man and his craft a sacrilege. Milton in his adaptation of the story elegantly refrained from saying any of this, but it is there in the scornful tone of voice in which he described the conception of yoking "the liberty of Greece," the farce implied by the picture of a man dwarfed by the ocean but scourging it with all his might.

It is here that the oriental theme may be seen turning round upon Satan. If the Cathay allusion seems to prove us impotent either to locate or to fulfil our highest hopes, the Xerxes analogy demonstrates the equal impotence of Death to overcome spiritual liberty, even after the Fall. Only Christ can walk on water. Milton's reference to the story of Xerxes scourging the waves (his first bridge having collapsed) also reminds the reader of Satan's role as God's scourge, who must himself shortly receive his just penalty. The paired similes catch us in a double emotion: of deep regret at our simple, vulnerable ancestors, "the hapless pair" (10.342) undergoing judgment and open now to the frozen-hearted malignity of Satan, Sin, and Death; of hope stirring beneath all this horror, born in suspicions that Milton sowed in the superimposed oriental narratives, that somehow Satan's Asia cannot ever fully destroy our Europe, for the two cannot be joined as Xerxes imagined. Only faith can move mountains.

The fact that everybody knew, and Milton had noted, that in the modern day, the language, customs, and personality of Greece had decayed subject to the Turkish variant on the Persian model, may sadden and perplex the reader who is caught up in this hopefulness. Xerxes, who did not accomplish the unrealistic aim of yoking Greek liberty, was succeeded historically by the Ottomans, who under Sultan Orcan in the four-

teenth century got their first foothold in Europe by capturing
and keeping Greece. Yet by this time, the Persians had turned
round upon the Turks, and during the Renaissance, Europeans
were gratified to notice that the very structure of the Turkish
state was a kind of self-collapsing mechanism, in which autocratic sons of efficient emperors might prove mentally defective
or voluptuaries—like the sixteenth-century Amurat III—or the
powerful janissary units (the root of military dictatorship, like
the Praetorian guard of the Caesars) might mutiny against their
leaders.[41] Rebels might arise like Timur; the Persians might dis-
tract that frightful vigilance of the Ottoman eye upon his European victim, or, in the seventeenth century (as Milton was to
record in his *Letters Patent*), European generals like Jan Sobietski might prove as effective as the Turks in skill, expertise,
and prowess.

In Book 1, the Turkish satanic empire had presented an image
of fearful concord at variance with the distraught and factitious
spirit of the Christian world. In Book 10, the chaos at the heart
of all Asiatic regimes is delicately revealed in a complex of military images. Satan, having completed his charming reunion
with Sin and Death, returns to Hell, to find nobody there to
greet him, the fiends appointed to guard the gates of Hell having all absconded in different directions:

> The other way Satan went down
> The causey to hell gate; on either side
> Disparted chaos over built exclaimed,
> And with rebounding surge the bars assailed,
> That scorned his indignation: through the gate,
> Wide open and unguarded, Satan passed,
> And all about found desolate; for those
> Appointed to sit there, had left their charge,
> Flown to the upper world; the rest were all
> Far to the inland retired.

(10.414–23)

The "indignation" attributed to Chaos at the structure erected
over it in contradiction of its own nature looks back to the "indignant waves" that so resented Xerxes' scourging of them, his
encounter with which preluded his destruction. Here is revealed the chaos that is Satan's native element, spiritually: it

resides like an inhering nemesis within his mode of government and is emphasized by the absence of guards at the gate of his empire. When the Sultan's back is turned, the janissaries cannot be trusted to keep their place. The concord that in Book 2 was envied among the evil spirits was significantly described as prevailing only within Pandemonium itself: outside, the innumerable legions were ruled by dread, untrustworthy in an army tempted to doze or stray in the absence of its leader's vigilance. Milton here demonstrated the fact that true concord can only be an attribute of liberty. The aristocracy of Hell, however, has preserved its unity:

> the grand
> In council sat, solicitous what chance
> Might intercept their emperor sent, so he
> Departing gave command, and they observed.
>
> (10.427–30)

The nature of this council, which should rather be assimilated to a royalist image than to a Parliamentarian or Cromwellian council of state, is explained by Milton's later allusion to it as a "dark divan" (10.457), the Turkish term for the privy council of the Porte, presided over either by the sultan himself or in his absence by the grand vizier.[42] The glancing allusion directs our attention to the absence of any democratic structure for intercourse under the dominion of Hell and asks us to assume that the vizier mind of Beelzebub controls and directs everything in his master's absence. Milton did not say so directly, because he had no need: *divan,* a word with corrupt associations, says it for him. It is dark because it reflects a consultation of evil minds communing in secrecy and craft, apart from the people and shadowed by the vizier and sultan. Because the word also has the extended meaning of a "hall of justice,"[43] there is implied play on the idea of equity and balance, and we may think of the scales hung in the night sky by a judging God at the end of Book 4, at sight of which Satan fled in a hectic panic of foreknowledge. We are aware that there is to be a judgment enacted in this great golden hall of injustice.

These orientalisms are focused, however, in the double pair of allusions—to Tartars and Russians, Persians and Turks—that informs the simile elucidating Satan's reentry into Hell:

As when the Tartar from his Russian foe
By Astracan over the snowy plains
Retires, or Bactrian sophy from the horns
Of Turkish crescent, leaves all waste beyond
The realm of Aladule, in his retreat
To Tauris or Casbeen. So these the late
Heaven-banished host, left desert utmost hell
Many a dark league.

(10.431–38)

This image is far more difficult in application than it appears on the surface, because a reader may not at first know to whom the terms of reference logically apply. It is so artful, indeed, that most critics do not attempt to trace point-by-point analogies, and so, for instance, Cawley, having traced in Spenser, Phineas Fletcher, and Milton's *Moscovia* the tradition attaching to the Tartars whose constant invasions of Russia were distinguished by their habitual trick of pretending to run away, only to turn in their tracks to ambush the enemy, only notes that this shows satanic deceptiveness.[44] It is true that the primary implication of the simile is one of destruction, linked with duplicity and violent extremes of temperature and behavior. The white wasteland of the snowy plains of Astracan recalls the white unreachable towers of Cathay, the icy river that cuts us off from the dream of fulfillment. But Milton's similes may almost invariably be elucidated more specifically than this. Milton has taken two pairs of immemorial enemies, both sides barbarians and continuously at odds with one another, morally indistinguishable from one another but implacably opposed. The Tartars had once made Russia tributary (*Moscovia*, 348); under Juan Vasiliwich "the *Tartars* of *Cazan* and *Astracan*" were vanquished, but the Crimean Tartars, being called in by the dissatisfied nobility, "burnt *Mosco* to the ground" (ibid., 353). And so the ebb and flow of pointless struggle between barbarous neighbors went on over the borders of their homelands, with each side using similar, and somewhat rudimentary, techniques of warfare: for Milton in the *Moscovia* reported that the Russians, too, were unwilling to fight save "by stealth or ambush" (338). If the fallen angels in their withdrawal from hell gates are held to be the Tartars, then the Russian foe who is tricked by them as they battle over territory can only be Satan. The next part of the simile is parallel. If the Persian sophy's (shah's) flight represents the retreat of the fallen angels, then the Turkish crescent must represent the advance of Satan into Hell. But the meanings of each retreat are in apparent conflict. The fallen angels as Tartars are imagined as preparing to defeat Satan. They hate him and will ambush him. But Satan as the Turk will defeat the fallen angels as Persians. He hates them and is inimical to them. His victory, however, will be hollow, for the purchased land has been laid waste and ruined. Milton has raised his readers to a dizzying perspective, high above the earth, whence we can survey two giant conflicts of barbarians, one in pursuit of the other. He has lifted the imagination to such a soaring height that it can view the great iced plains of Russia and the formation of thousands of men, whom we see not as individuals congregated but simply as a moving structure covering vast distances, "the horns / Of Turkish crescent." Monolithic cultures of the eastern world are seen in guileful conflict, whole nations aroused against one another. But the shock implicit in the simile lies in the fact that these mighty forces represent the relationship between a leader and his own creatures. As we are shown the oriental world cracking wide open and in its true state of discord, we see also how Milton has presented an unexpected but essential repugnance between Satan, the leader who pursues his own troops murderously, and his subjects, who elude him with a view to ambush. The poem uncovers an unconscious state of mind of a community under autocracy and predicts what in the ensuing scenes will occur: the anti-triumph, in which Satan and the fallen angels mutually defeat one another. Satan is hissed, the fallen angels diminished.

In this oriental dissension, according to Milton, our potential peace and security lie. The infidel Persians, through timely irruptions against the Ottoman Empire during medieval and Renaissance times, were indirectly protecting Christendom and scourging the infidel scourge. The unfaithful inhabitants of Hell are unfaithful also to one another. The poet, who studied Turkish affairs on behalf of the Commonwealth, in this final explicit image of the Turkish crescent in *Paradise Lost,* scoured it clean of any true danger to the soul capable of the "paradise within," for Turkish despotism is revealed here as a self-punishing engine, scourging the world only in the measure that God allows to Sin and Death, "My hell-hounds, to lick up the draff and filth" of human sin (10.630). The man-eating Massagetae of Herodotus, the blood-drinking Huns, the child-slaughtering Turks of Knolles all contribute to the image of Death, but just as Knolles had shown God using the military power of the East as a providential instrument of cleansing, so Milton's God uses Death as a purifier, until, his horrible activities complete, the cosmic barbarism may be itself eaten up by the "ravenous jaws" of Hell (10.637), barbarian consuming barbarian, reciprocally sealing those jaws.

Finally, in Book 11, Milton provided for us, and Michael for Adam, a vista of all the tyrannies of earth "and their glory" (11.384), a phrase full of irony and also of pain to the reader who has followed the barbarian images through the poem in their relation to Satan. Adam's humbled eyes penetrate all time and all space:

> from the destined walls
> Of Cambalu, seat of Cathaian khan
> And Samarchand by Oxus, Temir's throne,
> To Paquin of Sinaean kings, and thence
> To Agra and Lahore of great mogul
> Down to the golden Chersonese, or where
> The Persian in Ecbatan sat, or since
> In Hispahan, or where the Russian czar
> In Mosco, or the sultan in Bizance,
> Turchestan-born.

(11.387–96)

Milton need say nothing of the stain of blood that taints each empire, for nearly all have been glimpsed in the poem, in vile and intimate association with Satan. The reader of the catalog soon comes to an end. It is as if the verse scourges its own material by consigning it so cursorily to time. Like the digested travelogues from which the account was taken, there is no time to pause over details and reimagine the fabulous empires that are listed. Moments of astonishing beauty—"the golden Chersonese"—are fitful and seem caught in the very act of passing away. Each empire vanishes within a line, and there is a clear impression of the evanescence of worldly glory in the perspective of all time and space. In notes to 11.388–411, Fowler has shown how carefully structured the catalog is, centralizing the true "Ophirian gold" of the spirit mysteriously within each group of empires. More simply, each empire appears as a trap for its emperor—"The Persian *in* Ecbatan . . . / *In* Hispahan . . . the Russian czar / *In* Mosco, or the sultan *in* Bizance" (11.393–95, italics mine)—each is enclosed in his dwelling and dwarfed by the vastness of the panorama. The sultan assumes only momentary significance, static within his historical place as Michael's story flies over the surface of human history toward the final stasis, the reign of the King of kings. He looks almost harmless.

A last echo of the crescent image is a remote whisper in Book 11, tender and wistful in its memory of a physical paradise now fully lost to humanity. Michael prophesies that at the Great Flood the ocean will:

> usurp
> Beyond all bounds, till inundation rise
> Above the highest hills: then shall this mount
> Of Paradise by might of waves be moved
> Out of his place, pushed by the horned flood,
> With all his verdure spoiled, and trees adrift
> Down the great river to the opening gulf,
> And there take root an island salt and bare,
> The haunt of seals and orcs, and sea-mews' clang.

(11.827–35)

The barbarians are evoked by the image of inundation, the flood a punishment on human sins; that proud autocracy invariably associated with barbarism is also imaged in Milton's choice of the verb *usurp* to describe the covering of the landmasses by the sea. An image of gross violence is implied as Paradise is literally uprooted and carried down the Euphrates out to sea, but the poetry is simple, austere, reconciled. Paradise is not wrenched but "pulled," and it passively submits to the force of the sea, its motion represented in an almost wholly monosyllabic poetry. Transplanted, it is "salt and bare," unpopulated save by animals, and with no human voices (not barbarous even), the only sound the gulls' crying. It is an image that carries to the reader a sensation of deep but not intolerable loneliness, strangely accompanied by relief, as if a great cleansing had taken place. The site of the island scoured and treeless is the Persian gulf. The sea that was the resting place of this pure, terrible island is "the horned flood," the crescent.[45]

3

Imperial Caesar

Infamy and impiety characterize the Roman emperors treated by Milton in his *Defence of the English People*. The emperors appear there so frequently and in such numbers, accompanied by the most violent abuse, that the tract might almost be subtitled *A Defence of the Roman People*. This body of subject matter, wished on the regicide apologist by his opponent Claudius Salmasius, was entered into by the future poet of *Paradise Lost* with the greatest vigor, loaded with argument that everywhere declares the author's deep knowledge of Roman history and literature, as well as his conviction of its pertinence to the crisis of the English Parliament (figured by the Senate) under Stuart autocracy (imperial Caesar in his many diabolical personifications). The identification of seventeenth-century English events with first-century Roman ones, having its roots in the cyclical theory of history, shows the wheel of history revolving so that human experience duplicates the past exactly, until a nation's revolution against corrupt leadership becomes obligatory. Milton's characterization of the caesars is accompanied by the vengeance ethic that claims not the subject's right of rebellion but his duty to exterminate the caesar of the day. A subject is a criminal if he fails to do so. Milton penetrated with obvious relish into the unfortunate Roman people's miseries under imperial despotism: the breadth and exactitude of his classical scholarship, allied with the delightfully easy task of blackening the Stuarts by odious comparison, and the well-documented but well-nigh incredible bestialities practiced by Tiberius, Caligula, Nero, and Domitian, give these passages of the *Defence*, for all their clotted allusions, a violent momentum. Each exemplum of evil in the state hurries inexorably to an identical conclusion: criminality is only purged by the blood of the criminal. The prose carries a ritualistic power. Its incantation is a vehicle for the just violence that Caesar merited.

The earlier references to Caesar, in which this cry for vengeance originates, have a contrasting serenity, bespeaking

Milton's humanistic and Protestant dedication to the idea of man's liberty and dignity. Alluding to the problem of Paul's injunction to civil obedience in Romans 13, Milton says calmly:

> Our freedom belongs not to Caesar, but it is rather a gift from God himself given us at birth, and to surrender it to any Caesar, when we did not receive it of him, would be an act of shame most unworthy of man's origin. If any person should gaze upon a man's face and features and inquire whose likeness was found there, would it not be easy for anyone to reply, the likeness of God? Since therefore we are God's own, and indeed his children, we are for this reason his property alone, and accordingly cannot without wickedness and extreme sacrilege deliver ourselves as slaves to Caesar, that is to a man, and a man who is unjust, unrighteous, and a tyrant. (Yale 4, pt. 1: 376–77)

Milton here uses *caesar* as a generic term for the kings of this world, a king whose face on the coin identifies him with worldly trade rather than with spiritual commerce. He presents the antagonism between caesar and the freeborn soul of man as an archetypal confrontation. The prose is beautifully poised and assured, in setting the certainty that we belong to God, our faces still reflecting our divine origins, against the impossibility of our degenerating into the belongings of a caesar. This elemental antagonism is just that represented in *Paradise Lost* between Adam "with native honour clad" (4.289) and the design of Satan to turn this Godlike person into property of his in the service of "Honour and empire" (4.390), where honor is seen as worldly glory in the territorial expansion of autocratic power. The caesar of the regicide literature is a smaller, lethal image of the original enemy of human liberty: it is this identification that gives the first *Defence* so much of its rhetorical force.

From this deep persuasion of individual Christian liberty, Milton derived authority for his violently retributive account of the punishment of the emperors and of their Stuart successors. Chapter 5 is awash with bloodshed in retribution for the unnatural cruelties of the caesars, and it is as if the pen of the republican regicide cooperated in reenacting this bloodshed. Regicide is presented not only as an obligation but also as an act of piety and a positive joy, both to man and to God:

> The words of the tragedian Seneca may apply to Romans as well as Greeks:

> Jove on his altar can receive no sacrifice
> Of higher worth, or richer, than an unjust king.

For if you take these as the words of Hercules, in whose mouth they are placed, they show the judgment of the greatest Greek of his time; if you take them as the words of the poet who lived in Nero's age— and it is the custom of poets to place their own opinions in the mouths of their great characters—he indicates what he himself and all good men even in Nero's time thought should be done with tyrants; how righteous, how pleasing to the gods they held tyrannicide to be. Thus the best Romans did what they could to kill Domitian. (Yale 4, pt. 1:446)

Here we are offered a justification for attributing to Milton himself the sentiments expressed by the Divinity and Abdiel in *Paradise Lost* (since poets, especially under times of censorship, use central characters to deliver their own opinions) as well as an awareness of how historical events and personages may be incorporated into mythical literature (Hercules is a Greek Seneca, and Seneca a literary artist who was also a participant in history, advising and resisting Nero's tyranny until his exile). Greece and Rome are one, superimposing their patterns in the layers of history; England and Rome are one. Having studied Suetonius, Milton would also have known that Nero himself acted the part of Hercules in *Hercules Furens*,[1] so that Roman art and Roman history literally interacted, until the tyrant Nero's assassination brought him both just retribution and a kind of poetic justice. Seneca and Nero also feature in a play of doubtful attribution of this period, *Octavia,* in which Nero's incarnate malice, fear, lust, incest, taste for massacring Christians in the arena, and impious aspiration to godhead are described, and his punishment predicted:

> he will pay with his own poisoned life
> The forfeit of his crimes; the day when he,
> Ruined, abandoned, naked to the world,
> Will bow his neck beneath his enemy's sword.[2]

For Milton, the analogy with Charles I of late unlamented memory was so obvious that he expressed himself amazed that Salmasius failed to recognize it. "'Nero,' you say, 'killed his own mother' with a sword; Charles used poison to kill his father and his king! . . . Nero killed many thousand Christians,

Charles many more" (Yale 4, pt. 1:451). Here the regicide has extended the analogy, unsubtly but cunningly, to make his portrait of Charles into a superlative image of Nero, exhuming the old scandal about Charles conniving with Buckingham to murder James I and insinuating that Charles massacred his Christian subjects for reasons of a perverted sensual appetite like Nero's—making game of them—but also indicating that in putting an end to many more than had satisfied even Nero, Charles transcended the model of human tyranny so as to achieve a superhuman wickedness. In outstripping Nero, Charles drew level with Lucifer himself: "Thus the fiend is termed prince of this world," and at times "the very form of government itself, if it be unsound, or those in authority are both human and fiendish" (ibid., 384). Milton has here fabricated a monster composed of a threefold mating, of Satan, Nero, and Charles: this hybrid fiction overshadows the pages of the regicide literature, gorgonizing the reader with its violent, incongruous, and demonic appearance. From time to time it is shown exploding and disintegrating from the degree of poison in the compound: Nero the butcher is butchered; Charles the tyrant is executed; Satan the usurper is subjected to the judgment of Revelation. The nature of each, his career, and his providential ending are used to define the rest of the unholy trinity, and Milton was fortunate in the frame of reference that Salmasius bequeathed him, for it enabled him to demonstrate a favorite theme, that—in the end—vicious kingship begot, under the Providential arrangements of God, its own unpleasant reward. Most of the evil Roman emperors had come to a suicidal, inglorious, bloody, or otherwise disagreeable end.[3]

This potent image of evil was transferred by Milton from the political works to *Paradise Lost*, in which he allowed it to contribute to his characterization of Satan; to the identification of Satan's relation to "his" creatures, both the fallen angels and humanity, by attributing to him an *Imperium* based on conquest and governed from Hell; to the process according to which Satan achieves power (subversion of an apparent democracy and trial by ordeal in the conquest of our world); and to the mode by which in Book 10 Satan attempts to celebrate and institutionalize an autocratic power—the triumph. The imperial image therefore influenced not simply the characterization in

Milton's poem but, at a more fundamental and less obvious level, the plot and structure of his poem as well. He drew on the institutions of Rome, at that crucial period when Imperial Rome grew out of the ruins of the republic, and not simply on the characters of the emperors who violated the ancient laws and sanctities of Rome. Those characters may be glimpsed in *Paradise Lost,* giving extra depth, for instance, to the incest of Satan, Sin, and Death in its relation to their joint misgovernment of the universe upon which they prey. But more importantly, Milton's allusion to historical patterns and evolving institutions under the Roman Empire elucidates for us the pain of watching angels and humanity falling from grace in Milton's poem. Losing the republic was a grief felt by Romans as a kind of irreparable personal bereavement: it was a grief in which personal loss blended with public outrage and impotence, as in the years when the old cause—very like Milton's "Good Old Cause" under the Restoration—was felt to slide away under the control of mad but efficient tyrants. Milton was able to include this grief in his account of the fall into evil's tyranny in *Paradise Lost.*

The imperial image reveals a different aspect of evil government from that revealed by the oriental tyrant. Where the eastern sultans had ruled without law, they had also ruled without measure, and, as it were, in ignorance of law. Though each state rested upon military power, and the janissaries were not very different from the praetorian guard as representatives of rule founded upon the organized violence of the few against the many, the oriental tyrannies are described as formless, chaotic masses of beings on the borders of the human, barbarians who pour down upon civilization, fluid and protean, without form. They are like Chaos itself, through which Satan ploughs a passage with supernatural difficulty:

> a universal hubbub wild
> Of stunning sounds and voices all confused
> Borne through the hollow dark.

(2.951–53)

The sounds Chaos emits are "hubbub" like Babel, but also like the barbarian destroyers of all form, language, architecture, and reason. The Romans, on the other hand, are the embodiment of reason. They are civilization itself, in its profane state; the formulators of Greek law and its codifiers (Justinian); the bearers of this rational, architected rule, with its virtues of honor and glory around the map. Whereas the oriental sultans are used in *Paradise Lost* to represent despotic rule based on a sort of ignorant guile, hand in hand with inhuman violence, the Roman Empire, in directing its subhuman subjects where to "pour," stands for the quelling of barbarian cultures and the education of those cultures into a cosmopolitan empire of the just, the reasonable, the virtuous. This empire is based on measure in language, in politics, and in ethics; it comes not merely to destroy but to build roads between nations, both actually and metaphorically. The *Imperium* stands in contradiction to the forces of Chaos. Scorning the unlettered barbarian despot, it has no interest in hubbub or confusion. In *Paradise Lost* it may be imagined as represented by the bridge linking Earth to Hell in Book 10, constructed by Sin and Death with a more than Roman technical skill, in direct antagonism to the chaos it overrules:

> broad as the gate,
> Deep to the roots of hell the gathered beach
> They fastened, and the mole immense wrought on
> Over the foaming deep high arched, a bridge
> Of length prodigious joining to the wall
> Immovable of this now fenceless world
> Forfeit to Death.
>
> (10.298–304)

Practical efficiency and technical expertise are equally stressed in Milton's account of the architectural skill of the engineers. Mathematical skill is also postulated ("broad as . . . / Deep to"), but a mathematics so far within their grasp as to appear intuitive in the poet's account. He is as factual as they are efficient, and aside from the awed adjectives *immense* and *prodigious*, which in any case may be read purely as indications of size, the poet allows the practicalities of description to mime the industry of the protagonists. Only one detail, "Over the foaming deep high arched," gives us as readers pause, for in inviting us to look down to the sea of Chaos far below, it presents one of those vertiginous moments in which the poet takes the ground from under our feet and leaves our consciousness swinging above the abyss. The noun *deep* striking the adverb *high* shifts until it gains almost adjectival status and falls away. But the poetic brilliance of the description, in which the laws of grammar are stretched to their limits, leads us to the perception that the artifice described is not only extraordinary but specific.

The construction is clearly a triumphal arch, that classic celebration of Roman pride in victory, serving as a soaring statement of triumph over "the deep," quelled by the Romans and their superb building skills, and contrasting with Xerxes' pathetic effort to bridge the deep by building on it a flotilla of boats, the ephemeral causeway for an army destined for ruin seen above in Chapter 2. Just as Romans and orientals stood in opposition to one another, so the triumphal arch of Sin and Death in enduring monumental stone, proclaiming apparent victory and built to last, opposes the clever novelty of the Persians' wooden bridge. The allusion to this Roman archetype dramatizes that aspect of evil which is intelligent, constructive, and all the more terrible and dangerous because it directs its energies through stratagem. The building of the triumphal arch draws upon the corrupt aspect of the empire that Milton saw as partaking of sin and death: a hardened, militaristic culture dedicated to false gods, and even human gods, institutionalizing sinful practices like the deification of the emperor (voted through Senate in the time of Augustus) and violent illegalities under the cloak of *iustitia.* Imperial kingship thereby gave Milton material for the stealth of Satan; for his fabrication of autocracy by a native wit (native originally to Heaven) and his thorough knowledge of the heavenly constitution, so thorough as to be capable of brilliant travesty. No sultan could offer the poet such a wealth of allusive material to elucidate the depravity of abused reason in a tyranny.

The Roman Empire as representative of a materialism antithetical to Chaos, but which can use chaos for its own ends, stands in opposition to the barbarous riches of the east, showering gold upon her kings (2.4) like a prodigy of nature. In Milton's adaptation of the motif to his poem, the building of the infernal bridge is made to represent "art" opposed to "nature," for Death, striking the material dredged from Chaos, "fixed as firm / As Delos floating once" (10.295–96) the unstable substances of Chaos. Thus the triumphal arch, with its imperial association, refers to a higher power than that of the barbarian potentates, with all their murderous power. Invention, miming Creation, gives a more dangerous fixity to the rule of the evil that chooses this particular incarnation: Death can "fasten" us to hell (10.300); the orientals can only visit us from it. The image reminds us of the mining of Hell; the construction of Pandemonium; the invention of gunpowder in Book 6, and the all-too-human ability to turn reason into policy and, uniting it with violence, to invent war that makes pacific human beings "fenceless" (10.303).

But by far the most dangerous aspect of the Roman motif, and perhaps the most fertile poetically, is that it is not as morally simple as a reference point. There is no such thing, in European tradition, as a good sultan: they are all evil, differing only in degree, not in kind. In Milton's poem, therefore, the spaces they occupy are areas of darkness. The reader is safely assured of the vitiated character of any being who impersonates a sultan, and there is danger from the arousal only of fear (tinged with excitement at the shine of exotic gold) not of seduction. The poetic richness of the Roman imperial motif, however, is that it presents to the mind a complex and mesmerizing network of associations, according to which the patterns of history swerved from evil emperor to good emperor; from pagan emperor to Christian emperor.

Imperial Rome inspired in Milton a dualistic approach: after all, the *Aeneid*, written under Augustus, was one of the fathers of the tradition without which *Paradise Lost* could never have existed. In his *Of Education* (1644), having defined the function of education as being "to repair the ruins of our first parents" (Yale 2:366–67), Milton recommended to the young mind many Roman authors who were the products of the empire (390–391), among them the Emperor Justinian's codification of Roman law, the *Institutes* (399). Similarly, in his *History of Britain,* though he regretted the violation of "our" territory by the Roman conquest, he also recognized that the conquest brought to the woad-encrusted, Druid-enslaved Britons (ancestors we could hardly be proud of) the eternal benefits of civilization and just government, conferring reason on the irrational and rights on the anarchic indigenous population. Thus the Roman tyrant can be excused because he delivers us from a worse—because inner—tyranny. In the first *Defence*, Milton exempted a number of emperors from his disapproval: Marcus Aurelius who ruled "as had been done when the state was free" (Yale 4, pt. 1:360), Claudius, "an honest ruler and a decent man" (ibid., 385); "the Antonines, the best of emperors" (ibid., 392), and others. The rule of the meritorious for Milton could hypothetically nullify the evils of a defective machine in politics, so that despite misgivings he could allow the person to supersede the institution. Moreover, as he showed in the "Manuscript Digression" to the *History of Britain*, in which he demonstrated an astonishing (to us) parallel between the "rude and naked barbarians," the ancient Britons (Yale 5, pt. 1:443), and the Long Parliament of 1648, he was also able to elucidate a providential reason for the equally parallel fall of the Roman republic into the empire, a reason that acts as a kind of negative justification for that institution:

> For stories teach us that libertie sought out of season in a corrupt and degenerate age brought Rome it self into further slaverie. For libertie hath a sharp and double edge fitt onelie to be handl'd by just and vertuous men, to bad and dissolute it becomes a mischief unwieldie in thir own hands. (Ibid., 449)

Under this perspective, Nero, Caligula, and Tiberius were conceived, delivered, and nourished by their own subjects. Rome, the birthplace of that liberty of which civilization has dreamed ever since, found liberty to be a retributive instrument in incapable hands suicidally disposed, lethal as the "two-handed engine" of *Lycidas* (line 130) and the Sword of Justice of the *Tenure* (Yale 3:197) and *Eikonoklastes* (ibid., 584). The emperor emerges as an essential scourge of the people, like the sultan, and in a perverted way is "natural" to a degenerate epoch. In this limited sense, the institution may therefore be regarded as a "good."

Given these three perspectives—the predominant one implying malign corruption in the state; the image of the rare, good emperor who safeguards a state that is a republic in all but name; and the image of the emperor as scourge secondary but organic to the corrupt community that begets him—Milton had a rich and complex area of allusion upon which to draw. In *Paradise Lost*, many details of the first archetype attach themselves to Satan, under a providential structure. The militaristic and pseudodemocratic climb of Satan to power within his own

state in Books 1 and 2 ingeniously parallels the Roman imperial
model of gaining autocratic power, while the triumphal reentry
into Hell after the conquest of the earth by Satan in Book 10
again alludes to elements of imperial ritual in Rome. Yet this
"triumph" enacted by Satan after the fulfillment of his enterprise exists only within the larger qualifying framework of
God's greater spiritual triumph, which, spanning the whole
poem, offers a perspective within which Satan's momentary
triumph is revealed as derisory and ironic.[4] Sin and Death's
triumphal arch, awesome as it seems at the moment of building,
appears both inglorious and vulnerable beneath the consummate triumphal arch embodied in the very structure of *Paradise
Lost* itself, declaring God's glory in providentially judging
Satan, the false emperor, and redeeming his "empire," mankind. If we draw back from the poem as a process in time, in
which we are dwarfed by each event—the building of Pandemonium, the erection of the bridge to Hell—as it passes, and
if we ponder the poem as a great piece of architecture, a total
triumphal structure emerges. In terms of this structure the palace and the causeway seem small, as the poem soars to the
image of Christ in victory at the center:

> He in celestial panoply all armed
> Of radiant urim, work divinely wrought,
> Ascended, at his right hand Victory
> Sat, eagle-winged.

$$(6.760-63)$$

Here, Milton has incorporated the image of the rare good emperors into his poem, linking it with the unique Christ arising
in victory. His chariot shines with spiritual gold; his armor is
the effective brightness of his creativity and his omnipotence;
the "eagle-winged" emblem of victory, being the tawny bird of
the sun associated in Roman myth with Zeus and thus a symbol
of imperial majesty, casts all the doings of Satan around this
central focus of the poem into retributive shadow. When, contemplating this massive burst of divine energy in a measured
stillness at the apex of the poem, with its solar implications of
justice and the golden radiance of its details, we think of Satan
as *Imperator* or of the building of the bridge by Sin and Death,
these events seem tiny and spurious in comparison. The major

arch includes and transcends the minor arch, and the emperor de jure ironizes the antics of Satan attempting to establish himself as emperor de facto.

The assimilation of Satan to Roman imperial models begins in the first two books, which, simply by virtue of their position in the epic, are most influential in establishing the nature of the enemy in the poem. The presentation establishes his status as being founded on military power rather than on idealism. While the archetype of the classical epic hero in defeat is clearly implied,[5] there is also striking congruity between the presentation of Satan and the rise of the early caesars as recorded by Tacitus, Plutarch, Suetonius, and Herodian (authorities to whom Milton sarcastically refers his scholarly opponent, Salmasius, in the first *Defence*). The analogy tends to dissolve one's sympathies for the "epic" hero by relating Satan's position to the callous facts of history. Reading of Satan's opulence, we may remember the lavish and degenerate empire;[6] reading of his military status in relation to his emergence as absolute leader, we may call to mind the original meaning of the Roman *imperator* ("general") and the transference of the term from the executive to the legislative field. From Satan's "policy," we may be led to think of the stealth of the emperors in achieving power; from his retention of and verbal reliance on the old institutions belonging to Heaven (and liberty)—"Thrones, dominations, princedoms, virtues, powers," drawled out on every conceivable public occasion to flatter the egos and quell the suspicions of his followers—we may recall the farcical retention of a puppet senate by the emperors, along with an actual complete reduction in liberty. In Book 2, Satan's parliamentary success may suggest to us, for the moment, less the rigged Parliaments of the Commonwealth than the Roman Senate under Caesar, Tiberius, and Caligula. Such an identification is attested to by the accumulation of honorific titles by which Milton calls Satan during the first two books, both in reported dialogue and quietly in his narrative voice. These encapsulate the procedure through which Satan achieves power and focus the reader's mind on the kind of autocracy toward which Satan is reaching.

Milton was alluding in these two books to that historical process according to which the republican usage of the purely military term *cognomen Imperator,* signifying "commander-in-chief" (a title that was instantly dissolved when its bearer entered Rome, with the possible accompaniment of the granting of triumphal honor), gave way under Augustus, and later Vespasian, to *praenomen Imperatoris*, signifying absolute military dictatorship. This sinister transition among the earlier emperors was masked by the use of the honorific *princeps* (first among equals).[7] Milton turned this historical knowledge into poetic craft, tracking the guileful usurper through all the swerves, detours, sleights, rhetorical maneuvers, and political assumptions that are his footprints on the road to power and mapping Satan's secret route with an adroitness and poetic covertness that outstrips Satan's own. The forger of a new empire becomes the moral victim of the poetry that "places" him. Initially, the trail is dead, and the terms used to define Satan are statements of what he is not, since he is still stunned from his fall. At first he is "the arch-enemy, / And thence in heaven called Satan" (1.81–82). He is almost caught nameless, like those followers we saw in Chapter 1 whose names are erased from the Book of Heaven. It is a condition of dreadful nakedness, as though his being had been penetrated by void and negation. The new name, *Satan,* only derives from his namelessness. Lucifer is dead: something dark and antagonistic has survived, and it is only in his function as enemy that he may be described for the future.

In this way Milton has immediately indicated that much of the meaning of his poem will be conveyed by explicitly allegorical naming. The reader will therefore be disposed to pay close attention to poetic acts of naming and to the arrangement of honorifics. Low in the burning lake, Satan, "vaunting aloud" (1:126), is addressed by Beelzebub:

> O prince, O chief of many throned powers,
> That led the embattled seraphim to war
> Under thy conduct.
>
> (1.128–30)

This is nostalgia for status in Heaven, now irrevocably confused, and all to build again. As a prince in Heaven, Satan was not only the aristocrat but also metaphorically of royal blood: a royalty that is now quenched, along with the light he bore as Lucifer. But as a prince, he is also associated with *princeps*, "first among equals," the smug imperial lie. Beelzebub also draws our attention to the prime function of Satan as military commander, the shape in which he will rise again, and lose again. At line 272, Beelzebub calls Satan, "Leader of those armies bright"; at line 358, reemerging as army general to call his legions back into aggressive order, Satan is "commander"; but by line 378, he has metamorphosed in a most sinister way, into "their great emperor":

Say, Muse, their names then known, who first, who last,
Roused from their slumber, on that fiery couch,
At their great emperor's call.

(1.376–78)

From "commander," Satan has become "emperor." Both terms are translations of the Latin *imperator,* the second including but transcending the first and representing the transition, so easy in eras of crisis, between military leadership and absolute despotism. Satan has successfully crossed this unlawful bridge between meanings by securing the obedience of his armies, who have marshaled to his order.[8] The "great emperor" of Book 1, though his power is not yet formalized, unmistakably anticipates the figure of "hell's dread emperor" much more securely established in Book 2 (510).

After the roster of fallen angels, tributary kings to the rebel emperor within human history, Milton furnishes Satan with some of the accoutrements of empire, including a standard bearer (Azazel) and an "imperial ensign" (1.536) of the kind so dear to the hearts of Roman legions. The emblems of the emperor's power are beginning to be accumulated around him in readiness for the time when he shall appear as emperor de jure according to the new law that hell is inventing for itself. From here until the end of Book 1, Satan, like Caesar stealthily gathering power and territory, acts as the model general, a "chief" (1.524, 566), so that the darkening threat of imperial tyranny is concealed behind the impeccable actions of the commander on behalf of those in his care, until the time should be ripe for the assumption of the present "honor" of the state. This procedure was recognized practice among Roman emperors. Their courting of public opinion in apparent innocence became an essential factor in attaining absolute power. Tacitus reported the insidious means employed by Tiberius of surrounding himself with a loyal army and then winding himself into the hearts of the population, retaining only his old status as tribune, for show, "as though the ancient constitution remained and he were uncertain of his power." Tacitus stressed the importance of public opinion, for it appeared essential to Tiberius to "have the credit of having been called and elected by the state rather than of having crept into power."[9]

Milton shows in *Paradise Lost* a cynical awareness of the true source of Satan's fears for his troops when he represents the "dread commander" (1.589) as contemplating the losses sustained on his account by "The fellows of his crime, the followers rather" (1.606), where the verbal correction defines the function of Satan's armies in a manner more pleasant to his ego. His love for his legions is a ritualized affair: there is sarcasm in Milton's account of his highly rhetorical fit of tears (1.619–21). This cynicism, coloring the titles by which the poet identifies the adventurer, is just that with which a knowing people recognized the pretensions to republican fervor and civic zeal announced by each successive dictator. One of the masterly ironies implicit in Milton's use of this Roman archetype in his poem is that it illustrates the usurper's hypocritical respect for the legal formalities, mirrored by the people's cynical and equally hypocritical recognition of the underlying reality. Further, the emperor himself, in the very act of legalizing himself, *knows* that they know. It is an act; and Milton could draw on it in demonstrating the farce and sham involved in Satan's ritualization of power in Books 1, 2, and 10 of *Paradise Lost*. Commenting in his first *Defence* on Salmasius's garbling of Cicero, Livy, and Tacitus, Milton said drily:

> So far as dictatorships are concerned, they were but temporary and never instituted save in public extremity, when they must be given up within six months. What you call the rights of the emperors was no right but sheer force; the empire was set up with no right save that of arms. . . . [Tacitus] would have told you in book III of his *Annals*, whence come all your royal rights: When equality was ended and self-seeking violence began to take the place of decent moderation, then despotisms appeared and among many people remained forever." You might have learned the same from Dio . . . that it was brought about partly by arms and partly by the treacherous pretence of Octavian Caesar that the emperors were not limited by law; for

while Octavian promised before an assembly that he would give up the principate and obey the laws and commands of others, pretending to refuse the empire, he gradually seized it by keeping all the legions as his own to carry on the wars in his own provinces. (Yale 4, pt. 1:443–44)

He condemns Octavian's "personal assumption of the title of *princeps* or emperor or *autokrator* as though God or natural law had subordinated all men and laws alike to him" (ibid., 444).

In the *Defence,* the imperial titles to power are clearly relevant to the Stuart pretension to being *"princeps,"* "emperor," *"autokrator"*: the analogy discredits Charles I's pretensions to absolute power by assimilating them to the dirty political practices and unholy dealings of the Roman emperors. Its impiety also makes it infernal and easily adapted by the poet to the course pursued by Satan in the first two books of *Paradise Lost.* Autocracy based "partly on arms" is presented in Book 1; autocracy established partly by "treacherous pretence" is concluded in Book 2, and Milton dexterously shows "sovereign power" (1.753) exercised covertly by Satan until he and his colleague Beelzebub judge it prudent to accept such power openly. Book 2 swells to a crescendo in which Satan will declare total authority, beginning with Satan, isolated with the highest orders of angels like a senate secluded from the general throng, allowing the appearance of "free" debate. However, while in Book 1 Satan had appeared chiefly in his military function, there had been a stealthy buildup of images of royalty around him, and he appears at the opening of Book 2 upon a throne, to which he himself gestures in his first speech, presumably on the principle that to draw attention to a potentially unpalatable fact when it is in full view anyway is to disarm criticism:

Me though just right, and the fixed laws of heaven
Did first create your leader, next free choice,
With what besides, in counsel or in fight,
Hath been achieved of merit, yet this loss
Thus far at least recovered, hath much more
Established in a safe unenvied throne
Yielded with full consent.

(2.18–24)

This miasma of claims is a complex network of half-truths or lies, a bastard mingling of old and new authorities: Satan was only leader under Christ in Heaven; his claim to preeminence by success in arms does not impress when it is remembered that his fellows, or rather followers, suffered defeat through him; his counsel must therefore be thought suspect; the assurance he maintains of being established on a "safe unenvied throne" is invalidated by his later fear of competitors; and we have only his word for the "full consent" of the Senate. However, politicians do not necessarily suffer under the common responsibility of being logical or moral. Satan seems in this suave but intricate speech to be making a giant claim, yet in actuality he seeks no more motive title than *leader* through hereditary right, free choice, and military prowess. He only claims to be sitting on a throne: not to be a king. The throne speaks for itself: Satan does not, quite, and appears in the character of *imperator* in the old sense, or *dictator* "in public extremity," rather than as a perpetual occupant. The poet's virtuosity in presenting this transitional status is remarkable, lying more fully in what is not said than in what is. It is only later in the debate, when the very basic questions are asked, mainly by Beelzebub who has been primed with relevant material and has crucial lines to deliver, that the opportunity is created by Satan to declare himself openly as emperor. These questions concern the location of the empire of the fallen angels, its status and capacity for expansion, and the identity of the emperor. The latter problem can only be considered after the former have been satisfactorily answered.

Beelzebub intelligently opens the way to absolutism by locating the only viable empire not in Hell but in God's new world and by seeking a candidate for a new and special type of ruler: "whom shall we find / Sufficient?" (2.403–4). It is in this passage and in Satan's subsequent pretense to accept an elected imperial role, in the reaction of his followers and the preparation for the expedition, that the imperial affinities of Satan's rule crystallize:

> at last
> Satan, whom now transcendent glory raised
> Above his fellows, with monarchal pride
> Conscious of highest worth, unmoved thus spake.
>   O progeny of heaven, empyreal thrones,
> . . . .
> But I should ill become this throne, O peers,

And this imperial sovereignty, adorned
With splendour, armed with power, if aught proposed
And judged of public moment, in the shape
Of difficulty or danger could deter
Me from attempting. Wherefore do I assume
These royalties, and not refuse to reign,
Refusing to accept as great a share
Of hazard as of honour, due alike
To him who reigns, and, so much to him due
Of hazard more, as he above the rest
High honoured sits?

                                                        (2.426–30, 445–56)

Satan, who has previously only recognized the symbol of his monarchy (the throne) without laying claim to the royal office it symbolizes (a realistically absurd tactic), now graduates. First he plays king in his bearing, "*now* transcendent glory raised"; then, by circuitous mazes of rhetoric, he claims "imperial sovereignty" by feigning to accept it. The pompous tone undercuts him at every point: his charlatanism is never plainer than here, in the elevated diction in which he clasps power to him: "I should ill become this throne," "Wherefore do I assume / These royalties." It is a profoundly embarrassing speech. We may think on reading it of Caesar sitting "in a chair of gold, apparelled in a triumphing manner,"[10] being offered the king's diadem, which he longed for yet could not dare to take, a pantomime scorned by the regicide Milton in his first *Defence* (Yale 4, pt. 1:444); of Tiberius accepting office: "he gave way by degrees, not admitting that he undertook empire, but yet ceasing to refuse it and to be entreated."[11] Yet the satanic emergence has a drama lacked by the Roman emperors' knack of sliding into rule. It is as if Satan combined with the lifelong and immortal ambitions of the emperors that earlier Roman institution of the temporary appointment of a dictator to serve in crisis.[12] If this speech is ludicrous, it is also spectacular, and the reader may find the tide of rhetoric overwhelmingly easy to surrender to, though even the most captivated mind must surface when, reading of Satan's kindly resolution not to "refuse to reign" (2.451), it recollects that on no occasion has Satan been invited by one of his peers to inconvenience himself by doing so. Nobody has offered a diadem to Satan, but Satan has conjured one up metaphorically. He takes advantage of a situation that the mortified Caesar "in a chair of gold" could not command; he betters Tiberius's "ceasing to refuse" empire by accepting what has never been offered him. Milton's poem transcends the historical archetypes: the Emperor Satan jeers at the pale efforts of the human emperors. The sudden dramatic force of this irruption into majesty after Beelzebub has asked for a volunteer conqueror is paralleled and completed in Satan's triumphant return from the new world in Book 10, to appear in a surprising blaze of glory (again dramatically engineered) on the same throne (10.449–50). Here he will be welcomed back as full emperor, having finally accomplished the journey from *imperator* in its first meaning as military commander to its second as the holder of the *Imperium* (10.429).

It is, then, in Satan's manipulation of the institutions of the state, in snatching power while appearing graciously to receive it, that his likeness to the Roman emperor lies. Along with this accession of power into the hands of the one goes a corresponding diminution in the identity of the many. Books 1 and 2 represent a progressive narrowing down of the number, and reduction in the function, of the spirits in Hell possessing personality. This process, beginning with the isolation of the aristocracy in Pandemonium after Book 1, builds to a climax with Satan's "assum[ing] / These royalties" in Book 2. Individuality perishes in his peers, so that the scintillating personalities of Mammon, Belial, and Moloch, so richly established in the debate, are allowed to cease. They become "Others among the chief" (2.469), or just "they" (486), and their persons are not resurrected in the remainder of *Paradise Lost*. From the time of his assumption of absolute power, Satan *is* the state: he does not represent it or enact its wishes. His viceroys, fitly, become not Moloch or Belial but Sin and Death, aspects of himself allegorically represented. This political metamorphosis neatly coincides with the theological notion of Hell as a state of the inner being: "within him hell / He brings" (4.20–21). In political terms, his body *is* the body politic:[13] his subjects are reduced, for all the high talk of liberty, to a condition of slavery.

This morally annihilating subsumption of a whole nation into the body politic of the king, an image of which decorates the front of Hobbes's *Leviathan*, was deplored by Milton throughout the regicide literature but was recognized by him later during his career as the inevitable condition of a "nation not fit to be free." In his *Commonplace Book,* he had noted that the Romans who had become "slaves to thire owne ambition and luxurie" had lost in an organic way the ability to belong to a republic when they became externally slaves to Caesar (Yale 1: 420). This condition is peculiarly fitting to an analysis of the relation between Satan and the fallen angels: though they cannot be said to have "elected" him, they "begot" him, to their own bane. Tacitus tells us of Augustus, that "Stripped of equality, all looked up to the commands of a sovereign without the least apprehension for the present," and of Tiberius, that "people plunged into slavery—consuls, senators, knights."[14] Equally, hell's horror of its leader, as we saw in Chapter 2, above, cannot be mistaken:

they

Dreaded not more the adventure than his voice
Forbidding.

(2.473–75)

The pretense of open debate dies in an instant, and the great patricians among the fallen angels fade into their future roles as false gods to be scourged by Jahweh. Satan moves away from his "nation" altogether into the intimate circle of his "imperial family," Sin and Death, whose revolting incestuous couplings, regarded by Satan and Sin as a matter of glory and delight, recall the incestuous practices of the more berserk of the emperors of Rome.

In his first *Defence,* Milton specifically linked incest with autocratic power, showing how "that villainous Antoninus Caracalla" was beset by "the incestuous urging of his step-mother Julia" to place the emperor above the law (Yale 4, pt. 1:341); Caligula's enterprises with his sister need no rehearsal, and sexual perversion was almost a badge of office in the high times of the empire. In *Paradise Lost,* the portrayal of Satan, Sin, and Death is a reiteration of that theme, announced in relation to the god kings of history, of "lust hard by hate," where vicious sex and predatory violence, imaged in Death assaulting his mother with lust and rage, characterize the reign of evil. Power has drained from a puppet senate into corruption and terror personified, bred by imperial Satan.

But all these factors in Milton's characterization of Satan are subsidiary (though contributory) to the presentation of Satan less as a usurping governor than as a self-proclaimed god. If Satan's democratic claims are a mask for his imperial aspirations, then these in turn are a mask for his aspiration to divinity. In Book 5, Satan's motives for his rebellion are described by both the narrative voice and the rebel himself as being based on envy of Christ's new power and its diminution of those lower down in the celestial hierarchy, notably himself (659–65):

> New laws thou seest imposed;
> New laws from him who reigns, new minds may raise
> In us who serve, new counsels.

> (5.679–81)

Satan's confidences to Beelzebub are phrased in purely political (and here legalistic) terms, with an egalitarian insinuation that ascribes to God a violation of the heavenly constitution, with a consequent emancipation of his subjects from their old allegiances. "New laws" are doubled in emphasis by Satan's repetition of his allegation, and oxymoron is intended ("new laws" being a logical impossibility): there is a harsh edge to Satan's circumlocution for God as "him who reigns," and an attempt to deduce an organic relationship between "reigning" and "raising" (rebellion), reminiscent for the reader of Satan's assertion that God "tempted our attempt, and wrought our fall" (1.642). The speech is suave, artful, and overwhelmingly political: it treats Heaven as if it were *only* a state.

But against the political craftmanship of Satan and his unique oratorical powers; against, even, the narrative voice, the reader is obliged to credit God's definition of Satan's aspirations. Inspecting the gathering rebellion with that lidless eye of omniscience that never blurs reality, God gestures to the Son:

> Son, thou in whom my glory I behold
> In full resplendence, heir of all my might,
> Nearly it now concerns us to be sure
> Of our omnipotence, and with what arms
> We mean to hold what anciently we claim
> Of deity or empire, such a foe
> Is rising, who intends to erect his throne
> Equal to ours, throughout the spacious north.

> (5.719–26)

God echoes the military and political terminology adopted by Satan, but he does so ironically. The ensuing story reveals that God needs no arms to validate his title to reign, and this is explained within the speech itself, as God makes clear that Satan's ambition is to gain "deity or empire," that is, deity first, empire second. Satan's deepest yearning is to be a god: this is the significance of his palace at the Mountain of the Congregation, "In imitation" of the mountain upon which Christ's kingship was proclaimed; a "royal seat" (5.756) upon which he emulates not only Christ's kingship but also his divinity. This is also the significance of his claim to be self-begotten (5.860), as is made explicit in Book 6 by the narrative voice:

> High in the midst exalted as a god
> The apostate in his sun-bright chariot sat
> Idol of majesty divine.

(6.99–101)

In this exaltation from creature to divinity, Milton's image of Satan encapsulates all three royal archetypes explored so far in this work: the Stuart, the Turkish, and the Roman tyrannies. In *Eikonoklastes* Milton deplored Charles's confusion of himself with God and his continual attribution of his personal opinions to the Deity, "usurping over spiritual things, as *Lucifer* beyond his sphere" (Yale 3:502). Proverbially, the oriental potentate is adored as a god by his minions. But in the period of transition in the Roman commonwealth that coincided with and included the birth and death of Christ, a pattern of ascent in the direction of *godhead* may be measured over a series of generations, in which leaders limited by law swelled in aspiration beyond the limitations of mortality itself. The coincidence of this period of the empire with Christ's birth and death (which represents an opposite movement toward apparent humiliation, his side pierced by Roman soldiers) is noted in *Paradise Regained,* and the absolute opposition of the two kinds of empire is stressed. Book 3, the temptation to worldly glory, presents an invitation to Christ by Satan to emulate "Great Julius, whom now all the world admires" (3.39) and thus obtain glory; Book 4 requests him to out-Tiberius Tiberius, "Old and lascivious" on Capri (4.91), "Hated of all and hating" (4.97), and to liberate the world by force from his bestial rule. Christ's reply is exquisitely knowing and ironical, for in refusing the temptation to exterminate the emperor, he inquires threateningly of Satan:

> what if I withal
> Expel a Devil who first made him such?

(4.128–29)

The likeness between Satan and Tiberius is recognized, but they stand in the relation of primary and secondary causes of evil. Yet, through the rotten spirit of the leader of a nation dwelling (according to Satan) in "Houses of gods" (4.56), we may perceive the nature of satanic wickedness, reading from secondary to primary causes. Glory in the terms of *Paradise Regained* is just a species of violence; and the Romans are a vitiated, dissolute community waiting for dissolution, their triumphs standing in absolute contradiction to the gentle Christ whose beautiful conviction is that "Who best / Can suffer best can do" (3.194–95), a reigning quiet and pacifism that by their very existence mock the Roman glory culture and foresee its end.

Though *Paradise Lost,* resting on a dynamic polarity of energies and with war at its center, does not profess a quietism as absolute as that of its sequel, the same opposition is there. This is most clearly seen in Milton's integration into *Paradise Lost* of triumphal structures and images drawn from Roman history, the celebration of a formal triumph by the emperor being a crucial stage on the climb to the divinity that crowns imperial power. The triumph enacted by Satan in Book 10 of *Paradise Lost,* in which, having subdued the enemy (man) and established a colony in our universe under the vassal kings Sin and Death, Satan returns to Hell, is modeled on this principle. Though in Book 2 Satan had so condescendingly "not refuse[d] to reign" and had thereby declared himself emperor, he also recognized that the honor he did everyone the favor of accepting was contingent upon the hazard he meant to undertake. The transition from general to emperor was, in other words, not quite complete. After validating his claim by conquering man, Satan would be able to assume the rank of *Imperator* in the fullest sense. In Rome, *honor* and *merit* defined fitness for high office, and *virtue* was civic and racial rather than spiritual, aggressive and military rather than pacific. Renaissance understanding of the disturbing potentialities in these classical

concepts of virtue, honor, and glory (defined by Machiavelli as
the quality in the human will that can stun and defeat Fortune,
and underlying the ethos of popular plays like Marlowe's militaristic *Tamburlaine*)[15] would have made Milton's usage of such
concepts in the context of Hell quite clear to contemporary readers. Reading of Satan "by *merit* raised" to preeminence in Hell
(2.5) or juggling with terms like *honor* and its relation to *hazard,*
we might well recall the ritual proving of manly worth (*vis* by
vir) through extension of the empire, securing or advancing an
individual's hold on Rome, proving "virtue" by "hazard." The
honor normally chosen to celebrate this effort on behalf of the
Roman state was a triumph, which even the less ferocious emperors like Claudius aspired to deserve and enjoy as proof of the
validity of their power.[16] By analogy, Satan in *Paradise Lost,* the
very pattern of ferocity, looks for a spectacular honor in pay-
ment for establishing an alternative empire to the "dungeon of
our tyrant" (10.466), which in his triumphal speech he dismisses with a brief shudder.

The building of the triumphal arch by Sin and Death prepares
us to expect a festival celebration:

> Over the foaming deep high arched, a bridge
> Of length prodigious.

> (10.301–2)

It also expertly links the empires of Satan and the Romans with
the Caroline court, so that the reader's awareness (bred by the
Renaissance revival of triumphal architecture and pageantry)
can be drawn to the many-layered allusions of Milton's images
of monarchy. The triumph was incorporated into English civic
pageantry during the reigns of the Tudor dynasty, to be used in
processions and entries; it was assimilated into the masque
form, itself a court genre glorifying king and aristocracy by
linking them to heavenly counterparts.[17] Under Charles I, a
number of extravagant masques were performed for the king in
the form of "triumphs," up to the *Britannia Triumphans* of Davenant, Jones, and Lawes in 1637.[18] The late date of this masque
indicates that the display at the English court continued to the
very brink of the civil war, with the sun king's image as embodiment of law and order, unity and harmony, preserved in the face
of all the proof to the contrary that the country had to offer. In

fact, it may be said that a kind of self-multiplying inverse ratio operated according to which political failure was rapturously contradicted by triumphal eulogy. The closer the monarchy brought the nation to the brink of war, the more likely a *Triumph of Peace* was to break forth in astounding congratulation; *Britannia Triumphans* is real indication of *Britannia Furens.* Furthermore, there was in the Caroline court an emphasis on the authenticity of the triumph within the original Roman tradition, made explicit in the lengthy specifications that characterize masques, "All after the Roman form," "after the magnificent Roman triumphs."[19] The Stuart king is proudly represented as a modern caesar.

Such a genre coincidence, linking Satan, Caesar, and Stuart king, was a happy one for Milton. He spoke slightingly of "wanton mask" in *Paradise Lost* (4.768), and the ephemeral triumphal arches of the monarchy, erected for a day, along with the elaborate staging of the masques themselves, a baroque structure void of content, are obviously powerfully suggestive in relation to the "high arched" bridge of Sin and Death, which, firmly fixed as it is, belongs at both ends to worlds that are transitory. The bridge's mighty span from this perspective is made to look as frail as paper: an edifice of a day's duration.

But Satan is doing more than act out a vapid masque role. Milton returned to the ancient historians to furnish Satan with a reality both to copy and to travesty. Satan in his great returning violates all the conventions of the triumph:

> So these the late
> Heaven-banished host, left desert utmost hell
> Many a dark league, reduced in careful watch
> Round their metropolis, and now expecting
> Each hour their great adventurer from the search
> Of foreign worlds.

(10.436–41)

There is no public and ceremonious entrance into the city, flanked by armies and preceded by representatives and the spoils of the conquered. The "great adventurer," true to his shifty and vainglorious nature, forsakes tradition in order to achieve maximum sensation by discovering himself at the last possible moment, at the consummate point. Bathos, however, lurks in every detail. If, as John Demaray suggests in his perceptive study, *Milton's Theatrical Epic,* this bathos is linked only to the illusory perspectives of the traditional anti-triumph in the masque form alone, some of the depth and richness of this bathos is lost. Persuasive though Demaray's adaptation of poem to masque is, relating the emergence of Satan in his throne to glittering masque theatricals, his followers to an anti-masque mob, with a travesty dance as "they roll'd in heaps: (10.558), and a nauseous travesty banquet of bitter fruits,[20] the perspectives are reduced if you do not consider the historical origins of the triumphal structure. For instance, Satan's entry into Hell, according to tradition, can be expected to involve an external display of victory. But Satan enters Hell not as victor but as "plebeian angel militant" and, without any prior announcement, ascends "his high throne" (10.445). The ritual form of the Roman triumph is here not only violated but in fact abandoned by Satan: traditionally, the triumphator was *preceded* by a mighty array of heralds and trophies, announcing his achievements and building up suspense prior to his arrival.[21] Nothing precedes Satan, for, in terms he cannot himself understand, he has achieved nothing:

> he through the midst unmarked,
> In show plebeian angel militant
> Of lowest order, passed; and from the door
> Of that Plutonian hall, invisible
> Ascended his high throne, which under state
> Of richest texture spread, at the upper end
> Was placed in regal lustre.

(10.441–47)

The hall is like a theater, through which Satan passes disguised as a member of the audience; the raised throne is like a stage on which he will appear, to act. The action will be violated by a reality from outside the theater. But this surreptitious creeping into glory is a substitute for the political drama of the triumphal entry. This movement back into the heart of the city should demonstrate the completion of the imperial adventure. The throne Satan left as *imperator* in the first sense (its gorgeousness here recalling that of the allusive description in Book 2) he should be resuming as *Imperator* in the second. The canopy spread above the throne, an added detail, indicates the imminence of the coronation ritual. But Satan's paltry entrance, devoid of glorious accompaniment, is an authentic image of his real defeat: all the ironies, as God has promised at the beginning, are at the triumphator's own expense, and he cannot bring back to Hell a single captured soul as the booty of his enterprise.

Satan's entry into Hell disguised as "plebeian angel militant" has a deeper and more specific significance in connection with triumphal ceremonies. It was traditional for the triumphator to be accompanied by a common foot soldier as a reminder of his mortality at the supreme moment of his glory.[22] A comment by Tertullian in his *Apologeticus*—probably known to Milton—is powerful and apposite. When Tertullian explains the subordinate relationship of the emperor to God and the iniquity of his attempt to usurp divine authority, he can think of no better emblem of the emperor's essentially mortal condition than that image which has its place within the Roman ritual of power itself, the triumphal procession:

> Even in the triumph, as he rides in that most exalted chariot, he is reminded that he is a man. It is whispered to him from behind: "Look behind thee; remember thou art a man." That he is in such a blaze of glory that the reminder of his mortal state is necessary for him—makes it the more delightful to him. He would be less, if he were at that moment called a god, because it would not be true. He is greater, who is called to look back, lest he think himself a god.[23]

Milton would have been deeply impressed by this image of the Roman tyrant, whom Tertullian has ironically invited, as a test of strength, to "make war on heaven, carry heaven captive in his triumph,"[24] dogged by the whispering voice of his own transience and the silent prayers of the Christians of whom he makes game in the gladiatorial circus. This sarcastic, unterrified early Church Father spoke in a voice hauntingly close to Milton's own.

In the advent of the conqueror Satan to announce his victory, we are struck by the coincidence of the form in which Satan sneaks into his glory and the ancient emblem of the common soldier, whose sole purpose in being present at all in the triumphal pageant was to announce the vanity of glory. This silent declaration on the part of the poet to the attentive reader is emphasized by the fact that, upon reaching the throne, Satan vanishes altogether. There is no one there: no emperor, no empire. These subtle moments prove the theme stated by the Creator in Book 3, the symmetrical partner of Book 10, when, watching Satan's departure from Hell in search of an empire, he promised that all Satan's enterprises should "redound / Upon his own rebellious head" (3.85–86). In this final vision of Satan, we experience the fulfillment of that prophecy. As a common foot soldier, Satan reminds us less of his own mortality (since he cannot die) than of the mortality of that kingdom of which he has just boasted to Sin and Death (10.384–409), and of all the glory associated with it. Just as Tertullian defined the Christian triumph as founded on humility ("we are burnt. This is our garb of victory, the robe embroidered with the palm; this is our triumphal chariot"[25]), so Milton distinguished the "sorrow unfeigned and humiliation meek" of Adam and Eve's contrition, which rounds off Book 10 and is reiterated there at lines 1092 and 1104, from the vanity of satanic show. The gentle human couple who are supposed to be Satan's *Imperium* are the Christian triumphators, by virtue of their being able to do without the garb of victory, chariots of war. The vicious *Imperator* who claims them is also without triumphal paraphernalia, and he will burn, ironically, along with his followers, "parched with scalding thirst" for the ashy fruit (10.556).

History itself is often more potent than fiction as a source for ironies. The mighty applause expected by Satan from his followers in approval of his glorious deeds turns to hissing, recalling embarrassing imperial triumphs that fell similarly flat. Ludicrous incidents deflated Julius Caesar's grandest moments: "As he rode through the Velabrum on the day of his Gallic triumph, the axle of his chariot broke, and he was all but thrown out."[26] Tacitus recorded that Domitian's faked triumph over the Germans did not please the Romans: "the public had mocked at the sham triumph he had just celebrated over Germany, for which the markets had been ransacked to buy slaves, whose hair and appearance might admit of their playing the part of captives."[27] As Caesar's downfall drew nearer, his subjects were alienated by his triumphal display, especially the celebration of victory over Pompey's sons, for he had "destroyed the sons of the noblest man in Rome, whom fortune had over-thrown."[28] The triumph, therefore, worked ironically against the protagonist it aimed to glorify. Worldly glory as expressed in a single supreme ego was contradicted in the very form structured to declare it. It would hardly be surprising if Milton remembered such historical precedents when he wrote of Satan's triumph after securing dominion on earth, toward the end of Satan's political career in the poem and at the point that typologically foreshadows the final punishment of evil (10.575–77).

Historically, the triumph set the liberty of the Roman people under their victorious emperors against the enslavement of the "barbarous" nations they had conquered. The more difficult victory was the greater one, and involved a boastful mathematics such as that recorded by Augustus: "Nine kings or sons of kings were led before my chariot in my triumphs."[29] It was more noble, showed greater virtue, to be heavily outnumbered by a magnificent enemy than to capture defenseless or ignoble peoples with ease or through wiles. To cope with the fact that his apparent victory had been against nothing more challenging than two human beings—gentle, credulous, and young, subverted by charlatanism rather than power—Satan's triumphal speech to the admiring patriots of Hell makes much of the arduous character of the journey itself and recognizes the ludicrous pettiness of his own activities by inviting laughter at a God who plants his kingdom's safety in nothing more tremendous than an apple:

> Thrones, dominations, princedoms, virtues, powers,
> For in possession such, not only of right,
> I call ye and declare ye now, returned
> Successful beyond hope, to lead ye forth
> Triumphant out of this infernal pit
> Abominable.

> (10.460–65)

Satan signals a triumphal procession, but what he suggests is a confused reversal of the ritual. Triumphs are not "led out" of pits; they are led in to the native land, and its heart, the capital. The triumphator here refuses to recognize Hell as his *patria*. Furthermore, triumphal processions are received by the native inhabitants of the *patria.* Satan is proposing to remove all his followers from theirs. In boasting that he will lead the procession, he takes the wrong place, for the leader conventionally comes last. However:

> Long were to tell
> What I have done, what suffered, with what pain
> Voyaged the unreal, vast, unbounded deep
> Of horrible confusion, over which
> By Sin and Death a broad way now is paved
> To expedite your glorious march; but I
> Toiled out my uncouth passage.

(10.469–75)

True to his words ("Long were to tell"), the ensuing sentence labors on for a mortal twenty-two lines, structured upon the exploits of an unremitting ego: "I have done . . . I / Toiled out . . . / I found . . . / I have seduced . . . / Man I deceived . . . / my performance." A litter of adjectives extols his exploits, as the garbled narrative lurches toward its manic conclusion. Just as the Roman triumphator swaggered home manifesting the tokens of success, emblems of the aggrandizement both of himself and of his nation, so Satan rhetorically displays his exploits (having nothing tangible to show for them).

In Plutarch, Caesar's victories are shown to be hollow because they are not participated in by the people; the people *will not* praise. In the triumph of Satan, the people *cannot* praise. The poet's irony is directed against the whole empire of Hell, both him who rules and those who serve, emphasizing the subordination of all events to the will of God:

> So having said, a while he stood, expecting
> Their universal shout and high applause
> To fill his ear, when contrary he hears
> On all sides, from innumerable tongues
> A dismal universal hiss, the sound
> Of public scorn; he wondered.

(10.504–9)

The poet's insistence on a political model is attested by the phrase *public scorn.* Satan the demagogue is now imagined as diminishing from his monarchal status to that of a disappointed aspirant. We can no longer imagine his head as "fulgent" or his person as "star bright" (10.449, 450), for a look of the most genuine human amazement crosses his face (509–10) as he lapses into the serpent form that is his final metamorphosis. His imperial glory can last only as long as it is allowed to; monarchy is all in the eye of the beholder. Public scorn deflates him, erasing his high claims, as he always knew it would, and in this moment so replete with reassuring comedy, we remember that similarly ludicrous but also dark and chilling crisis in Book 2, when Satan, fearing that others of his "peers" might offer themselves as competitors for the errand to earth, "prevented all reply" (467) so that he would get sole credit for willingness to undertake "hazard huge" on behalf of the fallen angels (473). Milton offered the extra elucidating comment:

> But they
> Dreaded not more the adventure than his voice
> Forbidding.
>
> (2.473–75)

In Book 10, this dreadful voice sounds again, and we who have witnessed the terror it inspires in Satan's creatures (who would rather encounter the abyss he toiled through, Night, Chaos, Sin, Death, and God altogether, than dare to disobey him) are at first rendered just as confident as Satan of the "high applause" he expects. But awe of a leader is not love of him. Here the themes of English, Turkish, and Roman tyrants again interconnect. Tyrant and people are in fundamental opposition, a confrontation invariably ruinous in the ultimate sense. Milton ironically reflects within the anti-triumph this tendency to destruction on the part of such an empire. Satan is ironically exposed when his subjects do not freely allow him to stand as triumphator (revealing, metaphorically, their true but sublimated feelings toward him) and, by a further irony, when they are not permitted, by God, to do so.

In addition, the relationship of the victor (Hell) to the empire (our world) is ironically restated in terms of the triumphal imagery. By tradition, the victory must be shown as free, the vanquished as enslaved. But in this triumph, the apparently victorious nation is in fact less free than the nation subdued. Each of the allusions by the narrative voice to the term *triumph* in the account of the cosmic joke against the fallen angels reiterates this fact:

> Thus was the applause they meant,
> Turned to exploding hiss, triumph to shame
> Cast on themselves from their own mouths.

(10.545–47)

> so oft they fell
> Into the same illusion, not as man
> Whom they triumphed once lapsed.

(10.570–72)

The first of these quotations suggests a self-disgust forced on minds urgently attempting to congratulate themselves: their ritual becomes shame and anti-triumph, in the same way as anti-masque contradicts masque. Shame is in any case established as being natural to the inhabitants of Hell, who sprang into wakefulness "abashed" at the despotic call of "their great sultan" in Book 1; thus it is deeply fitting that they should now indulge in a festival of shame. In the second quotation, the relationship of their schemes to man's predicament is redefined. Man ate only one apple, once; the devils are reduced to innumerable self-defeating assaults on many apples. They are, therefore, much more enslaved than mankind, over whom they triumphed. Milton asserts that the fallen angels, in comparison to their relatively more innocent victim, man, will suffer greater degradation. Equally, the poet shows a movement on the part of man, woman, and God toward reunion after their alienation. The remainder of Book 10 is devoted to the enfolding movement whereby Eve's desolation and Adam's vituperative loneliness are abandoned in favor of mutual peace and prayerfulness, and the opening of Book 11 is devoted to Christ's intercession and a mediating wholeness achieved among woman, man, Christ, and God: a wholeness neither stronger nor intrinsically more valuable than that enjoyed before the Fall, but perhaps valued with a passion of gratitude that inspires a new sensation of its preciousness in the reader. The pattern of the remainder of Book 10, then, working toward reunion on the part of the impaired human beings and the offended divinity, opposes the pattern of Satan and his "nation" recoiling one from another, their experience being one of involuntary loss and self-division (for they are physically nauseated with both the fruit and their unchosen metamorphosis) and rejection of their leader. The

reader may perceive a subtle remembrance of that moment in
Book 5 when Abdiel, the faithful angel who dared to oppose the
policies uniting Satan and his armies in the war in Heaven,
turned away:

> From amidst them forth he passed,
> Long way through hostile scorn, which he sustained
> Superior, nor of violence feared aught.

(5.903–5)

"Hostile scorn" leaves Abdiel untouched: he holds the empire
within his mind intact, being free. "Public scorn" ransacks the
mind of any being so reckless as to locate his value and liberty
in an external *Imperium*. Suddenly, Satan is alone as Abdiel was,
but without the same defenses, painful to build but agonizing to
lack. In Book 6, Abdiel's return to his maker was greeted "With
joy and acclamations loud" (23); he was "high applauded" (26)
and led inward to the throne of God. This is a sort of triumph,
but not of egoism, for it depends upon the participant's
wish to mingle with his equals and, sharing with them, to accept his equality (21–22). Abdiel's triumph, celebrated in the
minor key, is dependent on his perfect ability to do without
such triumph, on his immunity, as God expresses it in his
speech of congratulation, to "scorn" and "Universal reproach"
(40, 34). In representing Satan's demeaning vulnerability to the
"universal hiss" of Hell (10.508), Milton has given a precise
analysis of the weak point in the tyrant's psychology, a weakness so glaring that it gapes in his mind like a great hole. The
reader has received hints of this potentially pathetic capacity
for combined isolation and servitude throughout the poem,
though pathos, which would be morally dangerous in connection with one whose evil would be soon resurrected, is avoided
here by the poet's insistence on the farce involved in Satan's
perishing into serpent form. The reciprocity of hostile emotions
between emperor and subjects is delectably revealed through
this pantomime:

> he would have spoke,
> But hiss for hiss returned with forked tongue
> To forked tongue, for now were all transformed
> Alike, to serpents all as accessories
> To his bold riot.

(10.517–21)

Far from the complacent accumulation of praise that might have led Satan to another fit of "not refusing to reign," Satan utters under his forced metamorphosis the venom he actually feels for his fellow patriots; to complete the joke, he may, Milton implies, be expressing himself thus at this very moment in Hell on an occasion of "annual humbling" (10.576). The poet will not claim that this is so, but he allows us a moment's pleasure in the possibility, before, the travesty triumph being complete, he removes our minds from this comic relief with that ominous "*Mean while* in Paradise the hellish pair" (10.585) to peruse the carnivorous monsters, Sin and Death, tracking prey on Earth. The barbarians are loose.

However, the image of imperial Rome is the first one we have examined that presents a fundamental moral dichotomy. The Stuart kings, according to Milton in the regicide literature, were evil; the sultans of the East, Pharaoh of Egypt, Nimrod of Babylon, all were evil. It was not possible to speak of "just instances" of these bad phenomena, though if the dedicated scholar inquired into English history with scrupulous attention, he might emerge with a handful of good kings—an Alfred, an Edward, an Elizabeth—exceptions to the general trend. However, Milton had been able in his prose works to distinguish a number of pious, excellent, and latterly Christian emperors, and, as our earlier references to Tertullian showed, he had Christianized Roman imperial and triumphal motifs and used them in opposition to the ethos of worldly glory.

The emperor Constantine (not a favorite of Milton's at any time, being a murderer, idolator, tyrant, and an "elm" round whose imperial wealth the "vine" of the Roman Church twisted parasitic arms)[30] was a transitional figure in this process of Christianization. The Arch of Constantine, set up in 315 A.D.,[31] was deeply influential on future uses of triumphal motifs in a Christian structure. While Constantine's statue at Constantinople shows him with the sun god's rayed crown, his triumphal arch bears reliefs of the *Sol invictus* and Mithras as divine protector of his army. Combining Christian and Mithraic elements to create a vision of himself as sun king, he projected himself as emblem on earth of solar justice and solar militarism.[32] The triumphal arch, as revived in the Renaissance, set forth this solar symbolism as a manifestation of the monarch celebrated;

as an extension of this came the emphasis on a central point as a focus of structure architecturally and meaning iconographically. Fowler has shown the way in which symbolism of the center in certain Renaissance works functions numerologically to assert images of cosmic (or solar) kingship, justice, and ascension or elevation, and he and Qvarmström have linked this interpretation to the triumph of Christ in Book 6 of *Paradise Lost* (in the first edition at any rate).[33] Under this interpretation the total epic structure of *Paradise Lost* is a colossal arch, soaring to the center at the image of Christ as the sun of righteousness, with a parody by Satan at 6.100.

Thus, Christ is the true emperor whose magnificence dominates Milton's epic. But what the poet has attributed to Satan in terms of the associations of the Roman emperors he rigorously denies to his triumphing Christ. Satan is the general of his troops: Christ is never *Imperator* in this first sense, this work being left to Michael. Satan's relationship to his empire is in continuous transition, while Christ is not related to the historical patterns of imperial tyranny. His people do not fear him, only his enemies. Uninterested in extending an *Imperium,* he is purely concerned with cleansing the existing state of impurity and filling up the existing vacuum after such a purge—with new creation. The poet has carefully detached the concept of the emperor from its roots in the clay, blood, and turmoil of the mortal world, allocating this residue to Satan, but he has given to Christ the unalloyed ideal of the image. Christ thus takes virtually no part in the warfare in Heaven in Book 6, for, although the "ten thousand thunders, which he sent / Before him" (836–37) are not encouraging to the now quailing hearts of the evil minority, it is less what Christ does than what Christ is that sends them hurtling down from Heaven. He does not need to touch them: his "ire" (843) has done so already; the "eyes" (847) of the apocalyptic chariot wheels send forth not just fire but pure terror. Christ does not push them over the edge of Heaven, for they are urgent to go. Milton describes their hectic withdrawal not in the passive but in the active voice:

> the monstrous sight
> Strook them with horror backward, but far worse
> Urged them behind; headlong themselves they threw
> Down from the verge of heaven, eternal wrath

Burnt after them to the bottomless pit.

(6.862–66)

The reader is well able to understand how mere abstract sight can produce a sensation so acute that it strikes the victim. The suicidal tendency of evil is again demonstrated in Milton's insistence that "themselves they threw" and in the anonymity of the individuals in that general rout. In that Babel panic, Satan is just one of many. A strange momentary silence seems to follow the expulsion, lengthened for the reader by Milton's description of divine wrath that "Burnt after them." The reader is left, in the new silence of the heavenly kingdom, to imagine the diminishing roar blanketed finally in distance. It is after this act unique to his being that Christ is received in his triumph:

> Sole victor from the expulsion of his foes
> Messiah his triumphal chariot turned:
> To meet him all the saints, who silent stood
> Eye witnesses of his almighty acts,
> With jubilee advanced; and as they went,
> Shaded with branching palm, each order bright,
> Sang triumph, and him sung victorious king,
> Son, heir, and Lord, to him dominion given,
> Worthiest to reign: he celebrated rode
> Triumphant through mid heaven, into the courts
> And temple of his mighty Father throned
> On high: who into glory him received,
> Where now he sits at the right hand of bliss.

(6.880–92)

Milton here presents the triumph of Christ, with each traditional element of the ritual observed in its decorous order; this celebration is what Satan in his hysterical return to Hell in Book 10 is clearly aching to have put on for him. There have been eyewitnesses to Christ's victory. It has been shown to be valid. His triumph takes the form of a reception of the triumphator by the faithful inhabitants of Heaven, who meet him as he moves from the circumference of Heaven toward its center. The armies "Sang triumph," as the Roman soldiers of history shouted *"Io triumphe"* upon the victor's entry to the capitol. If the palms the armies carry remind us of the approaching sorrows of Palm Sunday, they are also the authentic accompaniments of the Roman festival. Christ is defined not just as war lord but also as rightful heir. His entry is into the holy of holies. It leads into Raphael's (the teller's) present day, but it leads also into the reader's present, "Where *now* he sits at the right hand of bliss." This authentic, orderly, and gracious triumphal celebration confronts the mess, noise, and farce of Satan's triumphal efforts in Book 10.

The luminous brightness associated with Christ's triumph remains as a reflection in the reader's mind long after Book 6. It is the effect of the "radiant urim" of Christ's breastplate (6.761); the shining of his coming (768); the blazing of his ensign (775). Beautiful even in his violence, Christ appears through the transforming power of Milton's poetry as the sun of justice, with his radiance mirrored in the verse, while his just place of free equilibrium poised above everything is dramatized by his central position in the poem. In the parody in Book 10, in combination with a false numerological variant on the centrality of Christ, Satan is shown miming this refulgence. His triumph, occurring in Book 10 (appropriate since *ten* is God's number of commandment and completion), is enclosed, as we have said, by Adam and Eve's transcendence of their role as victims in the kind of humiliation that, since it is acknowledged freely in a meek way and without any pretense, becomes humility of the same family as Christ's. The center of Book 10, by line count at 552, is implicitly relevant to the imperial theme through the focus on the parodying trees that cause the devils their humiliating fall:

> laden with fair fruit, like that
> Which grew in Paradise, the bait of Eve
> Used by the tempter.

> (10.550–52)

The ascent we would expect at the center is contradicted; the sun of justice is seen not in its manifestation but in its effect (the punishment of the aspirants). No central light is found, only a dim falling off into the festival of shame.

But a passage containing related images of ascent and possible hidden solar symbolism in connection with the satanic triumph does exist, though way off center (violation of centralized structure for parodic purposes seems to have been quite common, particularly after Milton's example.)[34] Hence, in lines 443 to 452 (Satan's emergence into the underworld) there is implied

use of triumphal symbolism. Much of this is in terms of a reversal, for Satan had to go "down" (10.414) to get his triumph, back
to Hell, and there is no question of a triumphal entry because
nobody is waiting to receive him (419). This not-very-lively welcome is then deliberately exploited by Satan, who converts it
into a pageant all the more spectacular for having no beginning
and no middle, only an end. He ascends, but then:

> Down a while
> He sat, and round about him saw unseen:
> At last, as from a cloud his fulgent head
> And shape star bright appeared, or brighter, clad
> With what permissive glory since his fall
> Was left him, or false glitter.

(10.447–52)

His ascent of his throne is parodied by the inclusion of an act of
descent, bordering on bathos: "Down a while / He sat," with the
act of sitting, emphasized by the poet's artful presentation of
the verb at the beginning of the line, having an intolerably realistic air. When Christ "sits at the right hand of God," the act is
sublimed into metaphor. But Satan has been provided by the
poet with such a very material-seeming throne, solid and heavily tapestried. Besides, Satan's activities here are indecently
human in their pettiness. The childishness of being invisibly
all-seeing, with the relish of self-created suspense, is here allied
uncomfortably in the reader's mind with a feeling of sinister
behavior that is not pleasant to contemplate. Fantasy fulfillment, delicious to the individual dreamer, may not bring happy
consequences to those co-opted into minor roles in somebody
else's fantasy. Every person who has examined his own fan-
tasies of being invisible and springing a surprise upon an astonished audience knows this. Fantasy, safe when kept in the
head (like Eve's false dream, related in Book 5), involves injustice when put into action.

The symbolism of travestied solar justice that we would expect at a triumphal moment is present here only in a possible,
deeply buried, and equivocal form, underlining the injustice of
Satan's return. For Satan's head (when it does consent to appear) is "fulgent." His head seems, because of the chronology
implied by the narrative sequence, to precede his body into

visibility: "his fulgent head / And shape star bright appeared."
In Latin, *fulgor* and its variants all relate to flashes of lightning
and ideas of glory and renown associated with a sudden blaze;
and so Satan's head is to be imagined as a sudden, bewildering
flash of lightning. But there are subsidiary meanings. *Fulgor* has
a concrete meaning of "shining star" (Satan as Lucifer), and
fulgeo may be used in connection with the sun.[35] We have here a
cluster of elemental associations that we are invited to choose
among by a phrase in the next line, apparently casual or merely
evocative on a first reading. For this fulgent head belongs to a
shape not only "star bright" but, possibly, brighter. If from the
lightning imagery we have emerged with the impression of the
head as a kind of sphere of light emitting rays—a quite possible
interpretation—then we may be reminded of the rayed solar
crown of the triumphal emperor. Indeed, the phrase *or brighter*
seems specifically to suggest the sun.[36]

We suspect, then, that Satan, who has distinctly informed the
sun (and therefore the just God who displays the sun as his
symbol) of his irreversible hatred—its brightness was a reminder of his own former state (4.57–59)—here in his last theatrical appearance performs a hinted parody of *Sol invictus*. It is
only the gentlest of hints, but, as Satan's career in *Paradise Lost*
culminates, it is fitting that the imperial sun should emit its
waning false glitter under the brightness of the risen Christian
sun and that Satan should fall into a final unflattering travesty
of the light-bearing Lucifer who tried at the beginning of the
story to be the light-giver himself.

4

Feudal Lord

In Milton's Paradise, as evening comes on, and the sun's light declines, the reader is invited to look across to the west where the last color of the day is being poured out upon the still-innocent world:

Arraying with reflected purple and gold
The clouds that on his western throne attend.

(4.596–97)

In this ultimate outburst of light from the sun, Milton created a royal sky, with imagery drawn from the monarch's investiture. The clouds, like the courtiers of a western palace, are vassals who in doing homage receive the glory belonging initially to the monarch but "reflecting out" upon all who serve him faithfully. Both realistic and stylized, as well as theological, elements apply here. Milton gives us an impression of that moment of apparent stasis, of the sun just on the point of disappearance. The clouds of early evening are "arrayed," or invested, with the colors traditionally associated with the monarch, and in this classic conceit, Milton suggests the majesty conferred on Christ's subjects by his act of dying for them (his sunset), giving natural processes a ritual solemnity. We are spiritually robed in purple and gold by the pure sun, "cloudy" though the human spirit is and unfitted for kingship. The angels of Heaven perceive God's glory through "a cloud / Drawn round about thee like a radiant shrine" (3.378–79) and pass the filtered or refracted light outward as it pours from its source. In Book 3, circling the "Fountain of light" (375), the angels gain glory by proximity to this immortal sun; in Book 4, nature is glorified, raised to regal power, and metaphorically resurrected through God's symbol of himself in the Heavens. Within this context, we are meant to perceive Milton's attribution of royal symbolism to the deity as morally stainless.

Yet the purple and gold here attributed to innocence are colors that, whenever they appeared in the mortal world, arraying a human body, were anathema to Milton, as we saw in Chapter 1 with Charles's "purple robe" of spilt blood making up an appalling double garment topped by his purple robe of state. The human commonwealth is defined throughout Milton's prose works as a place where value is located in a spartan disregard of splendor, sumptuous clothing being a disguise (and, besides, expensive), and kingly regalia, thrones, courts, banquets, and courtiers being merely means of not very useful pageanting about on the part of an arbitrarily selected individual who turns his subjects into a nation of abject, servile idolaters.[1] On every occasion that the regicide pamphleteer mentioned these attributes of monarchy, there is ire and disgust.

One of the central problems created by *Paradise Lost*, therefore, lies in the reader's anxiety that images of kingship attaching to the corrupt world of the fallen should be apparently duplicated in an innocent context and that it is only by reference to context that we can judge the moral worth of this body of images. This perception informed the opinion declared by Malcolm Mackenzie Ross in *Milton's Royalism* that the poet was a covert Royalist all along.[2] It also underlies the opposite (Empsonian) point of view, which holds that Milton's republicanism was so strong that he was only pretending, or trying, to love Christ the King in *Paradise Lost*.[3] A possible way out of the dilemma is to center attention upon the theory of accommodation to which the poet has Raphael refer in Book 5, when (aware of the difficulties involved in making the state of Heaven and events there accessible to human understanding) he puts it to Adam that the things of earth may

> Be but the shadow of heaven, and things therein
> Each to other like, more than on earth is thought?

(5.575–76)

If, as Platonism affirms, we live on a copy, a shadow of the real world, smudged and difficult to discern correctly, it is yet an authentic copy whose experiences, rituals, and events do relate, however paradoxically, to the real. What we view with suspicion in our world may therefore be imagined purged and idealized in the heavenly world, and we should find it startling but not indecorous if the Christian poet transfers some "royal" ritual from this world to the other, legitimating it in the process of removing it from usurper to true possessor. The king of earth only coarsens himself with unmerited vanities when he triumphs in his coronation; on the other hand, true goodness may naturally be embodied in splendor.

This is the sort of conclusion that Leland Ryken arrived at in his *Apocalyptic Vision in "Paradise Lost."* Arguing from the theory of accommodation that Milton insisted "that when human qualities are attributed to God they must be divested of some of their usual connotations," Ryken repudiated Ross's theory of Milton's subconscious royalism, for under the contextual approach, "we are free to see that Milton could without contradiction use the royalist symbol to represent true spiritual perfection, despite the fact that he was hostile to the royalist image as it existed in the political situation in England."[4] This analysis does leave the reader with a temporary sense of liberation, by virtue of its simplicity. But its simplicity is the very thing that makes the theory unsuitable to convey the rich complexity of our experience of Milton's poem and its relation to his political assertions.

Milton does not include all aspects of earthly monarchy in his picture of the constitution of Heaven, only selected images. God would not be expected to impersonate a sultan or a pharaoh, or Christ to act out the role of *Imperator.* Adam as the undisputed king of Paradise could not be represented as wearing the long hair of the Stuart court, for his manly puritan virtue is embodied in hair hanging "not beneath his shoulders broad" (4.303). Christ is shown as a king, and there is a coronation ritual, but he wears no crown, occupies no throne, receives no unction. On the other hand, God is shown as presiding over a court rich in chivalric motifs as an absolute ruler over a rigidly formulated and militaristic hierarchy dressed with medieval splendor according to degree. Christ as king requires obedience and homage, but he reigns, as Abdiel later goes on to say (5.843–45) as *rex* under *lex.* God as king reigns above law but intends to surrender his rule to the pacific Christ at the end of time, when "regal sceptre" shall be unnecessary (3.339–41). Adam as king of earth rules under God's law, but the animals are required to pay him "fealty" (8.344), a feudal term implying absolute vassalage and paralleling his function in this lower sphere with God's in the upper. Milton extrapolated and mingled certain royalist motifs from this earthly source, rejected other features, and transferred the imagery to the heavenly sphere. The material he chose is, strangely, from the image of feudal monarchy, grafted onto the Jewish royal model for God upon which the Bible is based. The structure most closely associated with Milton's incorporation of the feudal image into his poem is neither that providential structure engendered by the image of the oriental despot nor the triumphal form associated with the Roman emperor, but a circular structure, the circle of the noblesse around the feudal lord, imaging the circles of angelic hierarchies around the Creator,[5] centering in Book 5.

However, it is not simply that Milton chose a certain kind of monarchy as his model for the monarchy of Heaven, but rather that, having chosen it, he emphasized some features at the expense of others. The image of feudalism is often taken as an innately offensive one, and Empson's objection to Milton's God appears to involve the Lord of Heaven's feudal character: Satan's people were the "serfs" of Heaven, and the heavenly army is there only to preserve the pecking order.[6] The assumption is that a feudal monarchy is just as repulsive as an oriental despotism, involving an automatic reduction of the many by the one. Yet, though feudalism is a conservative structure (and therefore perhaps inherently appropriate for the representation of a state of perfect changelessness), it is not identifiable with a condition of servitude, for in its pure form feudalism proposed a system of mutual responsibilities, a closely interlocking system of classes, each with its unique function, for all of whose good the ruler was responsible. Among the "peers," the sovereign was only *primus inter pares,* first among equals, and it will be noticed that Milton excluded from his class system of Heaven any of the serf or thrall class. His feudal structure, confined to a community of peers, each with heraldic emblems, does not rest upon any unfree element. Its leader is the guarantor of liberty. The emphasis in his poem is on God conceived as the great giver of good, endlessly passing out to his vassal angels the sovereignty that primarily belongs to himself. The angels reflect his light as the clouds above Eden reflected the purple and gold of the light they caught.

Feudalism supplied for Milton a model of stasis, toward which many revolutionaries, themselves productive of change, have yearned. Marc Bloch, in his definitive *Feudal Society,* explains the personal character of the bond between vassal and lord in feudalism, in a description of the ceremony by which a noble became the "vassal" (not a derogatory term but one implying dignity) of his lord. The ceremony is remarkably beautiful:

> Imagine two men face to face; one wishing to serve, the other willing or anxious to be served. The former puts his hands together and places them, thus joined, between the hands of the other man— a plain symbol of submission, the significance of which was sometimes further emphasized by a kneeling posture. . . . Then chief and subordinate kiss each other on the mouth, symbolising accord and friendship.[7]

The vassal commits his entire lifetime to his lord in this act of homage and then swears fealty (faith, *foi*) to endorse his allegiance. Homage was reciprocal and primary; by it the lord undertook to care for the needs and defend the rights of his "man." All who had done homage became the man of another man, implying a kind of equalizing tendency in feudalism, each person being simultaneously lord and vassal, in an intricate network of intense relationships. By the law of *seisin*, property was held only in fee rather than in possession,[8] by a grant reverting to the lord at the subject's death or if he broke allegiance. Vassalage was a sign of the highest virtue and freedom.[9] The chief owed the vassal liberality *(beneficium)*,[10] and, in return, the vassal owed service, but not that of the serf, whose service was hereditary and unfree and who paid no homage. This system, though Milton could not have desired it for earth, has an obvious beauty when transferred to the heavenly sphere. The lord is the Lord himself. In requiring homage from his vassal, he connects them organically to himself. What he gives he rescinds only if loyalty is withdrawn, as Satan withdrew his. He makes no serfs, though Satan imagined himself servile and broke God's peace with a baronial feud.

In Milton's *Commonplace Book* (Yale 1:459, 461) and in his *Second Defence of the People of England* (Yale 4, pt. 1:659), he cited approvingly two works by sixteenth-century French Huguenot authors—François Hotman's *Francogallia* (1573) and the *Vindiciae Contra Tyrannos* of disputed authorship—as defending the doctrine of tyrannicide. He used these works to defend himself against the equally French and equally Huguenot royalist, Salmasius. But each of these authors (living under regimes in which feudalism had not yet died) represented feudalism as an institution that, far from savagely repressing people, vested sovereignty in the nation rather than in the king and regarded the (elective) monarchy as pledged to guarantee the liberty and welfare of the people: SALUS POPULI SUPREMA LEX ESTO.[11] Under this view of feudalism, Hotman shows that the people have power of redress under the law, against persecution, and the author of the *Vindiciae* presents an image of feudalism that may be seen, in a certain light, as leveling the entire population to an equal value under God.

In the *Vindiciae*, the whole cosmos is viewed as a feudal structure, God being the absolute emperor through whom earthly kings, being merely contributory, hold their power in fee. The kings are vassals, and tenants, owning neither land nor people, and bound with their people in a debtor–creditor relationship, in covenant with God and one another. The people have the obligation of checking regal power, for the king is under the law. This feudal conception of the universe, superficially conservative, has radical implications for human beings. God guards the status quo not for his own sake but for ours and is the scourge of kings. Milton's account of the rebellion of Lucifer is marvelously elucidated if we compare it with the *Vindiciae's* conflation of the Bible with feudalism:

> So often, therefore, as any prince shall so much forget himself, as insolently to say in his heart, I will ascend into heaven, I will exalt my throne above the stars of God; I will sit also upon the mount of the congregation in the sides of the north; I will ascend above the heights of the clouds, I will be like the Most High: then on the contrary, will the Almighty say, I will rise up more high, I will set myself against thee: I will erase out thy name and all thy posterity, thy counsels shall vanish into smoke, but that which I have once determined shall remain firm, and never be annihilated.[12]

At length into the limits of the north
They came, and Satan to his royal seat

High on a hill, far blazing . . .
. . . .
Affecting all equality with God,
In imitation of that mount whereon
Messiah was declared in sight of heaven,
The Mountain of the Congregation called.   (5.755–66)

Such a juxtaposition gives a strange clarity to the different kinds of kingship involved in Milton's account of God and Satan. Satan is simply a rebel who has broken his covenant with his feudal lord. The Huguenot author directly assimilates the figure of an earthly prince to the rise and fall of Lucifer. God's implacable antagonism in the second half of the sentence, rising step by step to check the anarchic rush of satanic energy, can provoke in the reader no indignation, for throughout the *Vindiciae* we are aware that any anger in God is on our behalf. His conservative structure "shall remain firm," because order is the precondition of all good. In *Paradise Lost*, the poet thus attempts to demonstrate that we could not exist without order and that violence on the part of a feudal God may be essential to preserve such order. The remote, inhuman face of God becomes, under this perspective, if not pleasant then necessary, for it registers eternal vigilance against Creation's lapsing into the Chaos from which it was formulated.[13]

Book 5 of *Paradise Lost* is supremely a statement about the order upon which Creation is founded, focused against Chaos, which is raw and void. Milton made this explicit by having Raphael open his description of Christ's coronation and Satan's rebellion with a glimpse into the remote past, which formulates for Adam the chaos of prehistory but opens out for us a characteristically frightening abyss in relation to our own existence in time and space:

As yet this world was not, and Chaos wild
Reigned where these heavens now roll, where earth now rests
Upon her centre poised, when on a day . . .

(5.577–79)

Raphael guides Adam's mind back into a remoteness that is literally unthinkable, since it forces him to encounter a time before being existed all in our human terms. Raphael shows an emptiness, unpeopled by images, and in very plain terms insists on Adam's confronting the possibility that the firm ground upon which he stands might simply not be there: "As yet this world was not" opens the story and leaves the reader with that trembling suspicion that perhaps this nonbeing could come again, the delicate balance of things that the symmetries of the verse so exquisitely render ("where these heavens . . . where earth") being whipped away and the poise of human survival eradicated.

Yet the narrator has immediately introduced two major linked themes of this book: the idea of circularity, resting upon a center like the earth dependent upon its maker's ordering power, and the idea of monarchy, for a king antagonistic to cosmic order is introduced. Milton, with his capacity to uncover buried images with the transforming power of his poetry, shows Chaos (whom we have previously seen enthroned in Book 2) as having "Reigned." The two sovereigns, diametrically opposed as they are, shared the available space in the time before our time began, not in Manichaean equality, but in evident tension. It is only after this unthinkable thought has been presented that Raphael locates his story in one day. The Great Year of Plato "brings forth" one day in its wheeling cycle. To the human mind, this day looks initially frail and short, as does the mortal brevity of the human "life-day" compared to the immortal cycles of Heaven. The sphere of our world is dwarfed in the image of the eon in Heaven drawing to its close and the opening of a new age. Our thoughts about this image, given our ephemeral life cycle and our apparent irrelevance to this part of the story, may tinge our awareness of the perfect structure of heavenly history with apprehension. Raphael, speaking in the plot to Adam but in the poem to us, resembles a parent saying, "this all happened before you were born," evoking one's first prescience of mortality.

Under late English feudalism, however, though the calendar year was dated from Easter, there was also a so-called regnal year dating from the day of the king's accession. The day of the proclamation in Heaven, therefore, may be seen as a completion of the regnal year and the beginning of a new one,[14] for:

> the empyreal host
> Of angels by imperial summons called,
> Innumerable before the almighty's throne

Forthwith from all the ends of heaven appeared
Under their hierarchs in orders bright
Ten thousand thousand ensigns high advanced,
Standards, and gonfalons twixt van and rear
Stream in the air, and for distinction serve
Of hierarchies, of orders, and degrees;
Or in their glittering tissues bear imblazed
Holy memorials, acts of zeal and love
Recorded eminent.

(5.583–94)

This order is self-consciously chivalric, feudal, and old-fashioned. The assembly looks nothing like the muster of the Cromwellian New Model Army, attractive though that idea may be,[15] for the Puritan army did not appear like this; they were dressed, literally, to kill. C. S. Lewis thought that Milton loved the idea of social order for its own sake, but this theory is false and solves nothing.[16] The "true warfaring Christian" of *Areopagitica* (Yale 2:515) fights for a precious, unformalized "civill liberty" (ibid., 487), not based on disorder but also not fettered by any social preconceptions. Liberty for Milton preceded order and was a condition of it. Empson is indignant: "But why do the angels have to be organised into an elaborate hierarchy at all?";[17] he feels that the angels have no purpose save to serve Omnipotence and remind Omniscience of what it already knows.

But these angels, so carefully gradated, so archaic, and so apparently functionless, serve by their very existence a ritual function. It is the function of coronation. Psalm 2, upon which God's proclamation of his Son is based, is commonly known as the "coronation psalm," and Milton, whose polemical works show constant preoccupation with English coronation ritual (whose roots lie in the feudal past), grafted elements of this ritual on to the biblical source to render it accessible to human understanding. Milton the regicide and revolutionary committed himself, in his analysis of the Stuart king's usurpation of illegal rights, to a belief in the legitimacy of an original form of liberty-guaranteeing monarchy. The most important sources for this belief were coronation documents, in which the ancient English liberties might be discerned. In his first *Defence,* Milton defended the conservative law that forced the king to undertake an oath of allegiance to God, the law, and the people. The people were asked, "Are you willing to agree on this man as your king" (Yale 4, pt. 1:479). To the question, "Do you grant those just laws which the people shall choose?" the new king's reply must be: "I do so grant" (ibid., 482). Royal accountability, the binding character of the oath, and reciprocity of trust between king and people are all shown—in *Eikonoklastes* (Yale 3:592); *The Commonplace Book* (ibid., 1:435–36); and the first *Defence*—to be fundamental to English law, in its pure form. Milton had studied the ceremony in minute detail and concluded that it was the living vehicle of the people's legitimate, original rights under but against the crown.

The implications of accepting the coronation formulas as valid are unashamedly conservative. The ancient and original are seen as ideal; change is usurpation. The office is worthy, the man unworthy. But nothing could be more ancient and original than God ("As yet this world was not"); nothing more pertinent to this originality than an ancient ceremony containing archaic legal structures; nobody more fitted to enact and symbolize a legal relationship between sovereign and subjects than God himself, Law embodied, the Sun of Justice. Not all the features of the ceremony are included in Milton's poetic account, but even the omissions (of any worldly or corrupted elements) are enlightening. The "imperial summons" by which God gathers to him all the hierarchies of Heaven is, therefore, a representation of the calling up of "the feudal pyramid" to appear, as a historian of coronation ritual puts it, "in visible shape."[18] The purpose of the gathering was in itself not practical but mysterious and symbolic, and Milton used this mystical quality within English coronation ceremony to emphasize that far more mystical event in which angels witness the coronation of the Son of God. Milton's account lays simultaneous value upon the hierarchical classification of the angels and upon the emblems of "Holy memorials, acts of zeal and love" by which their bright personages are manifested. Though the caste system in Milton's Heaven is apparently rigid, all of the inhabitants are equally distinguished by these heraldic devices recording their virtue. It is a paradox that high and low may coexist without the low being degraded; nevertheless, the poet insists on it.

The striking thing about Milton's version of the feudal pyramid is the universal quality of its resplendence (all are glorified within an order in which each individual shines), allied with the positive application of the feudal image: nobody is left out. This universality and positiveness are in fact intrinsic to the feudal ceremony itself. At the coronation of Charles I, no one would have been so mad as to step up to inquire of the "spur-holders" about the practical usage of the spurs nor to ask what immediate purpose was served by their proceeding *after* the Earl of Warwick and *before* the canopy-bearers.[19] All these useless functions are symbolic parts of the intricate whole. In Milton's adaptation, there are no costly paraphernalia, no investiture, no actual anointing with unction. All are metaphorical. Redundant spur holders are replaced by the innumerable crowds of the saints, underneath "ten thousand thousand ensigns," symbolizing only what they are: loving, zealous, virtuous.[20] There is no practical reason for their being organized into "an elaborate hierarchy," but as they are not a barbarian horde, they cannot be allowed to "pour" around the throne. (Thus the radiance of their merit, reciprocated by divine love, is displayed in a structured form.) On the other hand, no one "'twixt van and rear" is borne down upon by the others.

Similarly, in the coronation service, rights were paraded and position identified by coat of arms, positively demonstrating the noble's inalienable position in the intricate order of things. Schramm explains that, with the growth of the Norman feudal system in England, the high day of the king became the high day of all the great men of his nation, grouped concentrically around their sovereign.[21] Likewise, the *promissio regis* by which a king binds himself to his people occurs before the ceremony; only in the later parts do the magnates bind themselves by a kiss of vassalage.[22] If Milton has depicted the Son's elevation as a vestigial coronation act, we should see no degrading of the angelic hosts. Under the transformation of his poetry, angelic heraldry symbolizes spiritual and moral virtue.[23] The nobles of Heaven—noble in the moral sense—are "high advanced," their tissues "glittering," their "memorials" holy.

This part of the account requires some labor of exegesis to make it comprehensible, but no amount could make the poetry beautiful. Milton's researches into coronation ceremony had been largely obligatory. Yet the poetry takes fire when the coronation structure meets the theological structure of angelic hierarchies, used so movingly by Dante in his *Paradiso* (xxviii) and so passionately by Pseudo-Dionysius in his *Celestial Hierarchies*. Christ's army has no crescent-jaws like those of the Turks; it occupies no phalanx formation like that of the Romans. It circles, and in the organic flow of this ancient symbol of eternity any jarring note of caste-bound militarism becomes silent. Here again, political and religious ideas fuse to the most perfect poetic effect. The concentric groupings of the angels around God are like the concentric circles of the nobility about a king, and each order, through closeness to its neighbor, renews its attachment to the sovereign, the fullness of whose power and love passes out from order to order:

> Thus when in orbs
> Of circuit inexpressible they stood,
> Orb within orb, the Father infinite,
> By whom in bliss embosomed sat the Son,
> Amidst as from a flaming mount, whose top
> Brightness had made invisible, thus spake.

(5.594–99)

The image is of an army displaying armorial bearings ("imblazed") in a kaleidoscopic pageant of color and a fiery burning of gold (for the heraldic word *imblaze* contains *blaze* and is associated with the term), with squadrons standing square to the view in an intricate pattern, like the interwoven tissues that the legions wear, and it is from this image that the mind moves to a dominant image of circularity. It is a movement toward an image of union rather than of linked details, and it is also a return, a circling back, to the images of the spherical earth, the circling Great Year, which opened this sequence. There is verbal reiteration, "orbs / Of circuit . . . Orb within orb," as if the poetry could mime these same circles closing around one another. The angels move in to surround the central point, having congregated "from all the ends of heaven" (5.586). Whereas initially the poet was careful to analyze the "hierarchies . . . orders . . . degrees" within the community of Heaven, here he synthesizes them into a wholeness that is made up of movement within stillness. The new image offers the reader sensations of security, safety, and love. In the enclosure of the encircling angels there is repose "inexpressible" because the angels bound the illimitable Father of all. They are "orbs" like planets around the earth, like the orbs of the chariot wheels of Messiah (6.828–30) or perhaps like the orb of a ring upon a hand, or like a world.

In the coronation service, the king is presented with an orb as part of his regalia, a globe surmounted by a cross, also known as a "mound." This orb represents his earthly power and his divine obligations. In Milton's poem it is the heavenly orb, unheld by God but held by the attractive power of love around him: in a sense holding him. Just as the chariot of Christ is alive with terrifying eyes staring like God's omniscience, so also his orb is not a physical object but a living community held together by love. Although the Father is described here as invisible by virtue of his brightness, the word *orb* may also refer to the ball of the eye, by which the community of Heaven investing the invisible Father with the power he already owns perceives the radiance of his being. From this bright, glittering enclosure God issues his proclamation, phrased by Milton in a variation of the coronation psalm. It is curious to reflect that Lucifer is among those angels who form the irradiating circle around God and the Son, inclining inward, toward the central point of the "flaming mount" and the throne of Christ. While the orb is offered to God in the persons of his sons, so also Christ may be said to be enthroned, "in bliss embosomed," his place of repose being not an object but a person. Milton as a poet stripped court ceremony of materialism. He gained his most spectacular effects by substituting persons for things, spirit for matter, while retaining structures recognizable in the material world. There is no sacramental oil for the anointing, only a deep, unseen act of the spirit; no throne for the Son save his Father; no crown save the thorns of his future death; no orb save his creatures; no investiture save with his Father's brightness; and a scepter—ultimately—only in his dying. Yet, in the deeper sense, all these coronation factors are present.

Christ's future dying is somehow envisaged by the poet and expressed to the reader in these scenes of coronation. This is the central paradox that must modify our response to the Messiah's exaltation. *Messiah* means *the anointed one,* and we have been shown in a brilliantly perceptive essay by W. B. Hunter that Milton's account of the begetting of Christ refers to three points in time: the beginning of things, when the Son was brought forth; the central point of human history, when the Son's voluntary humiliation made him a visitor of the grave; and the end of things, when Christ, in his Second Advent, and man, who shall have been made one in the incarnation, will be alike elevated. Hunter imagined the proclamation taking place on a kind of Maundy Thursday in the cycle of eternity, followed by the Black Friday of Crucifixion and extending to the Easter Sunday of Resurrection.[24] His point is that the reader of Book 5 of *Paradise Lost* has to imagine (against the pressure of mere logic) that all these occasions are superimposed upon one another.

In this context, the account of the clustering angels around the deity suggests a kind of pity, seemingly unaccountable but explained by Hunter's version. This is a coronation ceremony at which earthly expectations will be defeated at a very deep level. The Son's "bliss embosomed" is made out of the ache of his assumption of mortality, built on the agony in the garden, founded on grief yet to be encountered. His anointing is to a kingship that raises him above all others, but it is also (as Abdiel will later tell Satan) to a reduction that is at the same time a humiliation. The encircling angels, accepting their feudal obligation to the monarch, act as if to shield him from this uniquely grievous kind of kingship.

God's proclamation of his Son has aroused theological controversy of a harshness and multiplicity of argument painful to contemplate. Abstaining from full participation, I shall only consider the proclamation as a ceremony of kingly anointing. Milton's conceptions of the king's anointing in the mortal world and of the divine anointing of the Son are opposite in character and reveal a radical difference between earthly and heavenly kingships. Milton the political thinker rejected the sacred quality of the human king's anointing in favor of the biblical concept of mankind as "the anointed of God whom none may touch" (*Defence*, Yale 4, pt. 1:499). Sovereignty is seen as vested solely in the people, with an emotional insistence so vehement on Milton's part as to recall the beautiful confidence of Gerrard Winstanley, the Digger, calling for "The Kingly power of righteousnesse" that vests liberty and equality in the poor common people, as against the illegitimate "dark kingly power" of the oppressor.[25] We might almost mistake Milton for Winstanley, reading that "towns and boroughs are more ancient than kings, and in the very fields the people remains the people still" (*Defence,* Yale 4, pt. 1:486). In a sense it is an illusory likeness, for Winstanley was defending the people in the fields against the very people with whom Milton identified. But the feeling is there: a sense of the English as a nation of God's beloved children, especially anointed by Him, reducing the mysterious coronation unction to a mere jar of oil. The king's oath, being made to an anointed people, sons of God each one, therefore has a binding force of terrifying proportions.

Milton the theologian in his *De Doctrina Christiana,* commenting on Psalm 2, the basis of God's proclamation of Christ's begetting in *Paradise Lost,* says, "God begot the Son in the sense of making him a king" (Yale 6, pt. 1, sect. 5:207), linking to Christ's appointment a mediatorial function or resurrecting office (206–12). Milton the poet, in his metrical translation of Psalm 2 in 1653, emphasized the specifically kingly exaltation by translating the instrument of punishment, whereby earthly kings are to be destroyed, not as the more generalized "rod of iron" of the Authorized Version but as an "iron sceptre." The King James version has:

> Thou shalt break them with a rod of iron; thou shalt dash them in pieces like a potter's vessel. (Ps. 2:9)

Milton's metrical translation makes it clear that he sees the Messiah as the King over kings, reigning on behalf of justice:

> but I saith he
> Anointed have my king (though ye rebel)
> On Sion my holy hill. A firm decree
> I will declare; the Lord to me hath said
> Thou art my Son I have begotten thee
> This day; ask of me, and the grant is made;
> As thy possession I on thee bestow
> The heathen, and as thy conquest to be swayed
> Earth's utmost bounds: them shalt thou bring full low
> With iron sceptre bruised, and them disperse
> Like to a potter's vessel shivered so.

> (Psalm 2:11–21)

In God's proclamation in *Paradise Lost*, Milton refrained from using the word *king* but stressed instead the sacramental nature of the anointing and used the suggestive term *head* to express the character of the Son's leadership:

> Hear all ye angels, progeny of light,
> Thrones, dominations, princedoms, virtues, powers,
> Hear my decree, which unrevoked shall stand.
> This day I have begot whom I declare
> My only Son, and on this holy hill
> Him have anointed, whom ye now behold
> At my right hand; your head I him appoint;
> And by my self have sworn to him shall bow
> All knees in heaven, and shall confess him Lord:
> Under his great vicegerent reign abide
> United as one individual soul
> For ever happy: him who disobeys
> Me disobeys, breaks union, and that day
> Cast out from God and blessed vision, falls
> Into utter darkness, deep engulfed, his place
> Ordained without redemption, without end.

(5.600–615)

The poetry, founded upon the royal psalm used as part of Hebrew coronation ritual,[26] intermeshes other texts (Eph. 4:15, Col. 2:9, Gen. 22:16, Philem. 2:9–11) to expand the scope of meaning back toward the Creation and forward toward the Last Things. But we imagine the form of Psalm 2 continuing beneath the surface, counterpointing the poetry and emphasizing the ferocity and punitiveness that many detect (and normally dislike) in God's speech. The reference to the listening angels as "progeny of light," quiet detail though it is, honors them: it also links them into familial relationship with "my only Son," for he, as light or *logos*, created them. Through this intermeshing of dependent relationships, God's anointing of his Son gains a significance beyond the individual triumphal moment. Just as Milton in his political works insisted upon an anointed people from whom sovereignty issued and on whose behalf sovereigns reigned, so in this speech God suggests a kind of overflow of anointing from Messiah to angels; from Son to sons; by extension, from perfect God to erring man. If Christ is the head, the angels are the body. Organically related thus, their union is enhanced, and this is the great theme of the proclamation.

The insistence that the angels are to bow the knee and take an oath of allegiance is both a biblical and a feudal element, naming the subjects as vassals of the almighty. Again, the anger of Satan at being required to cringe and fawn upon a king whose reign must start with a display of abject servility upon the part of the subjects has been echoed by many provoked readers. Only an awareness of Christ's complementary bending down out of his deity to create symmetry with these subjects' own prostration, allied with an awareness of the universality of the anointing, can mitigate our anger at such a demand. Milton's poetry thus—by returning to the theme of the shared "blessed vision" of the unified angels, circling in orbs that body forth the "one individual soul"—suggests the beauty of allegiance. He attempts to show that the unredeemed fall of those too proud to become love's vassals is a psychological corollary of the rejection of such union, and it is interesting that he avoids the more human image that ends Psalm 2—the shattering of the pottery vessel that is earthly kingship by the Divine "iron sceptre." It is possible that he expected his reader to remember this image, however, for its very violence is reassuring to the "anointed" reader of the poem. Those image-doting, blood-stained kings of human history are the "progeny of darkness," bred by those angels who break union in Heaven. The persecuted may rejoice that God's anointed Son, daubed with no material unction but who has entered into a "vicegerent reign," will be able to disperse the heathen "Like to a potter's vessel shivered so" (Psalm 2:21). Further reassurance may filter to the reader through the structure of this speech. Its fifteen lines are equal to the number of steps upon a *scala humilitatis,* or ladder of humility: rising upon them, through humility, we attain the blessed vision. Christ, reducing himself through his humiliation, passes us on the way and, through lowering himself, insures our safe arrival at our unmerited destination.

But each of these responses in the reader is obtained indirectly, through an understanding of typology, through numerological interpretation of the lines. The poetry itself falls upon the ears like the voice of doom, and its dreadful call to obedience as the foundation of unity carries a kind of spiritual desolation that makes the reactions of a small portion of the listeners very understandable:

So spake the omnipotent, and with his words
All seemed well pleased, all seemed, but were not all.

(5.616–17)

These two lines (two being the number of division, breaking from the One) are bleak and oppressive. They record the first lie in Heaven: "All seemed . . . all seemed, but," and in the simplicity of the statement, with its sensation of inevitability, they toll in the mind like a direct fulfillment of fate. Union has now been broken, but celebration of heavenly union continues, certain hypocrites participating and mentally preparing for a feud.

Why these angels were displeased, however, is not yet said. We intuit the reason, but Milton passes on from his terse admission that "all" has become "not all" without any attempt at elaboration. Critics have assumed that this breaking with divine decree resulted from disgust at the grisly nepotism involved in a father elevating his son with such asperity and apparently unmotivated distrust of his peoples' response,[27] since this action may be felt to stand in contradiction to the superficially more attractive "democratic" approach made by Satan to his power. Yet Satan's claim is rooted more fully in pedigree than God's. Surrounding himself in Heaven and Hell with whatever vestiges of feudal rights he finds useful, Satan stakes his claim to equality with God by throwing it backward into the past, beyond the new edicts brought in by God to elevate his own. The speech that most clearly expounds this insistence upon the feudal basis of the nobles' power is the first "counterfeiting" utterance that he makes at the Mountain of the Congregation:

Thrones, dominations, princedoms, virtues, powers,
If these magnific titles yet remain
Not merely titular, since by decree
Another now hath to himself engrossed
All power, and us eclipsed under the name
Of king anointed.

(5.772–77)

Under feudal law, the nobles held their land and power from the king and had to return it at his will, but this was an issue between king and nobility that undermined feudalism to such a degree as to produce in England the Magna Carta defining nobles' rights against the crown. On first reading, we would expect Milton to be drawing with approval upon such a movement toward a balanced constitution (Empson sees Satan as a "grand aristocrat" appropriately defending rights originally his[28]), but Milton never showed any love of the English aristocracy, an aristocracy of the virtuous being the only legitimate lords. Once virtue in the form of personal and public allegiance to the good is gone, then so is nobility: titles become merely titular, labels divorced from reality. Satan inverts this fundamental feudal obligation and, in accusing Christ of eclipsing the nobles with his grand new name, fails to recognize, first, that what God granted freely Christ did not extort and, second, that the "name of king anointed," *Messiah,* has connotations rather of service than of government. In this speech, by resenting so fiercely the "prostration vile" (5.782), like a curdling taste in the mouth, that must be paid to the new feudal overlord, Satan revokes his metaphorical kiss of vassalage and his oath of obedience. In extolling the freedom of the angels according to the old constitution, he asserts that the invention of a new king represents the abuse

> Of those imperial titles which assert
> Our being ordained to govern, not to serve.
>
> (5.801–2)

In distinguishing between "governors" and those who "serve," Satan is pretending that there are serfs in Heaven, an invention of his own. In calling the angels "Natives and sons of heaven" (5.790), he ironically and unconsciously identifies himself with the feudal bondsmen *(nativi, niefs)* that sin has made them.[29] This denial of the reciprocal function of the king and nobility in feudalism, in favor of a literal interpretation of the titles of Heaven, contradicts the ethos in which Satan locates his title. For Satan, to be a "Throne" is to sit above all others; a "domination" dominates; a "princedom" exercises power; a "virtue" presides in virile strength; a "power" reigns. It is not at all clear, however, who is to be reigned over. Here the confluence of political titles and the traditional celestial hierarchy that Milton has brought together to define the rule of Heaven has a tempering effect upon the political material. The reader remembers that in Dionysius's *Celestial Hierarchy* all the orders receive love, justice, and power from the central and sovereign deity around whom they cluster for life: they pass the overflow of his glory outward, not servile, not governing, but each performing an individual mediation of divine bliss. It is the circle that we miss here in Satan's oratory, the failure to emanate loving presence and, therefore, to create organic union. The most beautifully ironic of the titles that Satan insists on is *virtue*, which every simple reader knows must be rested not on governing power but on sheer goodness.

As Satan's rule develops, the reader is aware of the disjunction of the feudal titles from their validating origins. The parodic events by which the fallen angel apes the divinity demonstrate the opening gap, which finally becomes a kind of catastrophic abyss like that down which he falls. After Satan's self-election to demonic kingship in Book 2, there is a travestied manifestation of his kingdom's feudal structure, along with a proclamation to the people and an acclamation. Satan in Pandemonium, according to the other fallen angels all the glittering titles they could possibly desire (on the principle that, the less the actual value residing in a title, the more profligacy a leader may assume in disposing of it—a principle well known to the Stuart court), emerges the monarch, with his peers:

> Midst came their mighty paramount, and seemed
> Alone the antagonist of heaven, nor less
> Than hell's dread emperor with pomp supreme,
> And God-like imitated state; him round
> A globe of fiery seraphim enclosed
> With bright emblazonry and horrent arms.
> Then of their session ended they bid cry
> With trumpets' regal sound the great result:
> Toward the four winds four speedy cherubim
> Put to their mouths the sounding alchemy
> By herald's voice explained: the hollow abyss
> Heard far and wide, and all the host of hell
> With deafening shout returned them loud acclaim.

(2.508–20)

The symbolism, deriving from the heavenly feudalism, has been turned inside out. In Heaven, angels are drawn inward by the persuasive power of love to encircle their maker (yearning back to him like the Plotinian emanations): in Hell, the parodied "maker," or inventor, moves, and the circle, or here "globe," of angels rather than turning inward toward the satisfying center are imagined with their backs to his turning outward in military formation.

The word *globe* here suggests the cold surface of a sphere, hard as earth; Satan's troops are not "orbing" as the angels of Heaven but are in a defensive–offensive posture. The ceremonies of Heaven have become militarized like their earthly feudal counterparts, and so have the heraldic emblems proclaiming titles, with the same clamor as the trumpets invading space with noise. "Bright emblazonry" looks forward to the coats of arms "imblazed" in Book 5 (592): what is signified by the emblazoned devices is not explained. In Heaven, heraldry immortalizes "Holy memorials, acts of zeal and love" (5.593); it belongs to peacetime and is a living inscription of goodness worn by the doer. In Hell, the value of the blazon, detached from source, is in itself or, more sinister, in "horrent arms." Acts of zeal and love are replaced by acts of impiety and destruction, commemorated in a meretricious tradition of emblems that is more like earthly chivalry, founded in blood, than the heavenly ideal from which it has fallen. Similarly, there is no emphasis on the intermeshing of devices, intricately weaving the feudal society together. Rather, trumpet sounds echo drearily out into "the hollow abyss," losing pitch as does all sound falling into empty space; and the angels, rather like an army off duty, straggle out in all directions, seeking not joy but "Truce to his restless thoughts" (2.526). The war is within, between incompatibles whose eternal opposition may yield only truce, never peace.[30] The horrible noise outside and the massive void around the angels mime the population's rootless loneliness. Satan has substituted his obduracy for God's heavenly form, and for the enclosing circle of security, a space opening out into hollow echoes. The epic games that follow are "wild uproar" (2.541), like natural calamities, in contradiction to the at once stylized and individuated dance of heavenly spirits in Book 5 (620–27), circling and uncircling. The Satanic feudalism, dragged up by the roots from the Creator, begets a process of disjoining and chaotic "wandering," in which the feudalism of Heaven draws the population toward a central focus and disposes them securely. The leader of such wanderers as Satan's has to be "hell's dread emperor" to terrify allegiance out of such vagrant units.

The proud nobles who were licensed brigands under European feudalism, and for whom fighting was "their whole purpose in life,"[31] are transferred by Milton to practice chivalry in Hell.

Milton presents Christ in the controversial exaltation of Book 5 not as a "dread emperor" but as *primus inter pares*.[32] If this were clearer, the offense at an apparently arbitrary violation of angelic liberty on the part of God, taken by many just-minded readers, might be minimized. Unfortunately, this revulsion is deeply understandable, for the elliptical brevity of God's speech sounds despotic, however sympathetically one attempts to read it, and the coronation ceremonial that follows may be alienating. Furthermore, the political framework in which the episode is offered involves a celebration of hereditary rule, anathema to many readers and to Milton himself throughout his political works. However, the poet successfully mitigated the moral flaws implicit in a hereditary principle in two ways. First, without giving Christ another father, Milton could not have gone further out of his way to show that Christ's merit rather than his birthright entitled him to rule: reciprocally, the angels' merit entitled them to receive him as their head. Second, as the first among equals, Christ guarantees "blessed vision" to the community of Heaven (5.613). Milton identifies the feudal principle of *primus inter pares* with Christ's appointment, through the anointing, to mediatorial office, the central function of Christ as it is defined in his *Christian Doctrine*. Some critics justify God's speech of exaltation by emphasizing the negative part of his injunction as a prohibition similar to that against the fruit in Eden.[33] But the positive aspect of the speech, poetically moving, is also full of substance in communicating to angel and reader alike the quality of what God is offering: the quality of a gift that is not in itself an exaction, but refusal of which will entail loss.

At the point when political and theological meet, the saving clauses are found: king and mediator (a mediator whom we as readers have met and learned to value in Book 3) meet in one:

Under his great vicegerent reign abide
United as one individual soul
For ever happy.

(5.609–11)

Isolated from the prohibition, this passage not only fails to offend the sensibilities but also carries a dignity within its measure; "his great vicegerent reign," a peace within its phrasing; "abide" contains "bide," to wait, and therefore encloses a promise, and there is a strangely simple and touching definition of the community's experience as "happy." It carries no harm to any creature. The status "vicegerent," a delegated power, suggests a bending down of the sovereign majesty to communicate with the people rather than an arbitrary promotion. The emphasis of these crucial lines is on unity, with one another and with Christ. The ensuing threat, therefore, only involves a kind of feudal forfeiture: God reclaiming his own.[34]

Milton's biblical scholarship made it possible for him to show Heaven as a political model in which the potentially corrupt principle of hereditary rule was absolutely tempered by the principle of meritocracy.[35] A striking parallel to the exaltation in *Paradise Lost* occurs in his *Commonplace Book*, in which Milton was attempting to evolve a way of modifying hereditary rule on earth so as to make it ethically acceptable, based on merit and not on blood. On appointing an heir,

> It is best, if a king expects to entrust his kingdom to his son after him, that he should so appoint his son that he will believe that his father establishes the succession of the realm, not on the basis of his coming of age, but on the basis of his deserts, and that he is to receive his father's authority, not as inherited spoils, but as the reward of worth; therefore, that the king should rather decide in his own mind and in secret than publicly proclaim whom he expects to leave as heir to the realm, and leave the succession, as it were, in doubt. . . . For this reason Elizabeth was unwilling to proclaim Mary of Scotland her heir. (Yale 1:433–35)

What Milton advocated in the terrestrial sphere, he was not above representing in the celestial one. God's Son is glorified late in time in order that he shall have accomplished acts of virtue to legitimate his kingship; at a ritualistic "moment in eternity" (the Platonic Great Year of the *Timaeus* [39D]), as if on a birthday.[36] The Son in his coronation is simply recognized as worthy, so that the elective principle supersedes the hereditary, as Milton had hoped it might for human kings "not on the basis of his coming of age, but on the basis of his deserts." "This day have I begot" may be read literally as the first birthday of the Son in eternity, a decorous moment to ritualize his creative goodness. This interpretation is compatible with the view—expressed by Robert Graves and Joshua Podro in *The Nazarene Gospel Restored* and accepted by most modern commentators—that Psalm 2 may be regarded as a coronation formula based on an older ceremony of adoption.[37] Milton's God, then, is revolutionary enough to adopt an only Son who must manifest his concern for the good of all before he is ceremoniously recognized as the Son who deserves kingship.

Throneless and crownless, but anointed, the Son is created king. Adam knows at this point what Raphael has told him, but we as readers entered the epic poem in medias res, and, knowing something of Christ's kingship in the future, should cast our minds back to Book 3 for illumination of the mystery of his reign and his anointing. Though Book 3 postdates Book 5 in real time, the circling movements of Milton's narrative keep insisting upon a basic wholeness of meaning within the poem. In the vision of Christian truth, there are no tangential experiences or irrelevant details; likewise, there is no real past, present, or future in a simple linear sense. The great circle of eternity; the recurrence of events, images, persons, postures; the looping movement of the narrative; the tight circles of human history repeating our fall invincibly—all forbid any merely chronological interpretation of the poem. In Book 3, God and Christ, being in dialogue, set Justice against Mercy, until Mercy is found to fulfill Justice. It is the book of Christ's sacrificial offering of himself for man. We cannot forget these events when we come to Book 5, for the key to the meaning of the exaltation of the Son, present in Book 5 in a buried form, has been offered directly in Book 3, the book of vision. Milton in his exordium asks for the mind to be "Irradiate[d]" (3.53) that it may tolerate, receive, and disclose this vision. God looks down, "bent down his eye" (58), upon creation. The encircling angels look upon God, lights receiving light; God foresees (79). In this strange give and take of vision, God's beauty is revealed in some of the most glorious poetry of *Paradise Lost*:

> About him all the sanctities of heaven
> Stood thick as stars, and from his sight received
> Beatitude past utterance; on his right

The radiant image of his glory sat,
His only Son.

(3.60–64)

This same structure is adopted by the angels in Book 5 when they stand "in orbs / Of circuit inexpressible" (594–95). The simile "thick as stars" suggests the same planetary orbit, in which each bright being has its own unique place, but the reader is struck with the quality of light burning with holy joy rather than with the circulating structure itself. The poet translates the angels from a personal to a transcendental status: sacred persons become "the sanctities of heaven," assuming an impersonal grace and dignity and participating in a life of which we can know almost nothing. They are remote and in stasis, as if held by the light of their beatitude. Christ himself is "the radiance" that can satisfy the poet's longing to be "Irradiate[d]." It is all "past utterance," and we remember this reading in Book 5 of the "orbs / Of circuit *inexpressible.*" This quality of a joy in light beyond the receiver's power to tell or the poet's power to express is directly experienced in Book 3. The poetry of light is so beautiful as to enforce participation. Though this feeling is not experienced in Book 5, it is remembered. The bare narrative echoes Book 3, and the patient reader is expected to know exactly what Satan rejects, not by receiving another outburst of light that might interrupt the narrative, but by allowing his memory to yield up the earlier images. The description of the mountain of God's declaration as, at its summit, invisible with pure brightness (5.599) recalls the angelic hymn rounding off Book 3:

> thee author of all being,
> Fountain of light, thy self invisible
> Amidst the glorious brightness where thou sit'st
> Throned inaccessible, but when thou shadest
> The full blaze of thy beams, and through a cloud
> Drawn round about thee like a radiant shrine,
> Dark with excessive bright thy skirts appear,
> Yet dazzle heaven, that brightest seraphim
> Approach not, but with both wings veil their eyes.

(3.374–82)

Nothing in Book 5 approaches the lyrical glory of this impression: the light hurting the yearning eyes of the beholder; the poignant detail of the seraphs shading their eyes from God's partial exertion of his light, which, though it is a kind of darkness in its extremity, is too intense to be borne. But this is what God's understated injunction to be happy in Book 5 entails: deep joy that is almost pain; stasis; light structured in circles of mystic song and dance. The inhabitants of Heaven, like the unstained human pair in Eden before the Fall, are presented as artists, poets, dancers, and lovers, whose creativity derives from their primal experience of God. The Christ exalted is the person whose voice we have already heard in Book 3 identifying himself as Son with man as son, "Thy creature late so loved, thy youngest son" (151), simply saying "Account me man" (238); though he is clear that "Thou wilt not leave me in the loathesome grave" (247), the adjective *loathesome* expresses the mortal contamination and deep loneliness that will characterize that lowest of all moments in Christ's agony: "My God, my God, why hast thou forsaken me?" This free, meekly made offer to surrender to the law is the condition upon which the first exaltation to kingship in the poem (though second in time) is made:

> Because thou hast, though throned in highest bliss
> Equal to God, and equally enjoying
> Godlike fruition, quitted all to save
> A world from utter loss, and hast been found
> By merit more than birthright Son of God,
> Found worthiest to be so by being good,
> Far more than great or high; because in thee
> Love hath abounded more than glory abounds,
> Therefore thy humiliation shall exalt
> With thee thy manhood also to this throne,
> Here shalt thou sit incarnate, here shalt reign
> Both God and man, Son both of God and man,
> Anointed universal king, all power
> I give thee.

(3.305–18)

Here God first explicitly repudiates hereditary rule in favor of elective rule on a meritocratic basis. Out of birthright in its ordinary sense are extracted rights based on goodness. Here also the anointing of the king is stressed, in close relation to the anointing of humanity, God's youngest sons. Christ's kingdom is seen as encompassing all time until kingship itself is rendered unnecessary, when the "regal sceptre" Christ "shalt lay by" may be dispensed with, after the Second Coming, "For regal sceptre then no more shall need" (3.339–40).

Few people have remained unmoved by the beauty of the poetry Milton gave to the Son here, the quietude of his demeanor and his gentle assumption of human nature. In Book 5, the poet refrained from setting Christ's kingship before us with the same degree of speaking brightness, perhaps expecting the reader's memory to supply the full picture that Book 3's dialectical structure and synthetic conclusion gave leisure to create. Book 5 is about action, at first ceremonious and ritualized, then powerful and dynamic, as Satan's army breaks the heavenly harmony and prepares for war. The modern reader must successfully actualize Book 3 in his mind while he reads Book 5 in order to feel the proper horror at the outbreak of "seeming" immediately after God's words of proclamation (5.616–17). We should also be able to recapture some of the power attached to certain conceptions within the ritual God performs, if we call to mind the rich significances involved for the contemporary Protestant reader within such phrases as God's "I / Him have anointed" (605), which emphasize that Christ's is a kingship devolving power endlessly from itself to its subjects.

The anointing is the central factor in this self-yielding structure of power. The pot of unction in the English coronation service was the subject of Milton's special loathing, both in itself as a derisory material object and because it was conferred by the imbecilic bishops with their rhomboidal hats (*Of Reformation in England,* Yale 1:612) to the accompaniment of meaningless jargon "that gives a Vomit to GOD himselfe" (ibid., 537), the bishops acting as anointed intermediaries who raised the king himself (through his anointing) to sacerdotal status.[38] All ceremonies connected with the "obscene, and surfeted priest" (ibid., 548) with his "many-benefice-gaping mouth," his "canary-sucking, and swan-eating palat" (ibid., 549), so vilified in the early anti-prelatical tracts, would be unthinkable and could not have legitimately derived from the Divine Principle. In *Paradise Lost,* Book 5, God himself anoints his Son, invisibly, and prior to the action. Milton's insistence on God's presence in the silent, inner life of man, the ceremonies that go on in the heart, unseen and private, is subtly expressed here. For Puritans, the anointing of Christ was the potential future anointing of all faithful souls as God's sons. The very word *anointed* seems to have brought a surge of trustful confidence into Puritan hearts. As Winstanley testified, Christ "indeed is the anointing, shall fill all, and all shall be the fulnesse of the anointing."[39]

The political implications of this theory of anointing were liberating and comforting to Christians; in the works of a majority of Puritan thinkers of the seventeenth century, this theory placed political sovereignty in the hands of the people rather than in the human king. This is so even, or especially, in a work with a feudal basis like the *Vindiciae Contra Tyrannos*. The king in his vasallage to God is under the people, for they are God's people rather than his. The oily daubings of unction on various portions of the royal anatomy are made only after the people have been asked "whether they desire and command, that he who is then before them, shall be their king?"[40] The Huguenot author consulted the coronation ceremony as a charter of human rights in all European countries and was not disappointed in what he found there: binding oaths upon the king; in Aragon, the king who "swears fealty, and does his homage" to Justice embodied in a person seated higher than himself; sacramental promises to obey law and God.[41] God's anointing of his Son in Milton's poem may likewise, in Puritan terms, be seen as a charter of rights to the faithful.

There is no crown, for a crown of thorns awaits Christ on earth, not mentioned but assumed by Milton in his terse account of the Passion in Book 12, austere because the poet was more interested in the significance than in the events of the Crucifixion, nailing up "the sins / Of all mankind" (416–17) so that they may never hurt Adam again. It is clear that God is glorifying and crowning for the future that part of himself which is pure love, transcending power, and before whose sacrificial nature the adoring angels have already in the poem been shown to cast down "Their crowns inwove with amarant and gold" (3.352), with the "weaving" metaphor emphasizing the intricate unity of Heaven. In general, in the celestial part of *Paradise Lost*, crowns are for throwing away, renouncing.[42] For similar reasons, there is no ritual enthronement of Christ in Book 5, in contrast to Satan whom we have already seen in Book 2 disposing himself with all imaginable complacency "High on a throne of royal state" (2.1–6). Satan's sense of the delectable character of the symbols of power is opposed to that speechless bliss in which the Son is "embosomed" with the Father in Book 5 (597). This is his throne. Likewise, there is neither oath nor any form of words on the part of the new king. We remember, perhaps, the "Beatitude past utterance" that God's creatures enjoyed in Book 3 (62) and are led to comprehend more fully the mystical quality of Christ's coronation, for beneath the threatening attitude of the Old Testament version of the royal psalm is a quiet presence preluding the New Testament and the love that repairs the destruction God predicts.

It is sometimes hard to discern and be open to the meaning of such silences. The boundless and intricate patterns of allusiveness both in Milton's work and in the works of other Renaissance Christian poets are so overwhelming when we begin to follow them up strand by strand that they awe the imagination.[43] In alluding to one area of Scripture, Milton automatically alludes to others, for the fulfillment of the prophecy of Psalm 2 in which God's elected king tramples down the kings of this world to exalt the faithful lies in the Gospels—the baptism of Christ by John the Baptist. "This is my beloved Son" (Matt. 3:17, and so on) points onward to the Crucifixion and the final exaltation at the Last Judgment. Many texts are interrelated, from Psalm 2 to Revelation, superimposed upon one another with automatic logic in the believer's mind. Just as in *Paradise Lost* there are three exaltations, so in the Scriptures there are a number of "coronations." It has been pointed out in this century that Christ's baptism appears to be a fragment of Jewish coronation ritual and that "the less easily disguised coronation rites, namely the award of the sceptre, the investment with a purple mantle, the crowning and ritual mocking"[44] were moved to the final act of Christ's life by later compilers who wished to conceal the politically subversive meaning of the messianic story. In Matthew we read:

> And they stripped him, and put on him a scarlet robe.
> And when they had plaited a crown of thorns, they put it upon his head, and a reed in his right hand: and they bowed the knee before him, and mocked him, saying, Hail, King of the Jews!
> And they spit upon him, and took the reed and smote him on the head. (27:28–30)

Milton may or may not have recognized that the mocking of
Christ was not a humiliation travestying the coronation rites
but (ironically) an intrinsic part of the Jewish coronation formula itself.[45] The tormentors would not know, according to this
reading, that they were literally glorifying the King when they
meant to degrade him. But Milton would certainly have recognized the coronation with the crown of thorns as the symbol of
Christ's redemptive function:

> he shall live hated, be blasphemed,
> Seized on by force, judged, and to death condemned
> A shameful and accurst, nailed to the cross
> By his own nation, slain for bringing life.

(12.411–14)

The plainsong of Michael's poetry in this final book hurries
over the episode, but we remember the reed scepter, the thorn
crown, and the scourge, the accoutrements of Christ's spiritual
status on which his claim to divine majesty rests.

A final vestige of European coronation ritual in *Paradise Lost* is
the celebration that follows God's speech. Much agreeable fun
has been made of all the eating and drinking engaged in by the
occupants of Milton' Heaven. Empson thinks such a bacchic
Heaven must be an ignoble and trying place in which to spend
eternity. Others defend the detailed descriptions of sensual
pleasures by Raphael as important thematically, explaining
Milton's doctrines of materialism and liberty.[46] These pleasures
also represent a vital feature of the coronation rite that must be
carried through to completion before the next phase of the action may begin. During the celebrations, the focus of attention
passes from God and the Son to the angels, who now participate in the kingship and demonstrate its meaning by fulfilling
equally their own natures and God's law:

> That day, as other solemn days, they spent
> In song and dance about the sacred hill,
> Mystical dance, which yonder starry sphere
> Of planets and of fixed in all her wheels
> Resembles nearest, mazes intricate,
> Eccentric, intervolved, yet regular
> Then most, when most irregular they seem,
> And in their motions harmony divine

So smooths her charming tones, that God's own ear
Listens delighted.

(5.618–27)

This is the image of "orb within orb" seen from another (double) perspective. First Raphael asks us to imagine the angels dancing around a center ("the sacred hill"), a kind of celestial ring dance. We cannot imagine it, and the narrator's definition of their movement as a mystical dance recognizes this impossibility. Raphael gestures for Adam's benefit to the spheres of the stars above and this indication also serves to delicately detach the reader's mind from any impertinent galliards or pavanes that might have intruded there and turn it toward a structure beyond his vision but within his imaginative capabilities—the cosmos itself and the Pythagorean dance of the spheres, wheeling upon the great axis of earth or sun (Milton refrained from stating a preference).

This vision is a relativistic one and involves the questionable principle of seeming, for from Adam's viewpoint, standing on one fixed place on earth, the stars must *seem* to perform no dance but to persist in serene stasis. The ecstasy of their dance could only be experienced if he were able to spend an eon watching the shifting positions of the cosmic bodies—immensely slow to human beings, quickening only from the standpoint of omniscience or the creative art of the imagination, to which Raphael appeals in Adam and Milton in his reader. Seen from below, the motions of the planets appear as "mazes intricate, / Eccentric, intervolved." Contemporary and ancient observations had revealed that the cosmic mathematics could fit a theory of regular circles round neither sun nor earth. *Eccentric* has many meanings: having an orbit without precise center; circles that fail to be exactly concentric; having no center (a misuse); an elliptic, curved, or parabolic orbit that deviates from the circular form; and, by extension, capricious, without central government. All these meanings may have been intended by Milton. The image is one of perplexity (reinforced by the attribute *intricate,* suggesting an entangling of the mind by complexity). Milton married a principle of individuality to an image of formal order: the universe, fitting no agreed mathematics, seen as static but actually in motion, representing the just government of the new king with its fine, incomprehensible balance—or tuning—of desirables. Here is a demonstration of the freedom that the Messiah's anointing yielded to his creatures; but at the edges of their freedom remained order, for none is without security, each is centered. By analogy with the human coronation ritual Milton had studied so deeply, the dance symbolizes the concentric groupings of the feudal order around the sovereign, but blessed here with that apparently eccentric freedom-of-being not necessarily enjoyed within the human structure.

Yet in this tuning and turning of the sanctities of Heaven, we should remember that all is not as it appears. Horribly, the form of the dance looks forward to the writhing coils of the serpent. The "intervolved" stars' courses, rolling and winding within each other's coils (the root suggestions of the Latin) pursue the involvement of the serpent in Book 9 in Eve's life, the involution of his rhetoric. Such terrible but fruitful puns are part of the dynamic force of *Paradise Lost*. The "mazes intricate, / Eccentric" take us to that

> Circular base of rising folds, that towered
> Fold above fold a surging maze.

> (9.498–99)

They also take us to the oblique movement of Satan, who makes by this sidelong process straight for his victim, unweaving her from Adam and innocence. This is not a merely verbal parallel. For within the ceremonies in Heaven themselves, the dance that celebrates the new union includes a serpentine intrusion: Milton has already told us very clearly that after the proclamation, "All seemed well pleased, all seemed, but were not all" (5.617). If this is remembered, then the coronation celebrations must appear a hollow mockery: "most irregular," for they contain participants whose hearts are centered elsewhere and who pay no more than lip service to the order they affect to accept. They are eccentric in this sense. But the poet's reassurance to the perplexed reader is beautifully, ironically, built into the treatment of his material, for the patterns of the dance are "yet regular / Then most, when most irregular they seem." Just as in Chapter 2 we observed Satan as sultan involuntarily cooperating with Divine Justice and in Chapter 3 Satan's followers were revealed as unable to accord him the triumphant celebration he sought, so here we discern an equally forceful irony against the breakers of original law. Those who have broken from the concentric groupings of the loyal around the sovereign still contribute, against their will, to the pattern of praise, to the supreme extent "that God's own ear / Listens delighted." That favorite and recurrent theme of *Paradise Lost,* of God's ability to draw good from evil, is here repeated in terms of the power of his royalty.

The final phase of the celebrations in Book 5 is the banquet, coinciding with evening. Milton seems to have attached special importance to this event; indeed, in the second edition of the poem he elaborated the account.[47] Yet readers have found the banqueting scene one of the most poetically and philosophically questionable or indecorous in the poem:

> Forthwith from dance to sweet repast they turn
> Desirous; all in circles as they stood,
> Tables are set, and on a sudden piled
> With angels' food, and rubied nectar flows
> In pearl, in diamond, and massy gold,
> Fruit of delicious vines, the growth of heaven.
> On flowers reposed, and with fresh flowerets crowned,
> They eat, they drink, and in communion sweet
> Quaff immortality and joy, secure
> Of surfeit where full measure only bounds
> Excess, before the all bounteous king, who showered
> With copious hand, rejoicing in their joy.
>
> (5.630–41)

The banquet may be justified as foreshadowing the Last Supper and Christ's request, "Take, eat: this is my body. . . . This is my blood" (Matt. 14:22–24). The "communion sweet" looks forward to the act of communion shared by Christians, a meal enjoyed without hedonism but one that, in making man sufficient, fills him with joy. The physicality of the act of eating, on which the poet insists, endorses the parallel between this act and Raphael eating with Adam and Eve, a meal prepared by the bounteous inferior and accepted with gratitude by the superior guest. This inverted parallel emphasizes the divine feudal lord's policy of granting self-renouncing titles to those in fee to him, modeled on his own humility. The poetry, with its determined ascription to the celestial community of alimentary canals, may be an initial shock but need not permanently alienate.

The banquet should also be considered as part of ancient human coronation ritual. From the time of the King Edgar *ordo*, or order of ceremony, of 973, a banquet was described as following the coronation ceremony, its scope being later enlarged to display the feudal hierarchy in terms of all the office holders functioning around the king.[48] Geoffrey of Monmouth's account of King Arthur's coronation also included a description of such a ritualized banquet.[49] Under this interpretation, the banquet in Book 5 may be seen as the consummation of a social ritual in a Heaven that is now established as a monarchy and, as such, is a manifestation and symbol of order. Milton intended something more ceremonious than the piles of food and well-set tables imply, for the banquet is a direct continuation of the symbolism associated with the Platonic-Pythagorean dance of the spheres that preludes it. The form of the dance is identical with the form of the meal: "all in circles as they stood, / Tables are set."

In fact, the circular structure associated with this phase of the poem is almost hypnotically reiterated: from the cycle of eternity, we have moved in imagination to the concentric rings of angels ("orbs"), the ring dance, the circling planetary spheres, the circle of tables. Round tables, as in the Arthurian myth, place no one in a position of directly inferior privilege. Communion as an act of absolute sharing, stressing common identity above individual rank while retaining order, is perfectly expressed through such a form. The dignity of the feast is further established when we read of the giver not as God nor as the Son or Messiah but as "the all bounteous king":

> full measure only bounds
> Excess, before the all bounteous king, who showered
> With copious hand, rejoicing in their joy.

> (5.639–41)

The implication must be that the giver of this joy is God in the person of his Son, through whom he will most frequently act in the remainder of the poem. This suggestion is reinforced later in Book 7 when Christ as the Word acts as the Giver (of life to the cosmos) and the dance of the stars is reiterated (7.374) to combine order with joy. The Son's loving-kindness is the seal of his kingship.

Traditionally, the coronation banquet represented the reciprocal bond between monarch and society—reciprocal because, while the sovereign proved his bounty by giving the banquet to his subjects, the subjects proved his kingship by serving the new ruler in their several offices.[50] However, the coronation banquet given by God the King requires nothing from the subjects save their pleasure. The king serves his people and not vice versa: "the all bounteous king" showers all possible enjoyment upon the participants, and Milton points out that the king's experience of joy is dependent upon theirs ("rejoicing in their joy" [5.641]). Though God's warning to the hosts of Heaven had been aggressive to the point (some might feel) of provocation, his subsequent behavior is assertively undemanding. There is certainly a delicate hint here of the Last Supper, a foreshadowing while still omnipotent of Christ, bending down to serve frail humanity—the clothing of Adam and Eve, the washing of the feet of the disciples (10.209–23).

Finally, a vestige of the Norman coronation ceremony may be mirrored in the revolt of Abdiel, the one just angel among Satan's followers. Schramm reports that, at the banquet of Richard II, one of the most significant symbolic events was the appearance of the King's Champion, who, in defense of the new king's right to rule, threatened to go into battle against anyone challenging that right.[51] This champion, whose actions incorporated the principle of ordeal by battle preserved in Anglo-Norman law as a relic of the Teutonic verdict of God, was a protector of the king's holy and dynastic claim. He stood in for him. Though Abdiel utters no such challenge at the banquet itself, he alone upholds and explains the validity of Christ's power against the challenger. Abdiel is a mediating figure, paralleling Christ. He mediates the divine message to Satan; in Raphael's narrative, he explains events to Adam; in the poem itself, he defines through his analysis the ceremony that we have just witnessed but whose implications are not all explicit. Through Abdiel, the character of Christ's kingship is clarified in rational terms; the obedience God had required is explained as having a basis in a twofold lesson; God's authority is validated by the fact that he is the author of all creation; the justice of the new regime is verified by its appeal to unity and its adherence to law itself.

It is here, through a seraph whose name signifies "servant of God," that Milton makes us conscious of exaltation to kingship as a species of reduction, prefiguring the time when Christ, laying down his life, shall show himself as king of the Jews and servant of mankind. The exchange between Satan and Abdiel at the end of Book 5 is an intense crystallization of meaning for the reader. Abdiel should therefore be thought of as fulfilling with a neat exactness the role of king's champion. The war is one of words, but no reader of Milton would doubt that word and sword are intrinsically related. Abdiel's words are powerful:

> Shalt thou give law to God, shalt thou dispute
> With him the points of liberty, who made
> Thee what thou art, and formed the powers of heaven
> Such as he pleased, and circumscribed their being?

(5.822–25)

Here is a challenge to Satan based not on God's superiority to law—the argument of English royalists detested by Milton—but on a relationship to law not capable of duplication by any earthly king: that of being its source and origin. "Circumscribed"—literally, "wrote around"—repeats the circular symbolism of the book, emphasizing the limitation imposed upon the laws of individual being by the hand of the surrounding Creator. It is an argument founded on God's eternity, omnipotence, omniscience, and goodness, applying uniquely to himself. The second argument is founded solely on the proof of God's love implicit in his concern for a greater equality among the community of Heaven. Here, Abdiel implies the feudal concept of a king as *primus inter pares*. In order to achieve such a closeness, the godhead must descend and reduce itself, while simultaneously exalting the community. Abdiel explains that Christ the Son created all the angels

> in their bright degrees,
> Crowned them with glory, and to their glory named
> Thrones, dominations, princedoms, virtues, powers,
> Essential powers, nor by his reign obscured,
> But more illustrious made, since he the head
> One of our number thus reduced becomes,

His laws our laws, all honour to him done
Returns our own.

(5.838–45)

In the final clause, Abdiel defines the circle of power, the circle of anointing that the formal rituals of coronation had symbolically dramatized. God who made law submits to law; he identifies through a perfect reciprocity with his creatures. "Illustrious" is a beautifully chosen epithet, for it demonstrates the light-bringing properties of true nobility, the capacity for true vision.

We remember here the Milton of the first *Defence* who insisted of the Old Testament God that "To the anointing, such as it is, of kings he preferred the anointing of his people" (Yale 4, pt. 1: 403), and, when Abdiel inquires scathingly whether Satan considers himself "all angelic nature joined in one" (834), we are reminded of the picture of the king incorporating a horde of people featured on the frontispiece of Hobbes's *Leviathan,* giving a horrible impression of the king having eaten them alive. Abdiel speaks against such megalomania and for the majority, as Milton held that he did in the *Second Defence:* "I speak, not on behalf of one people nor yet one defendant, but rather for the entire human race against the foes of human liberty" (Yale 4, pt. 1:557–58). As king's champion at the heavenly coronation, Abdiel is also champion of the entire race of God's sons, human as well as divine. Within the unlikely structure of feudal lordship, the poet has been able to demonstrate the deepest meanings of human liberty and equality.

5

The Father-King

When Milton engaged in the regicide controversy, perhaps the most potent royalist claim he had to answer was the conception that the king was not just the "healer" of his people (*medicus regni*) or its "husband" (*sponsus regni*), as the coronation service had it, but the father of his nation: *pater patriae*.[1] The king was thus in sacramental, organic relation to his people. Scripture called kings the "nursing fathers" of their people (Isa. 49:23). They were, as Sir Robert Filmer emphasized in *Patriarcha; or, the Natural Power of Kings*, direct descendants of Adam, the first father, and "as the father over one family, so the king, as father over many families, extends his care to preserve, feed, clothe, instruct, and defend the whole common-wealth."[2] Aristotle had also thought so;[3] Cicero repeated the idea in his *Republic*;[4] the Roman emperors sheltered behind its respectability, as "fathers" of Rome, implying a protective rather than a tyrannical function;[5] and the English constitution perpetuated the idea as having both a long pedigree and unusual emotive power, since, as the Royalist Judge Jenkins explained (in terms any child could understand): "the king and his people are obliged, one to another, in the nearest relation: He is a father; and the child (in law) is called *pars patris*."[6]

Judge Jenkins used the formula of the father-king to establish both the king's person and his office as sacrosanct and above the law, identifying both the "body politic" and the "body natural." The Royalist aim was to prove that killing a king is not only tyrannicide but parricide, the crime that of all others most offends against natural and divine law. This attempt typifies a favorite Royalist approach to the problem of defending the king against Parliament: no child may sit in judgment against its own parent. But the appeal of the idea was obviously much more than purely legalistic. The emotive quality of the idea of a father-king, of a sovereign personal in a way that a parliament, senate, or grand council could never be, worked powerfully for the Royalist cause: it suggested a love-relationship between the king and the people that reached down into the core of all the great and simple relationships that man feels as most sacred and right, and to which the most deeply felt taboos have traditionally attached. To kill a king was heinous and unthinkable, for the king was one's true father, and killing him hit at one's own identity, as well as at the identities of all those other countrymen who were linked and hierarchically limited by the blood-bond of the national family. Royalist poets in seeking images extreme enough to give form to their sense of shock at the monstrous nature of the crime reached out for ideas like cannibalism ("King-killers and men-eaters do agree"[7]) or (most commonly) the crucifixion of Jesus, but they found one of the most affecting to reside in the image of the violated paternity of the king.

A Roundhead had no emotional bait as alluring as this. While the Cavalier could summon the beautiful and aesthetic glow of easy images to attract the sympathy of the common man, the Puritan often seems to have felt that the plain truth he had to offer in return must appear austere or crude by contrast. *Eikon Alethine* and *Eikonoklastes* are felt to be vain and bitter by comparison with the gentleness of *Eikon Basiliké.* A number of alternatives presented themselves to Puritan defenders of the struggle against Charles I. They might accept the image of the king as father of the people but object that the person of Charles had parted company with his office, with the result that the "body natural" had vacated the "body politic" altogether. This was in itself a violation of the law of nature. In *England's Petition to Their King,* the people inquire whether, if the king's father had approached him with a drawn sword, he would not have resisted, for in this case, the father has broken natural law, and the son is released from the obligation to obey (*SCT* 5:35–36). John Cook in *King Charles His Case* answered in a coarse manner by reviving the old scandal that Charles and Buckingham had actually murdered James I: "Was he fit to continue a father to the people, who was without natural affection to his own father?" (*SCT* 5:219). In both these cases, the king's enemies take the royalist image of the king's fatherhood on its own terms and turn it against the king. The other possibility was to deny that an earthly king could rightfully be called the father of his people at all. This was the course Milton undertook.

The image of the father-sovereign came down to Milton—soiled by wear by corrupt Roman Emperors in Christian-hating times—in a contemptible tradition implying the persecution of the godly and the elevation of usurping mortals into "Idols of majesty divine." Early Christians had had to make perplexing researches into the catalogs of honorifics with which emperors decorated themselves, a perilous hunt to select allowable from sacrilegious titles, for the scrupulous abstainer might incur martyrdom: *"Principes pii, clementia vestra, aeternitas vestra . . . patres patriae . . . divinus animus vester, numen vestrum"* (sacred prince, your clemency, your eternity . . . father of the nation . . . your divine spirit, your divine authority) were mostly anathema.[8] All Milton's prose works show resistance to this blood-soaked and degraded tradition. In a crucial passage in the *Second Defence,* Milton wrestled with the problem of Cromwell's status in the government, resting his hope in the fact that Cromwell, refusing a kingship, had settled to be called *father* of his country. "The name of king you spurned," the poet said with mingled gratitude and anxiety (Yale 4, pt. 1:672). In other words, Milton was willing to concede the title *father,* but only if that of *king* was rejected. In an earthly monarchy, the conjunction of these titles was felt as threatening to the seemly order of affairs under heaven. The passage is alive with disturbed feelings, combining eulogy with a warning voice.

During his office as secretary for foreign tongues to the government, Milton was brought into extremely close contact with the notion of the father-king within an English situation and was obliged to repudiate the charge of parricide in his answer to the galling Salmasius's *Defensio Regia.* He had also answered Du Moulin's *Cry of the Royal Blood to Heaven against the English Parricides* of 1652, a hysterical condemnation of Milton, that "monster of a man and his co-parricides" (Yale 4, pt. 2:1051), for presuming to justify the murder of a Christ-like king. Du Moulin reported the celebrated forgiveness that Charles I gave to his murderers upon the scaffold, and, adding some suggestive imaginary details to enhance the drama of the occasion in the manner approved immemorially by pamphleteers, represented the response of the regicides on hearing of this Christ-like act of forgiveness thus:

> O king to be worshipped even by his murderers! O pious father of his people! O true disciple of Christ, who even after his death prays for his enemies!
>
> The sudden light of unmerited pity beat down the parricides and reminded them of their crime. On the faces of all shame and sad silence, as if they feared too late whom they had recently killed, and the very mention of the pity which they had denied to their king cast terror into the assassins. (Ibid., 1068)

This unhistorical account, rich in exclamations of awe at Charles, the son of God and father of his people, intermediary between Heaven and Earth, performing Christ's part toward his murderers, is typical of the Royalist interpretation of Charles I's passing. Bishop King saw that "Thy Thorny Crowne was still a Crowne of Gold";[9] Cowley later spoke of Charles I as crowning "the *Kingly* with the *Martyrs Crown*";[10] Thomas Shipman in "The Royal Martyr" spoke of the regicide as visiting a species of original sin upon the families of the murderers;[11] and the author of *Eikon Basiliké* begged, in Charles's own voice, *"forgive them, O my Father, for they know not what they do."*[12] Thus, the image of the father-king, sanctified in death, became assimilated to another, even more dangerous image, that of Christ the Son entering through death into perfect identity with God the Father. A complex of family relationships was exploited, until the English royal family began to appear as a branch of the heavenly royal family (the Trinity).

Milton's response to this dangerous association of king as father of his people and as son of God was both angry and rationalistic. In the first *Defence,* he refuted the charge of parricide by demolishing the mythic element in the father association and by refusing to admit that kingship falls within the law of nature:

> Indeed, you are wholly in the dark in failing to distinguish the rights of a father from those of a king; by calling kings fathers of their country, you think this metaphor has forced me to apply right off to kings whatever I admit of fathers. Fathers and kings are very different things: Our fathers begot us, but our kings did not, and it is we,

rather, who created the king. It is nature which gave the people
fathers, and the people who gave themselves a king; the people
therefore do not exist for the king, but the king for the people. We
endure a father though he be harsh and strict, and we endure such a
king too; but we do not endure even a father who is tyrannical. (Yale
4, pt. 1:326–27)

Milton reversed the analogy: in that the people beget the king,
they father him, and he is *filius patriae.* Any crimes he commits
against the state are therefore acts of parricide. With the dextrous doubleness of the argument in the last sentence, Milton
showed the familiar Janus face of the polemicist: accepting for a
moment the Royalist proposition, he argued from it to its own
confusion. Even fathers have merely limited authority over
offspring.

The pamphleteer was still marveling in *The Readie and Easie
Way* that one man could ever bear to set up "over his brethren,"
as the Revolution faltered to its close and newly minted Cavalier
poets were thinking up ways to greet the new Charles, the
"Banish'd David" who would as Astraea plant his foot upon
Dover Beach.[13] Milton produced a variant of his old argument.
We are brothers, in the same generation, none more venerable
than any other. He could not conceive how a mortal man,
"being a Christian, can assume such extraordinarie honour and
worship to himself, while the kingdom of Christ our common
King and Lord, is hid to this world, and such *gentilish* imitation
forbid in express words by himself to all his disciples" (Yale
7:429). The incredulous tone here in a man of fifty-two, with
twenty years' experience of public life, is quite unfeigned.
There was a genuine innocence, sustained over a lifetime and
bearing a deep imprint of the earlier humanist idealism, in
Milton's astonishment that a human being cannot see that as a
Christian, in adopting God's attributes on earth, he is pretending to be his own creator. The only kingdom he looked to in
political life was "hid to this world": looking away from this
perfection he could only conceive of a republic or protectorate
as being a viable copy. As the poet of *Paradise Lost,* he tried to
give some glimpse of what this celestial kingdom is like and
showed that in the hidden realm of God and Christ, the father-
king presides in his unique reality; in the brutal empire of
Satan, a bizarre forgery copies its uprooted and deteriorating

memories of this real kingdom. On earth in prelapsarian days, the father of mankind was able to govern on a paternal basis until Satan, transmitting to man his own distortions, bred worldly kings who copied in little his own poor imitation of the original. One of Milton's most difficult but most cherished aims in *Paradise Lost*—drawing upon his experience in public life— was to distinguish, with the power and subtlety of a poetic medium, between the Father-King in Heaven and these wicked plagiarisms.

The poet did this by associating the celestial monarchy with the creating principle, an association emphasized in Book 3 but developed and analyzed as the poem unfolds. Seen in his rela- tionship to his Son, and thence to man, God's royalty and paternity join. Christ celebrates this union of attributes in the first speech he makes in the poem, and in himself, of course, he is the visible embodiment and expression of the union, a reflec- tion of "Divine compassion" (141):

> O Father, gracious was that word which closed
> Thy sovereign sentence, that man should find grace.
>
> (3.144–45)

Here the epithet *sovereign*, which can mean both "healing" and "royal," poignantly echoes Milton's personal thanksgiving in line 22 for his Father's "sovereign vital lamp"—(the sun, which gives warmth, light, and fruitfulness to all created things and is, of course, God's animistic viceroy in the universe, fathering the creatures of earth and ruling the Heavens). The Son of God reveals that God is a healing king, giving eyesight to the blind, finding warmth for the alienated. The key word in defining Christ's kingship is *grace*, which as the Word of God he trans- mits to mankind who are his kindred. This allusive adjective *sovereign*, occurring in these two instances—the poet's invoca- tion; Christ's first speech—reminds us also that light was God's "offspring . . . first-born," a definition that occurred in line 1 of Book 3, perhaps to emphasize the Platonic One from which all phenomena overflowed.[14]

The Son goes on to plead, with gentle insistence on the fam- ily relationship between divine and human, for the extension of grace to humanity:

> For should man finally be lost, should man

Thy creature late so loved, thy youngest son
Fall circumvented thus by fraud, though joined
With his own folly?

(3.150–53)

It is not without meaning, though it may appear indecorous, to
call this pleading, in tone and manner, humane. Christ speaks
to the Father as a father. Man, "thy youngest son," is a kind of
Benjamin to God's Jacob, and to the Ancient of Days is attributed the capacity to embrace the youngest of his children
with that special feeling that human parents proverbially and
archetypally experience for the last-born of their old age, "late
so loved." Being born later than God's other sons, man has not
enjoyed his maker's care as long as the elder sons, so that there
is poignancy not only in the adverb *so* but in the double sense of
late as "lately" and "latest." Reiteration of the title *Father* ritu-
alistically throughout Book 3 further emphasizes the association that Milton is concerned to establish between God's
fatherhood (of the Son, of the angels, of light, of ourselves and
the whole of nature) and the untempered beauty of love. All are
sons, and Christ as the Son is best qualified to express this
affinity and belonging as intrinsic to the sovereignty of God.

In Book 3, the Father does not stand rancorously against this
filial bond. When the Son pleads "That far be from thee, Father" (154) to judge death to man, he is dialectically explaining
the nature of justice itself, not simply contradicting God's earlier exclamations of wrath and attempting to change his father's
humor. Milton based the dialogue between Father and Son
upon a projected presentation of an allegorical debate between
Justice, Mercy, and Wisdom.[15] Giles Fletcher structured *Christ's
Victory* upon a dialogue between Justice and Mercy, with Mercy
the victrix. God who fathered Christ also fathered (and essentially is) the compassion that shines in him, as a mirror reflects
light or as light belongs to the sun. Christ merely elucidates the
Mercy already implicit in Justice.

Although the hereditary principle of rule was detestable to
Milton on earth because of its arbitrariness and its proprietorial
designs upon personal liberty, in Heaven he was able to conceive of it as both morally viable and liberating. In hereditary
terms, the Good can only will and generate the good. God,
recognizing this quality in his Son, is mirrored in the Son's

recognition of the same quality in his younger brothers, whom he immeasurably dignifies by defining them in these terms. The hereditary principle in the higher world in *Paradise Lost* is made to appear benign by the poet's association of it with the Platonist frame of reference that shows the One desiring the joy of all possibles, without envy. The Cambridge Platonists, with whom Milton shared much, beautifully adapted this idea to the concept of rebirth through Christ. Ralph Cudworth, in *A Sermon Preached before the House of Commons* in 1647, spoke of Christ as "the standing constant, inexhausted Fountain of this divine Light and Heat. . . .he is always kindling. cheering, quickening, warming, enlivening hearts."[16] In *Paradise Lost,* Christ is the fountain of light, and Milton used the cheering effects associated in the natural world with that enlivening state of being bathed in sunlight as a way of showing the divine kingship as a source of joy. A political structure applied to Heaven was modified and made emotionally acceptable by association with an emotive philosophical tradition.

If, Milton pleasantly remarked in *Eikonoklastes,* kings were bred for excellence like stud horses, it would be our duty to obey them (Yale 3:486). But they are not, and we need not. However, Christ is shown in *Paradise Lost* to have been bred for excellence, so as to be the exact reflection of his Father "in all things" (6.736). All things include God's paternity, and this is the reason for that deep well of joy on which Milton's poem draws when it celebrates Christ's kingship. The prose works had equally celebrated the royal Christ in a very personal way, betraying no trace of disappointment that the Messiah had been presented in Scripture as a king. Salmasius taunted Milton in his *Defensio Regia Pro Carolo I* with the blasphemy of implying that if, as he has declared, all kings are tyrants, then "God himself should be called king of tyrants and even the greatest tyrant himself" (Yale 4, pt. 1:367, n. 92). This accusation may stand as a test case, for here Salmasius prefigures generations of critical accusers who think that because Milton did not like kings he did not like God. The fascinating thing is that Milton's reply in the first *Defence* displays no hint of the disturbance one would expect of a mind subconsciously at odds with itself. He dismisses the remark as mere blasphemy; it touches no nerve. For he had already declared, "'The Messiah is King'. This we recognize, it brings us joy, and we pray for his speedy advent: for he is worthy and there is none like him or resembling him" (ibid., 367). Christ's kingship is not reluctantly tolerated but willingly announced. "It brings us joy" because here is a king who will never impair our rights, violently assert himself, break the law, or defraud us of our own. Having fathered man, he will die for him.

Many readers of *Paradise Lost* will agree that the experience of joy in the poem is often most richly conveyed by the poetry of fertility and creation. My view is that by bringing Christ's kingship into close and deep relationship to this vein of poetic richness, the poet transforms our conception of kingship so as to scour the connotations of artifice, subjection, and sophistication and attach instead nature, birth, fecundity, and the simple shame-free joy of Eden. Initially, in Book 5, the Son is anointed king not only because it is his destiny to save fallen man and to harmonize the universe in an ultimate act of atonement but also because of the merit he has shown in the creation of the angels. This is Milton's poetic representation of his statement in the first *Defence* that "he is worthy." Abdiel explains to Satan that God used Christ to make "All things, even thee" (5.837): Satan scoffs, saying that he has no memory of being thus ignominiously given birth. This point of disagreement is crucial, for Satan is making ready to attempt a crime equivalent to parricide. In Christ's act of creativity he took upon himself the function of paternity: Son became father. His son, Satan, disputes his parentage and in doing so refuses to belong to the royal family. Looked at from this perspective, the opening words of God's speech proclaiming his Son's reign in Book 5, "Hear all ye angels, progeny of light" (600), take on an added significance—since the Son was the Light that, as God's agent, created the angels. It is from their king's creativity that the angels may derive their capacity to be "For ever happy" (5.611); it is by virtue of Christ's participation in God's paternal creativity, within the union of the Trinity, that God can legitimately announce that "him who disobeys / Me disobeys" (611–12).

The climax of Book 5, with the confrontation between Satan and Abdiel, lies in Satan's Promethean repudiation of his origins. The speech in which he refuses to consider the idea that Christ has fathered him is one of the most electrifying of the whole poem. It excites and simultaneously offends. Excitement is aroused by the sense we have of the exultation that might be found in total liberation from the past, from obligation and dependency. To be without a father is to be God. It is an immemorial need of the adolescent, sublimated in adult life. But it is also the breaking of a taboo. There is a sort of joy in Satan's speech, but it is a curdling joy, on the turn, and near to that hectic frenzy that leads the rebels to charge over the edge of Heaven into a fall of their own executing. Satan's destruction of the new king, if he could accomplish it, would be a triple crime of regicide, deicide, and parricide. Du Moulin had written of the killing of Charles I that "all the crimes which hell ever produced have flowed into this one crime" and that "Compared with this, the crime of the Jews in crucifying Christ was nothing."[17] Milton's ironic personal aside in the *Second Defence* dealt with all blasphemies of this order: "I always notice that the more enthusiastic a royalist a man is, the more he is inclined to bear any offence against Christ more easily than one against the king" (Yale 4, pt. 1:600). In *Paradise Lost*, Milton reversed the formula into its true application, for "all the crimes which hell ever produced" flow into Satan's rejection of his Father. His final speech in Book 5 is a parricidal outburst, in which an attentive reader might recognize the quiet beginnings of Milton's attribution to Satan of a tyrant's character. Plato in another context had also identified the despot as a parricide (*Republic*, 569B). Satan devalues the idea of Christ's fatherhood of him with an acid joke: he is inventing the art of sarcasm and invective that will have such a long and fruitless history on earth, an art that is very clearly the politician's tool. Taking strength from the silence of the rebels at Abdiel's elucidation of their origins, the leader, growing in confidence and power, rejoiced, inquiring:

> That we were formed then say'st thou? And the work
> Of secondary hands, by task transferred
> From Father to his Son? Strange point and new!
> Doctrine which we would know whence learned: who saw
> When this creation was?
>
> (5.853–57)

Abdiel's claim is made to appear ridiculous by Satan's reductive literalism. Put like this, it does sound foolish if fathers need surrogate progenitors in the form of sons. Milton knew that when mystery is hardened into doctrine it becomes distorted, and Abdiel makes no attempt to answer his adversary's objections. Satan is needled — "That we were formed then say'st thou?"—and from hurt pride he turns to crowing sarcasm. The idiom and the inflections of his phrasing, from the first spite to the pompous gesture "we would know" (embracing like a Leviathan all the rebels in himself), give this speech an especially dramatic stature. In one sense, his argument is so astonishingly childish that it is uncertain whether he really believes in what he is saying or whether this is a notion on which he has just alighted by happy chance. Crediting only the evidence of the individual's senses and memory, he discounts the authority of history, tradition, or any derived knowledge.

It was a Renaissance commonplace and it is always demonstrable that the senses lie. Satan rounds on Abdiel with petulant impatience:

> who saw
> When this creation was? Remember'st thou
> Thy making, while the maker gave thee being?
> We know no time when we were not as now;
> Know none before us, self-begot, self-raised
> By our own quickening power, when fatal course
> Had circled his full orb, the birth mature
> Of this our native heaven, ethereal sons.

(5.856–63)

Those who believe Milton's Satan to be a Promethean figure would pause here. Satan resembles far more accurately the tyrannical Zeus of the Greeks dethroning his just father, Cronos. Christ is a combined Prometheus ("universal benefactor of mankind"[18]) and Chiron (who shed his immortality to ransom him). Satan here disinherits himself in order to claim a new power: son of impersonal "Ether" controlled by anonymous fate, he rejects not only a father but any natural birth at all. The fallen reader consulting his own experience will scarcely doubt the fact of his birth simply because he cannot remember it. But there is a psychological pull in Satan's chant of "self-begot, self-raised" to which many readers must respond with excitement. It is an ultimate liberation, surreptitiously dreamed of in adolescence, to shed one's father as safeguard and authority and choose oneself as a preferable source. Aristotle in his *Nicomachean Ethics* expressed a recognition of this state of mind when he said, "Parents know their offspring with more certainty than children know their parentage; and progenitor is more attached to progeny than progeny to progenitor."[19] The very obviousness of this perception reveals the degree of psychological realism present in Satan's denial of the Son's paternity. Individualism denies its roots; the despot tears his up as an essential preliminary to self-assertion.[20]

The reader who experienced initial excitement at Satan's bravado draws back as the speech develops because it represents the violation of the most sacred taboo in human terms, the taboo insuring loving order in the community, in divine terms, sacrilege. The refusal to bear having a father is the crucial atheism that makes Satan, in Abdiel's words, "O alienate from God, O spirit accurst" (5.877). It is all the more dramatic that a spirit who is alone among a multitude should perceive the utter loneliness of Satan, alienated by having detached himself from his roots. Abdiel believes in the fact of his birth with a conviction born of reason and faith and possibly even memory. It is possible that Satan's lapse has actually vitiated his memory, through a corruption of his will, for Adam and Eve both do remember their birth and can describe it. To the question "Remember'st thou / Thy making?" Adam might have replied with the account of his infancy (8.250–333) and Eve with an account of her long, unborn sleep (4.440–91). Though both Adam and Eve are aware of the problem of identifying the true author, a shadowy and mysterious figure in both cases, their acceptance of the parent is represented as an act of trust, which is an initiation into their future life as children of God.

It is clear that, in the discussion between Abdiel and Satan in Book 5, the poet is carefully distinguishing between the two opposing kinds of kingship so that the reader shall be left with no doubt as to how to know them apart. Satanic kingship repudiates family love. Divine kingship is founded on family love and modified by it. This central distinction is explicitly made by Abdiel in the speech to which Satan so vehemently and preposterously objects, and it is linked to the feudal conception of a king as *primus inter pares,* a self-renouncing monarchy, which was discussed in the last chapter. In Milton's analysis, the feu-

dal image unites with the paternal image to define the divine
monarchy, so that children are elevated to become one with
their father. *Pater patriae* becomes *primus inter pares* in Abdiel's
definition:

> he the head
> One of our number thus reduced becomes,
> His laws our laws.

> (5.842–44)

Such a double union, of subjects with ruler and offspring with
father, was a paradox only capable of being enacted once, by
God, and not susceptible to reproduction by earthly monarchs.

Abdiel's defense of Christ's royal rule, however, has been
confusing to generations of readers. One generation is especially illuminating in the very mistakes it made. During the
Second World War, critics like M. M. Ross and G. Wilson
Knight, coming to *Paradise Lost* with their minds laden with all
the pressures and anxieties of the embattled British monarchy,
held that Milton was a Royalist at heart, so royal a person was
his Christ, so like Hitler was his Satan.[21] Ross's and Knight's
are sad, brave books, limited by the political circumstances in
which they were written. The authors cannot accept that Milton
saw the heavenly kingship as a unique and unrepeatable institution because it combined what it would be pure blasphemy
to attempt on earth: kingship and paternity. The famous passage in Milton's *Second Defence* in which he praises Cromwell as
transcending any real or legendary kings is misleadingly para-
phrased by Ross as "Cromwell is a greater king, even surpass-
ing Arthur."[22] But this is the most salient passage in Milton's
eulogy of Cromwell, a passage that leads the imagination far
away from human kings into the area of power conceived of as
care and solicitude, and dignity as ideal rather than titular, an
area Milton reserved for Christ-like men. Milton seems to recognize here in Cromwell a greatness that is different in *kind*, not
just degree, from the kings of the earth, just as in *Paradise Lost*
Christ is of a different order from his angels. It is significant that
Milton is very willing to endorse Cromwell's fatherhood of his
country, as long as it is not embellished with a crown:

> Such have been your achievements as the greatest and most il-
> lustrious citizen, the director of public counsels, the commander of

the bravest armies, the father of your country. It is thus that you are greeted by the spontaneous and heartfelt cries of all upright men. Your deeds recognize no other name as worthy of you; no other do they allow, and the haughty titles which seem so great in the opinion of the mob, they properly reject. For what is a title, except a certain limited degree of dignity? Your deeds surpass all degrees, not only of admiration, but surely of titles too . . . you assumed a certain title very like that of father of your country. You suffered and allowed yourself, not indeed to be borne aloft, but to come down so many degrees from the heights and be forced into a definite rank, so to speak, for the public good. The name of king you spurned from your far greater eminence, and rightly so. (Yale 4, pt. 1:672)

Milton's Cromwell is kingly in the higher sense (as God is in *Paradise Lost*) precisely because he is not kingly in the lower sense. If he added to his role of father a title of king, he would be violating his status both as a mere man and as a metaphorical father. This crucial passage, fraught as it is with anxiety over Cromwell's intentions and with uncertainty over the implications of the protectorship, preludes an important theme in *Paradise Lost*: the diminution in status that a title confers upon the truly meritorious.

Milton's republican beliefs deeply influenced his eulogy of Cromwell, who is seen as reducing himself from the status of citizen (very like the Roman republican *civis Romanus*) into a protective function such as that adopted by the immaculate Cicero as *pater patriae* fending off tyranny. Royalists during the Interregnum had tried to claim for the Stuart kingship a will to renunciation equal to Christ's. Henry King showed Charles I reaching out a kind hand toward the killer:

Inviting Treason with a pardoning look,
Instead of Gratitude, a stab he took.[23]

This reciprocity between the humble love of the king and the thrust of hatred in the regicide implies a historically fictitious habit of renunciation. Charles I died for his title; renunciation was involuntary. Milton in *Paradise Lost* contrasted the elevation of the earthly king above his brothers with Christ's *descent* into kingship, entering into the hierarchy to commune with his natural inferiors. All this comes about because Christ is, both literally and symbolically, *pater patriae*.

The emphasis on God's paternity in *Paradise Lost* is nowhere as obvious as in Books 6 and 7. These represent the great double center of the poem, realizing the paradox of God's nature—his anger and his fruitfulness—in a kind of diptych, the one side dark, elemental, and tending to destruction, the other a celebration of birth and cheerfulness. Books 6 and 7 confront one another as, in the Bible, the Old Testament confronts the New. Of course, the New Testament transcends the Old, just as Book 7 transcends Book 6, and love is vividly seen to fulfill and supersede law. Book 7 shows Christ as King compensating for the loss of the fallen angels, whom God relinquishes as no longer recognizably his sons. In *Eikonoklastes*, Milton had spoken of those who had ceased to fight for his conception of liberty under God as being "imbastardiz'd from the ancient nobleness of thir Ancestors" (Yale 3:344); in *Paradise Lost*, God symbolically repudiates his paternity of the rebellious angels and climactically disinherits them:

> Pursue these sons of darkness, drive them out
> From all heaven's bounds into the utter deep:
> There let them learn, as likes them, to despise
> God and Messiah his anointed king.

(6.715–18)

These children are disowned, and we may imagine them as being reborn of Satan, the father of darkness. Their "ancient nobleness" is violated, and the true stock (the Son) must drive them from the home in which they no longer belong. The loss of the "sons of darkness" is then in Book 7 compensated for by a new generation, God's youngest son, man.

However, although it is right to see Book 7 as transcending Book 6 in its account of Creation, it may also be appropriate to assign comparable importance to each book in establishing, as if simultaneously, the paradox of God's fatherhood and rule. The Justice that informs Book 6 is consolidated and reinterpreted (not disposed of) by the Mercy of Book 7, and it becomes clear that each attribute is essential to God's paternity. As I showed in Chapter 3, the central point by line count occurs in Book 6, in the first edition at lines 761–62, and in the second edition at line 766, providing a focus of attention at the point when Christ emerges to indicate his kingship in a supreme image of force:

He in celestial panoply all armed
Of radiant urim, work divinely wrought,
Ascended.

(6.760–62)

This image of force is essential to Christ's paternity: without it, the events of Book 7 would not be possible. As the ascending *sol iustitiae,* Christ is seen thundering into battle in a triumphal chariot whose details are based on the vision of Ezekiel,[24] but this is specifically "The chariot of *paternal* deity" (5.750, my italics). This phrase, I think, denotes not just that Christ has borrowed his own father's vehicle for the purpose of dispatching the rebels, but that he has assumed the role of paternal deity in order to enact the business of his kingship. In the last speech made by God to his martial son, so close at this point that its reverberations are still with the reader, the final injunction is to vindicate his status as "anointed king" (6.718).

It is clear that this scene of Christ in triumph is parodied earlier in the same book, when Satan is revealed in *his* chariot, poised in spectacular glory to initiate the war against God, and these two related triumphs are powerfully emblematic. Satan is revealed

High in the midst exalted as a god
The apostate in his sun-bright chariot sat
Idol of majesty divine, enclosed
With flaming cherubim, and golden shields.

(6.99–102)

The accounts of each triumphal moment—of Satan's, which begins the action, and of Christ's, which ends it—have a similarity in detail and effect that might easily lead us to an involuntary, spurious identification of Christ with Caesar, the heavenly and worldly monarchies assimilated to one another iconographically so that distinctions are not obviously accessible. Satan, however, is an "idol" because he is not legitimate, an illegitimacy revealed by close reading of the two symbolic presentations. Satan and Christ share nearly everything—chariot, ascension, and sun-analogy, centrality within an enveloping host of subsidiary angels (cherubs), and the acclamation of all. Each has a structurally important place in the poem—Christ at the exact center of the whole poem, and Satan, if I might add a modest numerological interpretation to the many that have been given to Milton, at the important line 100 of Book 6 in both editions. This number, an extension of the One and the Divine Tetractys, is the fountain of all being.[25] Yet it is here that Satan goes to war against unity, to destroy, and the implication is clearly parodic.

There are two important differences between the parallel accounts of Christ and Satan in triumph. The first is that Christ's chariot is a living one, Satan's a machine. Christ's chariot represents the Church, the body of the saints, by gracious use of whom he will conquer at the Second Coming. He is therefore both central and final. The destroyer can obviously have no such organic vehicle, for his associations are with death and not eternal life. His chariot is therefore reductive rather than exalted, for we are forced to compare it with those splendid but life-size ones we examined in Chapter 3, which habitually transported human emperors in a world in which time and mortality limit everything. The second difference between the two accounts of Christ and Satan is even more important, for it is the absence of reference to fatherhood where Satan is concerned that connects him to the debased secular government of earthly kings, of which Milton entirely disapproved. The poet therefore reveals Satan's absence of legitimation.

The context of the parody is significant here, for, as Satan appears "High in the midst" (6.99), we hold in our minds an image of the innumerable angels surrounding him, not only seeing them in their present state of rebelliousness but also remembering the deep satisfactions they have forsaken,

> who wont to meet
> So oft in festivals of joy and love
> Unanimous, as sons of one great sire
> Hymning the eternal Father.

(6.93–96)

The loud and glittering image of Satan enthroned now comes to mind, bringing with it all the images of kingship that will be rehearsed in relation to God, but with the one decisive exception. The missing attribute is given emphasis in the synonymous "sire" and "Father" and in the mention of the relationship in which the angels existed in their earlier state, as "sons," whose experience while it lasted had been a fellowship of joy. Their relationship to their present leader is not one of child to father (even an adopted one) but rather of worshiper to idol. The entire episode is enclosed within the consciousness of the narrator, Raphael, and the nature of his own participation in the events he describes modifies the feeling of the story. Raphael is a son of God: a mediating figure between Heaven and earth, like Christ. The loud apparition of Satan and his hosts "in terrible array" (6.106) confronting God's spirits when before they had met them peaceably was felt by Raphael as a shock and a sorrow. Attempting to describe their coming, he offers Adam an image drawn from terrestrial history. They marched as if flying:

> as when the total kind
> Of birds in orderly array on wing
> Came summoned over Eden to receive
> Their names of thee.

> (6.73–76)

In political terms, this image has a small but bitter irony within it (one I will take up again in the next chapter), for when the species came to Adam, they came to do him fealty and vassal homage, while Satan's army is bent on breaking fealty; they are oath-breakers who (though they too in a sense "Came summoned" by the all-embracing will of God) travesty in Book 6 their response in Book 5 to the proclamation. So also on earth the animal species will be released from fealty when Adam sins, and a predatory law will prevail. The image predicts the breaking apart of the cohering prelapsarian world, when man takes to wings and, as unrealistic as Icarus, is almost as completely lost. Raphael, we are aware, is speaking to a son of God who will break from his father, to be readopted as Satan will never be. The poet offers these hints delicately. But he makes explicit the pain of rupture and strife among a community of brothers. As the rebel armies come on, we watch them through the eyes of Raphael and sense the ugliness of the hard, sharp image they present, bristling with "rigid spears" (6.83).

This is a strange passage in which Milton conveys a sense of uncanny, eerie foreignness, essential to such a phenomenon in a Heaven that has previously been characterized by the flow and continuity of encircling forms. The satanic army is felt as an interruption to this flow, painful to contemplate because the poet intimates through a quality of inwardness and musing on the part of his narrator, how painful the sight of the army was for Raphael. Milton's description suggests a multitude of different archetypes: barbarian armies (the "furious" nature of their approach); the heraldry of a feudal past (perverted into the bearings on the shields "with boastful argument"); Homeric armies; grim Roman orderliness; the fratricide of the English civil wars:

> for they weened
> That self same day by fight, or by surprise
> To win the mount of God, and on his throne
> To set the envier of his state, the proud
> Aspirer, but their thoughts proved fond and vain
> In the mid way: though strange to us it seemed
> At first, that angel should with angel war,
> And in fierce hosting meet, who wont to meet
> So oft in festivals of joy and love
> Unanimous, as sons of one great sire
> Hymning the eternal Father.
>
> (6.86–96)

Surprise and sorrow at the previously unknown, unimaginable confrontation between the sons of God is uppermost in Raphael's reminiscence, and there is a strangely innocent quality in his meditation on how "strange to us it seemed" to receive fratricidal hatred where love had joined individuals in the past. The repetitions and symmetries of phrasing—"angel . . . with angel"; "meet, who wont to meet"—express the cruelty with which a first experience of hostility shocks the unsuspicious mind, presenting a simultaneous representation of lost harmony and current antagonism. The poetry places enormous emphasis on "Unanimous," literally "one spirit," the condition of true sons. The faithful angels have time to reflect on the dreadful consequence of that "breaking union" predicted by God, by looking upon the hostile posture of their brothers.

The image of Satan, utterly bare of paternal association, though surrounded by gold and noise, is a fitting emblem of his alienation from grace. It is not incongruous to imagine Milton looking back to the civil wars and reimagining the terrible first

confrontation between sons of God (the Commonwealth represented by "Abdiel stern" [6.171]) and idolators of the king, "the
grand foe" (149). Abdiel in the poem, as Milton metaphorically
in the civil-war and regicide period, declares: "my sect thou
seest" (147). It is also appropriate, considering the deep pathos
of this section of the poem and its insistence on the proverbial
truth that "few sometimes may know, when thousands err"
(148), to bear in mind Milton's isolation within Restoration society, a society whose king was, in the words of *The Readie and
Easie Way*, "ador'd like a Demigod" (Yale 7:425), Milton the poet
representing the conscious Puritan remnant, standing ground
with a conviction that the English people had forfeited their
allegiance to their true father, "imbastardiz'd from the ancient
nobleness of thir Ancestors." This experience within the civil
state of popular idolatry excluding a nation from participation
in true spiritual unity is apposite to the loss incurred by the
deluded angels in *Paradise Lost*, Book 6. Idolators confront sons.
Though it does not seem very fruitful to allegorize the War in
Heaven in order to parallel it to specific battles in the civil wars
(as Hill does in *Milton and the English Revolution*, likening the
first inconclusive battle in Heaven to Edgehill and identifying
the hurling of the mountains as a covert reference to "the levée
en masse in London in 1643," with the Son as the New Model
Army[26]), for such precise allegorization seems reductive to the
poetry and subsidiary to the theological meanings, there can
hardly fail to be a remembrance of the parricidal and fratricidal
civil war in which the poet had travailed. Such a remembrance
here is general and emotive rather than specific and allegorical.
There is a considerable pathos in Milton's glance back to the
time when the rebellious angels enjoyed the security of belonging to their father "as sons of one great sire." There is, conversely, exultation when the "chariot of *paternal* diety" emerges
on behalf of the faithful sons of God.

Readers have often objected that the joy of the unfallen angels
in response to their King is not truly demonstrated, that they
are presented as a kind of standing army kept in politic ignorance by a Machiavellian God, as spies and flatterers, dreary
epicureans in endless, vacuous holiday.[27] An honest reader of
the poem will probably admit to having been prey to such
doubts, reading of Uriel, etymologically "the eyes of God," mis-

apprehending Satan on behalf of omniscience; the sexual games of angels; their banquets; their inability to win against the enemy in open combat. These doubts are natural when Milton's difficulty in presenting the paradox of a heavenly community is taken into account. Many theoretical answers are feasible and helpful, such as that wonderfully sensible suggestion by Boyd M. Berry that the dilemma of the "strategic failures" of the virtuous angels is explicable in terms of the Puritan tension between providence and free will.[28] But such answers remain theoretical until it can be shown that the poem also demonstrates and embodies the meaning of the paradox. When Satan vilifies Abdiel in Book 6, he expresses almost the same criticism:

> At first I thought that liberty and heaven
> To heavenly souls had been all one; but now
> I see that most through sloth had rather serve,
> Ministering spirits, trained up in feast and song;
> Such hast thou armed, the minstrelsy of heaven,
> Servility with freedom to contend,
> As both their deeds compared this day shall prove.

(6.164–70)

From the occupation of "ministering," Satan ("lewdly" in Abdiel's opinion [6.182]) derives a class occupied with "minstrelsy." To his own free soul he opposes the servile flesh ("trained up in feast and song") of a slave-community. His taunt is that God's angels sit round doing nothing more liberated than singing and feeding, but the reader of the poem may reflect on the meaning of feasting and singing in Heaven, judging by what he has already perceived of these functions. The feast of Book 5 we have already shown as an act of participation, by all, in the divine nature; equally, the "minstrelsy" of Heaven is something more than casual warbling. The planets, "orbing," are not lazy in creating the music of the spheres; the songs of the just angels are represented within the poem (itself a song as characterized by Milton) and are works of art. In their "minstrelsy," God's filial angels are taking part in his own creativity. Abdiel, recognizing this, denies his serfdom and labels his opponent a *thrall*, "to thyself enthralled" (181).

The power of angelic song, luminous with joy, is nowhere more profoundly felt than in Book 7, where Christ's kingship, secure from the violence that established it, is explained by the poet through Christ's actions and the subtle beauty that informs the great circling hymns of praise sung by the delighted angels in response to the creating function of Christ the King. The angels are spectators at the birth of time itself. Both they and the poet who sings "with mortal voice" (7.24) take part in Genesis.

Book 7 makes it very clear that Christ is King by virtue of his power to create. The form of this book is based on the sevenfold structure of Genesis 1, which divides each level of Creation day by day, and the given structure allows Milton to overflow into a poetry of unparalleled lyricism and abundance. I think, however, that there is yet another structural principle at the basis of Book 7, this time a dual one, again founded upon Scripture, that provides a simple but effective key to Milton's image of the divine kingship in the poem. This key is supplied by the visionary excitement of Psalm 24:

> Lift up your heads, O ye gates; and be ye lift up, ye everlasting doors; and the King of glory shall come in.
> Who is this King of glory? The LORD strong and mighty, the LORD mighty in battle.
> Lift up your heads, O ye gates; even lift them up, ye everlasting doors; and the King of glory shall come in. (Ps. 24:7–9)

The image of the opening gates, into which the victor is about to enter, occurs, then, twice in the psalm, at verses 7 and 9. It occurs twice also in Book 7, before and after the Creation:

>   heaven opened wide
> Her ever during gates, harmonious sound
> On golden hinges moving, to let forth
> The king of glory in his powerful Word
> And Spirit coming to create new worlds.

(7.205–9)

> Open, ye everlasting gates, they sung,
> Open, ye heavens, your living doors; let in
> The great creator from his work returned
> Magnificent, his six days' work, a world.

(7.565–68)

In both psalm and poem the King of Glory is announced, though in the poem the first occasion is not an entrance but an exit from Heaven. Enclosed by these two announcements in the case of the psalm is the question as to the identity of the mysterious King, and the answer is given in terms of omnipotence and earthly power, "the LORD mighty in battle."

In the same way, between the two parallel allusions in the poem the identical question as to the King's identity—"Who is this King of glory?"—is *implicitly* asked and answered. Yet in *Paradise Lost* the answer is a different and almost an opposite one. Whereas the psalm identifies a warrior-king, "the LORD mighty in battle," the two echoes of Psalm 24 in Book 7 of the poem enclose a celebration of a creator-king, expressing his glory not in the destruction of war (which he has already accomplished in the previous book) but in the act of fathering a world. The psalm itself is not solely concerned with God's force (it establishes his liberality and fertility in verses 1 and 2), yet, in *Paradise Lost*, within the formal echoes of verses 7–9, Milton used the passages that structurally parallel verse 8 to embrace a redefined conception of the Messiah's royalty. The first allusion to the psalm is a simple narrative directive, and the second is part of a hymn of celebration, sung by the angels at the completed fact of Christ's glory and preluding the mighty hymn of Creation that rounds off the seven days of Genesis.

Within the Genesis structure, the angelic "minstrelsy" has an important part to play. The function of the singing is not made explicit by the poet, but he devotes a significant portion of his verse to describing it:

> Thus was the first day even and morn:
> Nor passed uncelebrated, nor unsung
> By the celestial choirs, when orient light
> Exhaling first from darkness they beheld;
> Birth-day of heaven and earth; with joy and shout
> The hollow universal orb they filled,
> And touched their golden harps, and hymning praised
> God and his works, creator him they sung,
> Both when first evening was, and when first morn.

>   (7.252–60)

The birthday of the universe, paralleling the birth-day we examined in Chapter 4 of the Son as king in Book 6 and its consequence, also echoes the birthday of the angels themselves. The Word, here witnessed fathering our world, proves by this act its claim (accepted previously on faith) to have created the off-spring of Heaven. Light is imagined by the poet as a breathing out ("Exhaling") from darkness itself, and the spontaneity of the watchers' delight, expressed with sudden "joy and shout," is a very human reaction of marvel at this uniquely beautiful event. The exquisite skill of Milton's account of the angels' song is revealed when we consider that the song is expressed as a kind of filling of void, a contribution to the creation of plenitude, and therefore an act of original creativity in itself; otherwise the poet would not have devoted a whole line to insisting that "The hollow universal orb they filled." This filling of the pristine heavens by active choirs (not minstrels lolling in a feudal court) suggests to the reader a positive participation necessary to the great scheme of existence.

In this most personalized of universes, the angels may then be said to be human in their vivid reaction. They are also in some sense royal, with Christ's fathering royalty, for when "creator him they sung" it is as if they name their maker, as Adam named the creatures and God named the angels at the beginning of things. The reciprocity of king and subjects, father and children, is very clear in the identity of purpose in these acts of naming. Milton does not present this reciprocity on a purely theoretical or abstract level, for the quality of the poetry he bestows on God's creation has such lyric perfection, mingling sublimity and sweetness, that few readers could have abstained from exclaiming upon the loveliness of the vision. It is an awe that finds expression in the reascent of the angels singing of the work of art that has been produced as "Magnificent, his six days' work, a world" (7.568) with the measured dignity of the phrasing, the deep stasis on each caesura. The freedom of the returning angels is expressed in the threefold imperative of their hymn, "Open, ye everlasting gates . . . Open, ye heavens . . . Open, and henceforth oft" (7.565, 566, 569). As God commanded the world to be, through his Word, so the angels command the heavens to act, according to the living laws within them. We hear again the shout of exultation that welcomed the first day of creation into being. Liberty and not servitude informs and structures their song, and the reader of the prose works, remembering Milton's statement of recognition to Salmasius—"The Messiah is king. It brings us joy"—may feel that the quality of this joy, different in kind from any terrestrial pleasure, is the fundamental experience of Book 7.

Christ's kingship is not only redefined but changed between his exit from Heaven and his reentry. The Sabbath hymn that completes the book makes explicit that it is in his creativity rather than in the passion of his revenges that Christ is magnified. The angels sing:

Great are they works, Jehovah, infinite
Thy power; what thought can measure thee or tongue
Relate thee; greater now in thy return
Than from the giant angels; thee that day
Thy thunders magnified; but to create
Is greater than created to destroy.
Who can impair thee, mighty king, or bound
Thy empire?

(7.602–9)

The kingship of Christ is shown as a kind of evolution, for it is greater now than when it scoured Heaven clean of cruelty in a gesture of supreme power. The poet plays on an internal rhyme of *create* with *greater* to emphasize this. In Book 7, though the poet consciously comes down to earth, he soars for the first time from the notion of earthly kingship to a new vision of the nature of the heavenly King, which absorbs and transcends all the images accumulated in the first six books. This image is achieved through the avoidance of all emblems that could possibly suggest earthly monarchy: there are no thrones, scepters, swords, or palaces here. The poet's imagination fastens upon the one function that distinguishes God from every other entity: his power of original creation, a power that is met by extemporaneous but patterned outbursts of joy from all of God's creatures. If we remember Satan's relationship with his subjects, the contrast is startling, for contrary to the normal rule in the poem there is no parody. No attempt is made to establish Satan as *pater patriae*.

Satan's rhetoric in speaking to his subjects is lofty, impersonal, and impressive, and their relationship to him is that of grand servants to grander master, at best as comrades in arms. One is jolted to remember that the poet never shows them calling him "father" or "brother"; he never reciprocates with "my sons" or "my brothers." It is in this barren lack of kinship between Satan, Beelzebub, Belial, Mammon, and the insect throng of fallen spirits that we perceive their rootless and joy-less condition. Satan's ephemeral tears for their losses (1.619–20) have not the lasting comfort associated with a father-king. Even in relation to Satan's "royal family," a parodic trinity in-volving an element of love, the familial image is grotesquely stripped of all emotion by being an incestuous love between monsters, each hostile to the other and locked in an aggressive relationship ("my inbred enemy" [2.785]) or a lascivious one ("Thy daughter and thy darling" [2.870]) in which none is capa-ble of satisfaction. The "royal family," detached from the larger family of the state, exists as if in vacuo like an absolutist mon-archy on earth and swells in Book 10 to a spurious epic grandeur only to distintegrate from its own self-punishing corruption.

By contrast, the divine family extends itself infinitely out-ward, by new creation of entities loved for their own unique quality, like the "spawn abundant," the "fry innumerable" that fill the seas in Book 7 (388, 400). By including the ancient image of earth as mother earth warmed into fruitfulness by father sun, the poet is able to embrace an image of maternity in his pre-dominantly masculine structure, with the benign and kindly suggestions that maternity must bring. The teeming earth with seas like amniotic fluids and her "fertile womb" (7.454) opening like the gates of heaven to give forth new creatures, none too microscopically small to be undeserving of a mention, "Minims of nature" (482), suggests a cosmos that breathes, feels, smiles (502), and cares. The poet was immensely prudent to withhold any such emotive images from the satanic kingdom. Earth and Eve, increasing, pregnant with new life (though wayward and mistaken), and finally redemptive, healing agents, are emotive evidences of God's paternal love for his creatures.

Whereas in Book 6 we were made aware that it was the Son (Messiah) who was the agent of justice, in Book 7, though it is sensible to see Christ as the Word, in company with the Holy Spirit, the being who comes forth to create the universe is more of a composite God. The "omnific Word" may speak to the waves (7.217), but it is in *"paternal* glory" (7.219, my italics) that He rides into Chaos, and the Creator is from that moment known only as *God.* The Trinity does not seem as personalized as it had been, and the Son's image melts more absolutely into that of the Father.[29] Milton was following Genesis, of course, but he also appears to be offering a presentiment of that era predicted in Book 3 when time itself should have an end, the conventional symbols of monarchy should be laid aside, and "God shall be all in all."

Book 7 is the happiest book in the poem, the least flawed by pain or bad omens, combining a visionary poetry expressing with sweetness and dignity Milton's vision of a golden age with his celebration of God's creation of order out of love. Neither civil wars nor empires are relevant here, for we have left behind the lords of the earth. Paternal tenderness overflows into the warm fertility symbolism of days one and two, the dance of vegetation and spheres of days three and four, and the teeming life of the animal species on the fifth and sixth days. It is a vision of becoming, not just being: all is motion and appetite. God's whole existence seems poured into the act of fatherhood, and through this concentration of himself in this one function, the great paradoxes of his nature are aesthetically and theologically suggested and reconciled. Just as within each single day of Creation infinite variety is brought into being, so also Milton reconciles in general terms the finite with the infinite (7.169), order with plentitude,[30] animate with inanimate. During this act of creation, the mind is liberated from all familiar symbolism associated with royalty, so that the hymn that accompanies the reascending Christ, "Open, ye everlasting gates," quite redefines our notion of the heavenly kingship. Milton varies the words of the psalm here, supplying "creator" for "King of glory," yet the listening reader hears silently the echo telling that the "*King* of glory" may come in and knows that the cycle is complete and that the question he also heard counterpointed between the two echoes of the psalm—"Who is this King of glory?"—has been finally answered. After this, the term *empire* in the Sabbath hymn cannot be interpreted according to the customary materialist meaning. All political terminology associated with the Father-God assumes new mystical significance, to be apprehended by the heart as much as by the mind.

The radical nature of this vision is emphasized by the fact that the invocation to Book 7 deals with a world at an opposite pole from that which I have described. In the invocation, the myth of Orpheus and the Bacchantes is generally recognized now as representing a thin veil of allegory over the predicament of a Puritan poet under a Restoration monarchy that understands nothing of the ideal monarchy Book 7 will reveal. The use of the myth looks back to the yearning moment in *Lycidas*, before the civil wars, when Calliope was helpless to prevent her son's destruction (lines 58–63). There the state of nature itself had been the subject of Milton's grief, but here it is natural to suppose that the death force incarnated in "Bacchus and his revellers" must have precise political relevance to the new Caroline court:

> But drive far off the barbarous dissonance
> Of Bacchus and his revellers, the race
> Of that wild rout that tore the Thracian bard
> In Rhodope.
>
> (7.32–35)

Such allegorical attribution seems unavoidable when we consider the terms in which Milton in *The Readie and Easie Way* foresaw and evaluated the nature of a new monarch, "with a dissolute and haughtie court about him, of vast expence and luxurie, masks and revels, to the debaushing of our prime gentry both male and female" (Yale 7:425). The Royalist pamphleteers were seen as "diabolically" creeping out of "thir holes, thir hell": they were "tigers of Bacchus . . . inspir'd with nothing holier then the Venereal pox" (ibid., 452–53). When we remember that Bacchus, in addition to his orgiastic qualities, was always shown in a chariot drawn by tigers and lions, "and, like a king, he has his guards" in the form of satyrs, maenads, and the rest,[31] that he had been imaged as a law-giver and civilizer,[32] and that he was associated etymologically with Nimrod,[33] we have no hesitation in identifying him with the returning Charles II. The pamphleteers are the tigers who draw back Bacchus (Charles II) to tear the natural order apart with "revels." No myth could express more poignantly than the Orphic Milton's sense not only of the fragility of the Creation in confrontation with its enemy, Satan, but also of how paper-thin poetry is, even divine poetry, in conflict with the irrational. But the myth has immense political relevance to the whole subject of Book 7. Renaissance commentators on the Orphic inheritance, especially the Florentines, valued Orpheus chiefly for his monotheism, his supposed belief in the Trinity, and his corroboration of the Creation as recounted in Genesis.[34] The dissolute and unnatural court of a king who rules by reveling stands against Book 7's conception of the ideally powerful Orphic God who belongs rather to Heaven than to an earth dominated by the dark and savage reality of the present Dionysian reign. Thus Book 7 could be seen as the product of the dissolution of Milton's millenarian ideals: his placing of Christ's kingdom beyond time, leaving "evil days" to the fallen earth.

After Book 7 has expressed the theme of God's royal fatherhood in a blaze of lyrical poetry, this lyricism fades, to lie quietly beneath the surface of the remaining narrative as a memory and a promise. Such visions are not the material of life either during or after the Fall, for they lie outside man's immediate experience, and he does not deserve them. The poetry of this theme becomes muted over the second half of the poem, as both author and reader become subdued to the inevitability of the loss of Paradise. The glory expressed in Book 7 is no longer intrinsic to the mood of a poem in which our representatatives, Adam and Eve, become so rapidly and subtly detached from access to the vision of the heavenly crown. Christ also becomes a being whose glory and triumph are tempered by sorrow at events in the world beneath, and as man loses sight of perfection the poem's temper is moderated in response to that loss. It is not that God or the Son becomes any less royal or fatherly: rather, these attributes have been immutably established, and all that now remains is that they should be acted out, without a great deal of relish, to punish and redeem God's youngest and erring children. For instance, though God at the beginning of Book 10 sits on his "throne supreme" (28) thundering out judgments as "the most high / Eternal Father" (31–32) and the Son as his Father's expression manifests himself to his fallen subjects as a "sovereign presence" (144), the accoutrements of power and the titles indicating majesty seem largely obligatory and not emotive.

Kingship is not really important here, and the Son descends to single man out for justice and embrace him in mercy, without regal train or pomp, as a premonition of his later descent into human form and then into the grave. Stripped of ornate majesty, Christ, sober, rigorous, and austere, gives judgment with the imprint of his future mercy and pain stamped all over it. It is as if he tastes mortality for the first time in dispensing it, though seeing beyond it he can picture the triumph of the Resurrection with powerful optimism (10.182–92). Yet that triumph does not appear as real to him or to the reader as does his sense of the pity of what *now* is, and through the premonition of his own coming manhood and death, consciousness of his kingship is buried by the poet in the emotions associated with human fatherhood:

> then pitying how they stood
> Before him naked to the air, that now
> Must suffer change, disdained not to begin
> Thenceforth the form of servant to assume,
> As when he washed his servants' feet so now
> As *father of his family* he clad
> Their nakedness with skins of beasts, or slain,
> Or as the snake with youthful coat repaid;
> And thought not much to clothe his enemies
> Nor he their outward only with the skins
> Of beasts, but inward nakedness, much more
> Opprobrious, with his robe of righteousness,
> Arraying *covered from his Father's sight.*
>
> (10.211–23, my italics)

The two italicized phrases suggest that at this stage in the history of man's fall and rising, with the disintegration of original order, so also the fatherhood of God has split into two distinct phenomena, only to be fully reconciled when history has come full circle and the final triumph is attained. Until this ultimate reintegration, the first form of fatherhood must protect man from the second Fatherhood. The Son, as "father of his family,"[35] performs his first identifications with human beings in a domestic image of cherishing concern, and this concern (though the tenses are interestingly confused) is shown by Milton as foreshadowing the later menial role Christ would adopt in dramatizing the nature of love for his disciples' sake. Such an image must remove this kind of fatherhood from association with the regal, an association still attached to the terrible God of omniscience, whose staring, never-sleeping eyes forge their way into man's vulnerable soul. (The emblem of the all-seeing God is first introduced very early in Book 10, at line 6, to prepare the way for this symbolism.) A similar pattern is repeated at the opening of Book 11, when the Son presents himself once more as intercessor for man, as though he were fading from the heavenly monarchy toward sharing man's nature:

> let me
> Interpret for him, me his advocate
> And propitiation, all his works on me
> Good or not good ingraft, my merit those
> Shall perfect, and for these my death shall pay.

(11.32–36)

It is only through withdrawal into a paternity so human as to be willing to suffer for and with the dregs of humanity, shedding glory, majesty, and even kingship itself, that with the completion of history these attributes may all be reassumed and the Father-King may ascend the throne in a perfected universe:

> he shall ascend
> The throne hereditary, and bound his reign
> With earth's wide bounds, his glory with the heavens.

(12.369–71)

6

Naked Majesty

The kingship of Adam in Eden before the Fall is one of the most poignant images evoked by Milton in *Paradise Lost,* for it leads us into the heart of his Golden Age vision, tasting freedom, power exerted without force, and dignity without ornament; and out again, with a mortal taste in the mouth, it leads us into the world of "all our woe" (1.3), where we are all subjects, whatever local and temporary titles we hold, where power is coercion and violence, and where mankind elbows its way up a Chain of Ambition such as Philotime held in *The Faerie Queene* (2.7.44–49).

The kingship of Adam is in one sense closer to the reader than any other image in the poem. We would not wish to be near Nimrod; we abhor the barbarian, regret the emperor; we could not approach the mighty, salvific feudalism of heaven save on bended knee and covering our eyes; though we are by grace God's sons, we only fitfully participate in his majesty by fostering kingship within the mind through temperance and faith. The cosmic figures of the poem soar beyond human reach, but Adam is humanity itself, rather more than life-size, but recognizable, approachable, and identifiable. It is as if Milton held an idealizing mirror up to our eyes and, inviting us to look in and admire, made accessible to us a knowledge not only of what we might have been but also of the power we might have enjoyed. Yet it is also an image of a condition in the past, at the primal source of human life, and reaches us like light from a distant planet that has only a past and never a present. A great sadness accrues to the image of Adam's kingship because of this, and a sense of its vulnerable character, too, because at every point the physical nakedness that is Adam's strength and an index of his inner purity speaks to the fallen reader of the frailty of the power he holds.

The experience is paradoxical. Adam as king of the terrestrial world is free of all the heavy items that represent the vesture of monarchy in the reader's fallen world. There is liberty in his naked majesty, exempting him from cares of state and social obligations, the mere trouble of dressing that fills up the monarch's day in the postlapsarian world. But because the fallen reader, as Milton in Book 4 shows himself deeply aware, has never been in a position to contemplate nakedness without some uneasy stirrings of "dishonest shame" (313) or feelings of exposure to judging eyes that bring either ridicule or prurience, we must also contemplate Adam with a sense of his potential exposure. The pathos within the experience is present from the first moment of description. It is different in kind from the pathos of the cluster of similes that precedes the description, but it is reinforced by the fact that it is first presented through the unloving eyes of Satan:

> Two of far nobler shape erect and tall,
> Godlike erect, with native honour clad
> In naked majesty seemed lords of all,
> And worthy seemed, for in their looks divine
> The image of their glorious maker shone,
> Truth, wisdom, sanctitude severe and pure,
> Severe but in true filial freedom placed;
> Whence true authority in men.
>
> (4.288–95)

This is a composite image of naked majesty, undifferentiated in terms of gender, which Milton will split off into male and female only after making the essential point that both Adam and Eve (whatever the specializations in their nature that God thought fit to introduce) are fundamental participants in the divine nature and dispensers of an earthly form of the divine justice. There is no element in the description that does not relate to their function of governing and judging, and this not in a tangential or allusive way but explicitly and specifically. Their upright stance indicates not only the rectitude of their minds but also an erect will, to be exerted in judgment, distinguishing them from the animal species whose lords they are. They are clad, like noble savages or like the Britons described by Milton in his *History of Britain* as "the native and the naked *British valour*" (Yale 5, pt. 1:66), in "native honour," that is, their clothes are nothing but themselves, a kind of nobility bearing no emblem but in itself an embodied emblem. It is this

that constitutes naked majesty and confers lordship in the
edenic world. When the angels flock in to the inauguration of
Christ as king in Book 5, they bear heraldic indications,
blazons, blazing forth their virtue. They are a huge army of
individuals surrounding their sovereign. In Paradise, Adam
and Eve are the corporate sovereign; they should be compared
not to the adoring army of angels but to God and to the Christ
who is clothed in nothing but light (5.577–99). This identification is endorsed by the poet's statement that "The image
of their glorious maker shone" in Adam and Eve, a radiance
like that of Christ receiving and reflecting the light from its
divine source.

Adam and Eve's nakedness, then, is their power. It enables
an unveiled reflection to occur from God to man. In the reiterated "severe," this same rigor of seeing and judging is maintained but elucidated in the qualification "Severe but in true
filial freedom placed." This is the heart of Adam's kingship: its
roots take vitality from the liberty involved in being a son of
God, linking Adam with the angels as sons and with Christ as
Son. Eve is also in a metaphorical sense a son of God, since
Milton has not chosen to break the unity of their majesty at this
point, and we should assume that he was enacting a serious
intention in postponing the gender classification until such
time as he had established their joint responsibility, dignity, and
freedom. Their power to govern is derived from a filial freedom
without which Eve could not have been considered fully
human, for the poet explains that it is from this condition that
"true authority in men" derives. The word-play in *authority*,
simple though it is, is rich and clarifying, for the word contains
the source word *author*. Adam's power stems from being the
true son of his Author, God: as son, he receives from the source
the right and ability to be an author himself, *pater patriae* on a
limited basis as the acknowledged and subordinate heir of God.
The government of the unfallen earth is therefore defined in
very cogent terms from the very outset as a form of patriarchy,
tempered by obedience, in which both male and female
participate.

The poet never subsequently denies this joint authority in
Adam and Eve, but he drastically (some think violently)
qualifies it as soon as it has been set forth:

Whence true authority in men; though both
Not equal, as their sex not equal seemed;
For contemplation he and valour formed,
For softness she and sweet attractive grace,
He for God only, she for God in him;
His fair large front and eye sublime declared
Absolute rule; and hyacinthine locks
Round from his parted forelock manly hung
Clustering, but not beneath his shoulders broad:
She as a veil down to the slender waist
Her unadorned golden tresses wore
Dishevelled, but in wanton ringlets waved
As the vine curls her tendrils, which implied
Subjection, but required with gentle sway,
And by her yielded, by him best received,
Yielded with coy submission, modest pride,
And sweet reluctant amorous delay.

(4.295–311)

When Milton acknowledges the gender difference, terminology associated with the exercise of power enters much more massively into the poetry. To Adam's "Absolute rule," Eve responds with "Subjection." Both phrases were odious to the poet politically. In *The Tenure of Kings and Magistrates* and *Eikonoklastes*, he had repudiated Charles I's prerogative over the law as a kind of usurpation; in the two *Defences*, while exclaiming that he did not oppose kingship as such, only its abuse, he limited those eligible to a maximum of one when he told Salmasius that the only one who could reign on the pattern of God is "some person who far surpasses all others and even resembles God in goodness and wisdom. The only person, as I believe, is the Son of God whose coming we look for" (First *Defence*, Yale 4, pt. 1:428). Milton here ignored Adam whose eligible qualities were presumably too far in the past to be appropriate in the current political quarrel. The political prose writings display an equivalent personal dislike of any political model based on the subjection of the worthy. What distinguishes the human community of Paradise, however, from any other political phenomenon is, first, that it is a community of two (the number of division but also that of balance and equipoise) and, second, that it uniquely enables a political analysis based on an innocent "Absolute rule" reciprocated by an answering "Subjection," founded in those innate and natural human differences uncontroversially assumed to be present in the sexes. In Milton's *Tetrachordon* and his *Doctrine and Discipline of Divorce,* he had been able to argue toward an unconventional conclusion (the allowability of divorce under certain circumstances) by emphasizing a conventionally acceptable premise of female inferiority.

Incorporated into a poem with important political strands, this conventional relationship between ruler and subject, distinguished from a coercive relationship by its framework of mutual love uniting and identifying the higher and lower partners, was an emotive and crucial emblem for the poet of civil concord based on the uniting of disparate elements. The flight of Eve from her husband, given in her account of her first meeting with him, may therefore stand as an emblem of the commonwealth, where lord and subject are one. In marriage they are one in a very literal sense: one flesh. They are essential to one another in a more than utilitarian fashion, and they are fruitful in their union in a manner that unites productivity with divine creativity. In Eve's account of Adam's first words to her, we are aware that he, who is her legitimate "author" and therefore has natural "authority" over her, also experiences a need of her and a high valuation of her that is intrinsic to his being:

> Part of my soul I seek thee, and thee claim
> My other half: with that thy gentle hand
> Seized mine, I yielded, and from that time see
> How beauty is excelled by manly grace
> And wisdom, which alone is truly fair.

> (4.487–91)

This highly rational opinion on the part of Eve, expressed with sober good sense, is the product both of her "sanctitude severe," born in her, and of her association with that quality in Adam. The paradox of rule and subjection in a world where force would be a contradiction in terms is beautifully dramatized in the tension of meanings in Eve's statement that "thy gentle hand / Seized mine." Nothing gentle may be said to engage in an act of force, yet to *seize* is to exert force. The only experience in which this semantic conflict could not occur would be in an erotic situation, where yielding is a positive and voluntary action rather than a negative one, melting boundaries that in political terms are only more strongly delineated by terminology like *rule, subjection, seizing, yielding*. The same paradox is posited but immediately solved within the first description of Adam and Eve's relationship, when Eve's hair is compared to the abundant, curling tendrils of the vine:

> which implied
> Subjection, but required with gentle sway.

(4.307–8)

In that the vine requires a prop and cannot function without one (see 9.432–33), it is subject: given the prop, however, the vine—whose luxuriance and defiance of arbitrary form the poet superbly evokes, "as the vine curls her tendrils"—is free.

The description of Eve's hair, though clearly important as erotic detail contributing to the feeling every reader has of the sensuous joy of Milton's Paradise, also contributes to his political analysis in an extraordinary way. Subject as Eve is, her beauty is energetic, individual, and free. Milton went to considerable lengths to redefine political terminology by associating it with the controlling metaphor of love between man and woman, in his qualifying clauses ("implied / Subjection, *but*"). We may read what follows in two ways. Either Adam "requires" Eve's surrender "with gentle sway"; or Eve requires that he shall exert "gentle sway" over her subjection. The noun *sway* suggests an interesting subsidiary meaning of motion to-and-fro, which echoes the reciprocity within the relationship that the poet is aiming to suggest. In the union of Adam and Eve, it is not easy to perceive subject and object, when we consider that "by her yielded, by him best received." The line sways in balance upon its center, its symmetry mirroring an implied equality in which dominance is never an active enforcement but rather a passive receiving of the gift given. Here, Eve, the yielder, is so in two senses: she surrenders; in doing so, however, she yields fruit and is the giver. Her "coy submission, modest pride, / And sweet reluctant amorous delay" (310–11) are paradoxes along the same lines. Sexually, they may generate uncertainty in readers, who feel that Eve plays sexual games of a wanton character not consistent with the purity and straightforwardness of Paradise. But considered in the political terms

offered by the poem, this trinity of gestures only enacts the <u>real
freedom of Eve's subjection</u>. "<u>Coy submission</u>" increases <u>her</u>
own gratification; "modest pride" is the exact balance or <u>mean</u>
<u>of behavior</u> to which man, angels, and God in *Paradise Lost*
<u>point as the aim of human life, attained here by Eve</u> effortlessly
and in pleasure; and "reluctant amorous delay," exciting as that
may be to the masculine imagination, also emphasizes the
power with which Milton's God has blessed woman: power to
sustain her lover's excitement if she chooses, but power also not
solely to delay but to stop altogether if she so chooses.

[marginalia: inclined to love, being in love]

The relationship between the two in its pristine form is therefore in name a kind of monarchy, but in nature (through the
motifs of marriage and androgyny,[1] and through the deep re-
definition of the terminology of power that Milton's poetry allows) it resembles more a little republic of two. As Christ's
kingship is self-renouncing toward both angels and mankind,
so Adam's is to Eve. <u>The ideal Milton postulates is a cooperation between differences so intense that the two may think of
one another as</u> "Part of my soul . . . / My other half" (4.487–88).
These different natures are grounded in identity. As Milton
showed in *The Doctrine and Discipline of Divorce* (Yale 2:272),
"Gods doing ever is to bring the due likenesses and harmonies
of his workes together." Married, the two parts of this miniature commonwealth are king and queen, and in her own right
Eve shares the exquisite quality of the moon ascending over
Paradise:

> the moon
> Rising in clouded majesty, at length
> Apparent queen unveiled her peerless light,
> And o'er the dark her silver mantle threw.

(4.606–9)

Whatever premonitions of ensuing danger the reign of the
moon might bring—bearing memories of the lunar deities I
discussed above in Chapter 1, such as Astarte introduced in
Book 1—here the intimacy is all innocent as the moon discards
the cloudy vesture that is like Eve's veiling hair (4.304), to be
put aside in the act of love, and sheds a luminous quality over
night as a kind of covering, comforting "silver mantle." Arche-
typal associations of maternity with the queenly moon are *[marginalia: original pattern, model]*

clearly present in the poet's imagination, as is the chastity of Diana. The fickleness to come is held by the poet in abeyance. In Book 7, he shows the moon taking all her light from the sun, holding her place "opposite in levelled west" (376). Unequal in radiance, she is equal in poise and balance; a sort of just equivalence that is like Eve's, essential to the scheme of things.

Milton's opinion of queens in the political sphere had not been high. He considered them unserviceable and unnatural: it was a sign of barbarism in a nation to subject itself to a woman. His *History of Britain* gloats over the treacheries of Roman empresses displaying the expected "female pride" (Yale 5, pt. 1:71); over the British effeminacy in accepting Queen Cartimandua, whose husband and people came to hate "the uncomeliness of thir Subjection to the Monarchie of a Woeman, a peece of manhood not every day to be found among *Britans*" (ibid., 74). Even that national heroine Boadicea is vituperated as an index of British barbarism, scorned by the Romans "as if in *Britain* Woemen were Men, and Men Woemen" (ibid., 79), her armies "the wild hurrey of a distracted Woeman, with as mad a Crew at her heeles" (ibid., 80). The unspeakable dreariness of this historical survey of England's deplorable ancestors is quite livened up at these moments of sardonic misogyny on the author's part, and one could wish for more of them.

When in the Interregnum Milton came to consider the queens of modern history, he naturally said what he could against them; but when he found qualities so undeniably virtuous that there was no obvious way to detract from them and when they were needed to furnish valuable exempla, he had grudgingly to cite them with approval. This frequently happens with Queen Elizabeth in the *Commonplace Book,* when Milton was bound to record her religious and constitutional policies as setting correct precedents. These queens are generally labeled "Exceptions." In Milton's *Second Defence,* the reader who has learned to live with Milton's misogyny by constant proximity must almost laugh out loud reading the eulogy of the Protestant Queen Cristina of Sweden, which Milton undertook on behalf of the government, for it is so extreme and fulsome that it must have blistered the hand that wrote it. The queen who had applauded Milton against Salmasius is flattered thus:

> As for you, *most serene ruler of the Swedes,* he could not long deceive you and that keen judgment of yours. You have proved yourself the

princess, and I might almost say the heavenly guardian, of that course which prefers truth to the heat of partisans. . . . such a glorious, such a truly royal defender of my honesty. . . . How magnanimous you are, Augusta, how secure and well-fortified on all sides by a well-nigh divine virtue and wisdom. . . . plainly of heavenly origin. (Yale 4, pt. 1:603–5)

This effusion of flattery to the royal lover of Athene and her vigorous intellect, by the holder of the published view that a woman's place was not with her head in a book, is the product of political exigency. It sounds like Adam over-praising Eve in Book 8: "All higher knowledge in her presence falls / Degraded, wisdom in discourse with her / Looses discountenanced" (551–53), a piece of excess that transports the speaker perilously near to the abyss, and to which the admonitory angel Raphael must retort with a sharp lecture on refraining from subjection to the beloved inferior (570).

Yet it is in his *Second Defence* that Milton gave voice to that beautiful and memorable aphorism according to which he explains that he wrote *Eikonoklastes* "not, as I am falsely charged, 'insulting the departed spirit of the king,' but thinking that Queen Truth should be preferred to King Charles" (Yale 4, pt. 1:628). Here, the regicide turned from the punitive violence of his characteristic apology for the events of 1649 to an explanation formulated upon a high, just valuation given to the feminine principle, Queen Truth. The feminine personification, Platonist and Spenserian—like the saving Una of *The Faerie Queene* and the embodied Mercy of Giles Fletcher's *Christs Victorie*—symbolizing a goodness that is also attractive and lovable to a human being, is placed above the male person and his brutalities. This high valuation of the feminine in its proper place is characteristic of Milton in a way that his eulogy of Cristina is not.[2] It is this reverence that informs and tempers the presentation of Eve in both the earlier and the later parts of *Paradise Lost,* an awareness of her worth that draws her level to Adam though not fully equal to him, a genuine version of Queen Truth though ephemeral in her reign.

It is because of this quality, which may be called equivalence, not equality, with Adam, that Eve can form a kind of miniature commonwealth with him. The character of such a commonwealth, as a guide to future ages, is pleasingly shown by Milton in that book of *Paradise Lost* where one might least expect to find political ideas, Book 7. It is no accident that the emblem of such a community is framed within the book of fertility and creativity, during the sixth and final day of Creation, at the end of which man, the masterpiece, will be made. A commonwealth is set in a background of beauty and enchantment; the reader's perception of it is sweetened by the pleasure of the poetry with which, despite hints toward the Fall, Milton enacts Genesis, presenting shapes, colors, and movements in a verse that is prodigally rich and virtuoso. It is when he brings his vision from vast expanses down to creatures of microscopic smallness that Milton introduces the double emblem of the ideal community, designed by God as supernatural artist, described by the poet who mimes his inspirations, and capable of being copied by human beings who can share that inspiration:

> First crept
> The parsimonious emmet, provident
> Of future, in small room large heart enclosed,
> Pattern of just equality perhaps
> Hereafter, joined in her popular tribes
> Of commonalty: swarming next appeared
> The female bee that feeds her husband drone
> Deliciously, and builds her waxen cells
> With honey stored.
>
> (7.484–92)

By "just equality" Milton does not mean equality on a democratic or utilitarian basis in which each social unit weighs equally with the rest but rather a community in which justice is distributed according to merit, in a state whose members are all meritorious but not equally so.

Such a commonalty is defined in the *Second Defence* as being the rule of the greater over the lesser for the common good: "Those whose power lies in wisdom, experience, industry, and virtue will, in my opinion, however small their number be a majority" (Yale 4, pt. 1:636). The great advantage of the commonwealth of the ants from the point of view of political argument is that its members are small enough to be viewed all at once in their cooperative exercise. There is humor and sweet temper on the part of the poet who teaches us to look down on the republic of ants toiling at their common purpose by supplying the tiny insects with the elephantine epithet *parsimonious,* laboring along the verse line to convey the enterprises of the colony. It is a great deal of fuss to make about the building of an ants' nest, and perhaps the poet smiles at the tremendous effort put in by human society to such little effect, particularly in his bestowing of the ironic *perhaps* to the old emblem of the providential ant culled from the bestiaries. More seriously, the poet celebrates every tiny detail of the divine creation, marveling at the light-reflecting wing of a fly, the great-heartedness in the heroic instincts of an ant that the eye must strain to perceive. The mystery of plenitude, the art and care of the Maker, are celebrated.

If Eve had continued provident, the gardening of the commonwealth of Eden would have continued eternally; just equality would have been preserved by the kingship of Adam and Eve, under the guidance of their own "wisdom, experience, industry, and virtue." The adjective *provident* contains a rich and most unexpected seed of further meaning, for it translates the name *Prometheus,* which, as we saw in Chapter 5, means foresight, prudence. The giant virtues of Adam and Eve cooperating with providence in Paradise could have secured a happy future for man without the stealing of fire, the torture, and the expiation. Eve could have learned about Promethean matters from the example of the ant. Adam could have learned from the bee, to avoid being a drone dependent on the "delicious" offerings of his wife. The poet enacts the lesson preached by Raphael to man in Book 8 about being "lowly wise," for to look downward at the little creatures of earth brings deep knowledge, and the gently humorous, joyous quality of the poetry teaches the fallen reader how to look for knowledge in this humble way, to hope that, perhaps, even postlapsarian man may build his commonalty upon it.

What fallen man can never recover, however, in Milton's vision, whatever makeshift constitutions he may devise for himself, arguing from Scripture, Aristotle, or nature, is the "naked majesty" that the poet celebrates in Adam. Eve's nakedness, though theoretically sharing in this attribute, is more obviously a function of her innocent sensuality. When she leaves Raphael and Adam to ponder astronomy together in Book 8, her "lowliness majestic" (42) and "goddess-like demeanour" (59) make her a "queen" (60), but, more obviously, a Venus-figure inspir-

ing amorous love. Adam's demeanor, harder and more bare of
sensual association, links him with the divine kingship in an
explicit way. This is made clear in Book 5, in which the Mer-
curial figure of Raphael enters our world, linking it by his presence with Heaven. The encounter between Raphael and Adam
is a meeting of kings. Traditionally, Mercury (or Hermes) carries
a caduceus, which, reproduced in coronation ritual, appears as
the king's scepter, suggesting that the king is a mediatorial
figure between Heaven and earth.[3] Milton offers no caduceus
but refers to Raphael in terms emphasizing the royal associations of this Christian Hermes, associated, through the image
of the "phoenix" (272) that he resembles, to the kingship of
Christ. In his descent he offers paradoxically a pattern of
resurrection:

> six wings he wore, to shade
> His lineaments divine; the pair that clad
> Each shoulder broad, came mantling o'er his breast
> With regal ornament; the middle pair
> Girt like a starry zone his waist, and round
> Skirted his loins and thighs with downy gold
> And colours dipped in heaven; the third his feet
> Shadowed from either heel with feathered mail
> Sky-tinctured grain. Like Maia's son he stood.
>
> (5.277–85)

Of all the gods, Maia's son, Mercury, was said to be the closest
friend to man. Milton's Raphael brings with him not only the
love of their common "Father" (5.246) but also a royal message,
as his own person is a royal one. While the blue colors of his
wings symbolize the entrance of Heaven into earth and the gold
and silver ("a starry zone") relate to his source in God, the
upper wings are specifically described as covering his breast
"With regal ornament." *Ornament* is a curious word for the poet
to select, given its connotations of display extraneous to the
wearer; *regal ornament*, with the suggestions of courtly magnificence, is even more strange. But it is this very incongruity that
turns the reader back to the text, to discover why Milton adorns
his royal angel with a robe reminiscent of that purple robe so
detested by Milton in the affairs of human kingship.

But, of course, there is no robe at all, extrinsic to the wearer.
Milton says that Raphael "wore" six wings, but the usage is

metaphoric, for his wings are himself. Raphael is not encumbered by any of the "troublesome disguises which we wear" (4.
740), the clothing both mental and material behind which fallen
humanity protects itself and declares its shame, which it must
clumsily shed to love or communicate. He is dressed only in
himself. For the noun *mantle,* Milton substituted the participle
mantling for the action of those great, beautiful wings that
"came mantling o'er his breast / With regal ornament." The
poet's puritanism transforms the meaning of the word *ornament,* so that from the crucible of his imagination it emerges to
denote a beauty intrinsic to the pure, plain, and thence kingly
spirit. Raphael brings to earth an embodiment of heavenly
royalty.

In order to encounter this phenomenon, Adam as king of the
lower world rises to meet the visitation in its own terms:

> Mean while our primitive great sire, to meet
> His godlike guest, walks forth, without more train
> Accompanied than with his own complete
> Perfections, in himself was all his state,
> More solemn than the tedious pomp that waits
> On princes, when their rich retinue long
> Of horses led, and grooms besmeared with gold
> Dazzles the crowd, and sets them all agape.

> (5.350–57)

Both figures, the "godlike guest" and his human host, are active. Raphael does not descend upon Adam by way of patron-
age: on the contrary, Adam, never a passive occupant of the
Eden over which he reigns, walks forth to meet him. The poet
offers a movingly simple description of this action on the part of
"our primitive great sire," moving partly because this naked
figure might be a vulnerable one if it were more insecure or self-
conscious: as our sire, Adam is linked to our fallen nature, but
he, through his family relationship, confers on us something of
his own dignity. He is presented as being bare of all ornament,
and Milton signals his kingship by contrasting the glory of the
absence of extraneous adornment with the contemporary experience of a royal progress. The presence of a cluster of rhymes
and half-rhymes in the passage—"meet / complete / state /
waits"—may alert us to the crucial importance of the distinction that is being made here, the simple and dignified measure

describing Adam's progress as if enacting the tenor of his mind's "Truth, wisdom, sanctitude severe and pure" (4.293), in contrast to the satiric eye that Milton casts upon the pageant of modern royalty.

In the modern pageant, the horses seem to be the major protagonists, the most glorious courtiers being grooms; and the procession passes along in equine majesty admired by open-mouthed crowds who cannot see the princes for the horses and the horses' servants. Time is wasted here; the gold is an unusual sort of dirt ("besmeared"), highly suited to the grooms' occupation; the crowd is composed of fools, "agape," so that one can almost see the expression upon their faces.[4] The dirty, contaminating gold that belongs to the Mammon world of lucre and the animal world of the irrational is wholly foreign to Adam's solitary "complete / Perfections." His kingship is unvisited by the voyeurism Milton had always associated with the crowd, "a credulous and hapless herd, begott'n to servility." Adam greets Raphael without fear but with respect, and in the interchange of greeting, each recognizing the worthiness of the other as "Native of heaven" (361), their mutual courtesy is not an exercise of etiquette but a due acknowledgment of the unadorned truth. This theme of naked majesty is reechoed in a minor key when Eve is introduced as "Undecked, save with her self" (380), though the associations here are more sensuous than political. The encounter of Adam with Raphael involves the meeting of king with king, different in appearance and in degree, but equally mirroring the divine kingship that each as true son of God reflects. The poet's introduction of a picture of the degenerate modern monarchy, which is not simply a distortion of the original but its antithesis, informs the meeting with poignancy.

Adam and Eve are king and queen over the terrestrial world, but they must not bring into it coercive power or force. It is essential to the paradox of prelapsarian existence that the hand of justice be stayed; there can be no rigor of law because order is the precondition of paradisal existence. Exertion of any control other than self-control must imply that a lapse has already occurred. Therefore, Adam receives the fealty of the animals, but there is no suggestion that the lower species would ever offend him:

> each bird and beast behold
> Approaching two and two, these cowering low
> With blandishment, each bird stooped on his wing.
> I named them, as they passed, and understood
> Their nature, with such knowledge God endued
> My sudden apprehension.

(8.349–54)

The natural world yields freely to Adam, echoing the liberty enjoyed by the heavenly spirits under God. The poet insists on divine rule as a cooperation between ruler and ruled, a reciprocal keeping of faith (fealty deriving from *foi*) between the two parties. The details characterizing the act of homage on the part of Adam's subjects are quaint, even comic, in keeping with the lightheartedness of God's dealings with Adam as he brings this youngest child into his inheritance. Animals bow; birds on the wing, with a prodigious contradiction of their airborne nature, stoop. The latter detail darkens with a sadder implication when we remember that Raphael in his (somewhat desperate) attempt to portray the oncoming legions of evil spirits in the war in Heaven had compared their flying march to this very event, "the total kind / Of birds in orderly array on wing" (6.73–74) coming to receive their names. We are made aware that if a peaceful and orderly gathering may be used as a parallel for a rebellion, such disturbance of the natural order may be at every moment potential.

However, Adam's account is serene. His part as king is twofold: to name and to understand. It is not to command, since coercion would only be consistent with two powers at enmity with one another. The God described by Adam in Book 8 is a smiling God, playing with Adam as if he were a young king still in infancy and actively enjoying his creation as a human parent spares time to enjoy his child's experiments with the art of reasoning:

> the vision bright,
> As with a smile more brightened, thus replied.
> What call'st thou solitude, is not the earth
> With various creatures, and the air
> Replenished, and all these at thy command
> To come and play before thee, know'st thou not

> Their language and their ways, they also know,
> And reason not contemptibly; with these
> Find pastime, and bear rule; thy realm is large.
> So spake the universal Lord, and seemed
> So ordering.

(8.367–77)

God is teasing and playing with Adam. Even he will not "order" in this pristine time, travestying for Adam's benefit and for the purposes of the game his own posture as King of kings. Adam is allowed, even encouraged, to argue with the architect of all Creation; the Creator will allow himself to tell partial truths so as to strengthen Adam's independence and reasoning. What is clarified here is the fact that there is no real joy to be found in "bearing rule." Adam rightly wants a companion rather than a kingship. Milton suggests the ethical rightness of this desire by showing a God who gives every appearance of enjoying the company of his offspring, despite his claim to being "alone / From all eternity" (405–6). The God who thus plays with Adam proves the fitness of what Milton had so passionately pleaded for in *The Doctrine and Discipline of Divorce:* laws framed to exclude the probability of "God-forbidd'n loneliness" from human experience (Yale 2:247). In this tender interlude, God puts aside both Justice and Mercy in order to enter into the smile of human recognition that the poet sees as the source of joy and thence of goodness itself. In a sense, God abdicates his kingship here, to share the liberation of a comic release, until he restores the status quo by announcing to Adam that he had from the beginning planned a "likeness, thy fit help, thy other self" (450) for him to enjoy. God as loving father creates for Adam a nearly equal companion, and Adam perceives absolute proof that his maker is "creator bounteous and benign" (492).

A lesson to be drawn from this last refreshing episode recounted in such dreadful proximity to the Fall is the emptiness of power unrelated to love; in a state of innocence, power cannot be enacted, whereas love can. Adam does not enjoy having inferiors, in a positive sense. There is no emotional charge in the issuing of commands and no necessity to do so. Power is largely passive, since obedience is received rather than extorted. Love in the garden of innocence is charged with emotion, active, untainted with power. Yet in this lies Adam's danger, as Raphael goes on to explain to his host in the admonitory lecture, for love untempered by reason implies "thy subjection" (8.570). Coercion has crept in by the unexpected route, and the king who has the power to order but who must in a state of innocence refrain from exercising rule becomes himself a subject.

The dilemma faced by Adam in Book 9 is an infinitely subtle one. He faces it less as one torn between reason and passion than as one held by conflicting arguments of nearly equal validity, based upon the correct relationship between love and power in the state of innocence. Eve, determined to leave Adam's protection in order to pursue ends imperfectly known to either of them, would require a restraint little short of physical coercion to be kept from fulfilling her desire. Adam comes to the limits of the active possibilities of prelapsarian kingship. His injunction to her to go is a painful last statement of that kingship.

> Go; for thy stay, not free, absents thee more;
> Go in thy native innocence, rely
> On what thou hast of virtue, summon all,
> For God towards thee hath done his part, do thine.
>
> (9.372–75)

The rhetoric—"Go . . . Go"—is flawlessly noble.[5] The argument, based on the definitive role played by inner states of mind in human conduct, is irrefutable; but the tragedy is that this authentic voice of paradisal kingship is expressing a kind of foregone epitaph upon itself. When Eve is tempted by Satan it is into becoming "Empress of this fair world" (9.568), a kind of consort to Satan's *Imperator* role, an empress who follows the course of evil (626) and is subject in a way that she cannot conceive. Her brief command to Satan, "Lead then, said Eve" (631), parodies Adam's "Go . . . Go" to an almost ludicrous degree, so bathetic and inartistic is her new style of utterance as empress. Her fall is into the *dominium* Wycliffe had defined as entailing as essential corruption.[6] As "Queen of this universe" in Satan's final speech of temptation and "Goddess humane" (684; 732), Eve passes out of the Paradise into which she was born into the fallen world that lies beyond it. The pastoral crown Adam is weaving for her cannot belong to her, for she no longer exists within the pastoral world:

> From his slack hand the garland wreathed for Eve
> Down dropped, and all faded roses shed.
>
> (9.892–93)

This harvest crown, symbolic of rule exercised without force, is the first object in Paradise to die.

But Adam does not degenerate into a Nimrod, a Caesar, or a grand seigneur. Milton's prototype for Adam is King Solomon, wise beyond mortal expectation but betrayed by his own concupiscence to false religion and idol worship. Though there is more than a little of the nimrod-spirit of vicious inhumanity in Adam's acrimonious recriminations of Eve—"Out of my sight, thou serpent" (10.867), lethal words that must be seen as proof of Adam's corruption—and although Nimrod and the kings of this world are in lineal descent from Adam, inheriting a sin for which he was responsible, the poet emphasizes the continuing humanity in Adam, which links him with Solomon rather than with Nimrod and thence Moloch and Satan. We do not feel that there is or could be blood on Adam's hands; nor is he subject to temptation to the worldly power, gold lust, or violence that characterize the satanic principle when it entirely overwhelms human nature. The poet presents him to us under an image of barbarism that is pitiable (the Indian herdsman [1108], the American Indian [1116]) rather than aggressive.

Though a reader may be provoked to moments of hostility to Adam after his fall, he far more entirely pities him as an erring man, astray and frightened, than dislikes him as a dangerous criminal against his maker. King Solomon, as I showed in Chapter 1, is the perfect archetype for expressing this lapsed nature that equally retains its humanity and our sympathy. Milton had, in his prose, repeatedly cited the oracular Solomon whose wise prescriptions and *"morall precept"* were pertinent to modern experience and whose actions might be cited as legal precedents for just behavior in the state.[7] Though in his first *Defence of the People of England* he did not deny that Solomon might have acted tyrannically toward Israel and that Israel would have had the right to execute him if it had so judged, the tyrannical aspect of Solomon's behavior was minimized and Milton offered mitigating explanations to justify it. When he said, "Solomon was lured to crime, but it is not said that he lured others" (Yale 4, pt. 1:372), he expected his reader to associate the king with the secondary sin of Adam and of every man rather than with the primary sin fathered by Satan. However, Milton was far more interested in Solomon's sexual fallibility than in any of his other attributes, as he shows in his treatment of that king in relation to David Rizzio in the first *Defence* (ibid., 371–72).

In *Paradise Lost,* however, the identification of Adam with Solomon is somber and tragic. It is introduced at the beginning of the poem, where it keeps hideous company with the cults of the false gods, especially the gory Moloch:

> the wisest heart
> Of Solomon he led by fraud to build
> His temple right against the temple of God
> On the opprobrious hill, and made his grove
> The pleasant valley of Hinnom, Tophet thence
> And black Gehenna called, the type of hell.

$$(1.400–405)$$

The effect of the juxtaposition is to create an awareness of the dangers implicit in that uxorious nature which is commonly felt to be so forgivable, so remote from the destructive violence whose very ugliness declares it to be an obvious evil. Solomon's "wisest heart" is a remembrance of that most moving passage in the book of Kings in which, deeply acknowledging his own inadequacy to follow his father David in ruling as king of Israel, Solomon turned to God with the confession, "I am but a little child: I know not how to go out or come in" (3:7) and requested of God an "understanding heart" (3:9). It was on the foundation of this absolute and childlike admission of human helplessness, opening the door to the guidance of the divine fatherhood, that Solomon, who "knew not how to go out or come in" built the temple in Israel, gave judgment, and accrued incomparable power and wealth. This wisest heart also links him in Milton's poem with Adam, the "goodliest" man ever born (4.323), to whom the admonitory angel imparts the intelligence that he should "be lowly wise" (8.173). The suggestion is that it was by virtue of the very openness that made it possible for Solomon so freely to yield himself to God that fraud could enter him. He is emotionally accessible. Milton's syntax in line 402, whereby Moloch's temple confronts "the temple of God," implies the deadly character of the vulnerability, in both Solomon and Adam, which when creatively used results in a richly yielding virtue but when relaxed becomes a channel for the forces of hell to pour their evil through so that a "pleasant valley" becomes a graveyard. Hell is founded on earth by the weakness of the builder of the temple of God. The moral duty of inner strength is reinforced by the vision of the nightmare power of the fallen angels in the catalog of false gods to exploit human frailty.

In Book 9, as Satan approaches Eve in that penultimate hour of her freedom and innocence, the poet remembers in an allusive simile the meeting of Solomon and Sheba that in the biblical account comes so close to the fall of Solomon. Eve within the garden is seen as inhabiting a lovelier place than

> that, not mystic, where the sapient king
> Held dalliance with his fair Egyptian spouse.
> Much he the place admired, the person more.

(9.442–44)

It is as if the Temple of God, in the radiantly innocent person of Eve, is confronted by the temple of Moloch. Gehenna itself, the hell on earth of the satanic consciousness, approaches what is pleasant with what is black and makes ready to take over. The pathos in the phrase *the sapient king* is that, alluding as it does both to Adam and to Solomon, it is not necessarily ironic. The dalliance Solomon enjoyed with Sheba was of the educative sort, leading her to admire the place—Israel and the temple—and the person—Solomon—who ruled so justly with what was still "the wisest heart." She was moved, in the account in Kings, to acknowledge that "thy wisdom and prosperity exceedeth the fame which I heard" (10:7), and she recognized the true God through Solomon's account. Christopher Ricks notes that *he* in line 444 has a potential ambiguity, denoting Satan standing in for Adam's uxorious admiration for his wife.[8] I should prefer to read it as Satan ironically replacing Sheba, who admired the sapience of Solomon to such excellent effect. For once in the Bible, Egypt is held in captivity to Israel: without force and by spiritual power. The sadness is that this episode in both the epic poem and the biblical account should stand so close to the protagonist's fall, as if—as is the case—no earthly power, not even God-given wisdom of heart, could defend humanity.

Adam's fall, like Solomon's, is swift in the telling. *Sapience* and *dalliance* again occur as allusions, but this time in an irrecoverably tarnished context. Having gorged the fruit:

> in lust they burn:
> Till Adam thus gan Eve to dalliance move.
>   Eve, now I see thou art exact of taste,
> And elegant, of sapience no small part,
> Since to each meaning savour we apply,
> And palate call judicious; I the praise
> Yield thee.

(9.1015–1020)

The burning is of hell-fire. The praise bestowed upon Eve by Adam is a reversal of the biblical story's acceptance by Sheba of Solomon's superior qualities. Solomon here yields to Sheba, calling wisdom a form of appetite on the basis of a verbal quibble. The true parallel is to Solomon's willingness to give himself to strange women and false deities: to the downfall of David's son. The babble of Adam's logic foreshadows Babel. The hatred he conceives for Eve soon after their intercourse issues from an "estranged" Adam (1132) whose punitive malevolence makes Eve rather than Satan the enemy; it is an abdication of the justice of his prelapsarian kingship.

We also remember the figure of Solomon when we follow through the final quarter of the poem the process of regeneration and the new kind of rule provided as a possibility for Adam and his sons in order to replace the original loss. The new form of kingship relies on no externals. In this respect it is only a restatement of the form embodied in Adam when "in himself was all his state" (5.353). Though in Books 11 and 12 Milton follows through the cycles of history to the davidic kingship and the self-renouncing triumph of Christ, little if any trust is placed in history. The Gospel's powerful optimism is presented austerely, and human nature may not hope for certainty on this planet. But Solomon's virtue is offered as the saving attribute, according to which each man may create an inward temple of God (the Holy Spirit), behaving according to the principle of wisdom that is universally available:

> To whom thus also the angel last replied:
> This having learned, thou hast attained the sum
> Of wisdom; hope no higher, though all the stars
> Thou knew'st by name, and all the ethereal powers,
> All secrets of the deep, all nature's works,
> Or works of God in heaven, air, earth, or sea,
> And all the riches of this world enjoyed'st,
> And all the rule, one empire; only add
> Deeds to thy knowledge answerable, add faith,
> Add virtue, patience, temperance, add love,
> By name to come called Charity, the soul
> Of all the rest: then wilt thou not be loath
> To leave this Paradise, but shalt possess
> A paradise within thee, happier far.
> Let us descend.

(12.574–88)

The sentence labors in its accumulation of virtues: "add . . . add . . . add," enacting the herculean task of the Christian soul as it pursues a form of happiness not based on outward "rule . . . empire," nor on dependence upon any human loved one, but on the aggregate sum of wisdom. We may feel that it is a grim, impersonal happiness. But it represented for Milton that arduous Christian liberty and kingliness within the soul which more than compensate for the fall and may ultimately temper any individual into a power more potent than that of "the wisest heart / Of Solomon."

Notes

Notes to Introduction

1. See, for example, G. Wilson Knight, *Chariot of Wrath: The Message of John Milton to Democracy at War,* and Malcolm MacKenzie Ross, *Milton's Royalism: A Study of the Conflict of Symbol and Idea in the Poems.*
2. A. L. Rowse, *Milton the Puritan: Portrait of a Mind,* pp. 25, 101.
3. Hugh M. Richmond, *The Christian Revolutionary: John Milton,* p. 154.
4. Christopher Hill, *Milton and the English Revolution.* Robert Hodge's "Satan and the Revolution of the Saints" represents a less creative Marxist analysis. Andrew Milner's *John Milton and the English Revolution* (London and Basingstoke: Macmillan, 1981) takes violent issue with Hill in an appendix over the sociological approach to literature, but his work does not in general have Hill's literary awareness. See for other studies of the political themes of *Paradise Lost,* Stella Purce Revard, "Satan's Envy of the Kingship of God: A Reconsideration of *Paradise Lost,* Book 5, and Its Theological Background"; Joan S. Bennett, "God, Satan and King Charles: Milton's Royal Portraits"; Joan Webber, "Milton's God" and *Milton and His Epic Tradition.*
5. Walter Raleigh, *Milton,* p. 135.
6. Knight, *Chariot of Wrath,* pp. 127, 134.
7. William Empson, *Milton's God,* pp. 76–77.
8. J. B. Broadbent, *Some Graver Subject: An Essay on "Paradise Lost,"* p. 115.
9. Hill, *Milton and the English Revolution,* p. 372.
10. See Merritt Y. Hughes, "Satan and the 'Myth' of the Tyrant," p. 131.
11. Hill, *Milton and the English Revolution,* p. 405.

Notes to Chapter 1

Kings of This World

1. See, for example, Jack Goldman, "Insight into Milton's Abdiel," p. 251; Peter Malekin, *Liberty and Love: English Literature and Society,* p. 93.
2. For closer discussion of the relationship between *Eikonoklastes* and *Paradise Lost,* see Stevie Davies, "John Milton on Liberty"; Joan S. Bennett, "God, Satan and King Charles: Milton's Royal Portraits." The relationship between Milton's Puritan political experience and *Paradise Lost* is ably analyzed in Boyd M. Berry's *Process of Speech: Puritan Religious Writing and "Paradise Lost"* and, with superb insight, in Christopher Hill's *Milton and the English Revolution.* Its connection with epic, analyzed as a subversive form, may be studied in Joan M. Webber's (sadly, posthumous) *Milton and His Epic Tradition.*
3. For this reason, I do not concur with Donald F. Bouchard's opinion that "*Paradise Lost* is a meta-text of pamphlets like *Eikonoklastes* and *The Ready and Easy Way*" (*Milton: A Structural Reading,* p. 59).
4. Isa. 14:12.
5. The rhetorical method employed against *Eikon Basilikè* is analogous to that later used against Salmasius. For analysis of this technique of point-by-point

refutation, combined with an overall device of *indignation,* see Anthony Robin Bowers, "Milton and Salmasius: The Rhetorical Imperatives." Milton (not without qualms) accepts the author of *Eikon Basiliké* as King Charles; in fact, it was probably mainly the work of Dr. Gauden.

6. Charles I, *Eikon Basiliké: The Portraiture of His Majesty King Charles I,* pp. 129–30.

7. See Chapter 3 for study of this triumphal structure.

8. Louis L. Martz ably expressed the human application of the rollcall of the angels when he said that it gives "a summation of human vice, depravity, and irreligion. . . . It is the world we know" (*Poet of Exile: A Study of Milton's Poetry,* p. 189).

9. See, for example, First *Defence,* Yale 4, pt. 1:310, 346 ff.; *Second Defence,* Yale 4, pt. 1:599, 603 ff.

10. See Chapter 6, below, for a discussion of the significance of this episode.

11. Galbraith Miller Crump, in *The Mystical Design of "Paradise Lost,"* offers a useful account of circular structure in *Paradise Lost.*

12. See *Paradise Lost,* 1.397–99, n.

13. See Chapter 4, below, for Christ as King.

14. *The Tenure of Kings and Magistrates,* Yale 3:197 ff.

15. See Milton's *Tenure,* Yale 3:234; John Cook, *King Charles His Case, SCT,* 5:233; Junius Brutus, *A Defence of Liberty Against Tyrants: A Translation of the "Vindiciae Contra Tyrannos,"* p. 81.

16. See Chapter 5, below.

17. See *A Remonstrance of Fairfax and the Council of Officers* in A. S. P. Woodhouse, ed., *Puritanism and Liberty: Being the Army Debates, 1647–9,* p. 462; Thomas May, *The History of the Parliament of England, which began November 3, 1640 . . . ,* p. 163; Cook, *King Charles His Case, SCT,* 5:226; *Englands Petition to their King, SCT,* 5:36, and so on.

18. See, for example, Grant McColley, *Paradise Lost: An Account of Its Growth and Major Origins, with a Discussion of Milton's Use of Sources and Literary Patterns,* and George Wesley Whiting, *Milton's Literary Milieu,* pp. 55–56, for valuable material.

19. Joseph H. Summers, *The Muse's Method: An Introduction to "Paradise Lost,"* p. 209.

20. Dennis H. Burden, *The Logical Epic: A Study of the Argument of "Paradise Lost,"* p. 179.

21. Compare Isabel Gamble MacCaffrey's analogous interpretation of Milton's epic similes as "loopholes into history" in *"Paradise Lost" as Myth,* p. 133.

22. *Englands Petition to their King, SCT,* 5:34.

23. See Marcia Vale, *The Gentleman's Recreations: Accomplishments and Pastimes of the English Gentleman, 1580–1630,* pp. 27–33, and D. R. Watson, *The Life and Times of Charles I,* p. 75.

24. See C. V. Wedgwood, *The Trial of Charles I,* p. 148.

25. Cook, *King Charles His Case, SCT,* 5:235; *Eikonoklastes,* Yale 3:361.

26. *The Doctrine and Discipline of Divorce,* Yale 2:247, 251.

27. James Howell, *Englands Tears for the Present Wars, SCT,* 5:42.

28. See Geneva Bible, "Brief Table of the Interpretation of the Propre Names."

29. See Christopher Hill, *Puritanism and Revolution: Studies in Interpretation of the English Revolution of the Seventeenth Century,* pp. 58–125; A. E. Barker, *Milton and the Puritan Dilemma, 1641–1660;* Don M. Wolfe, *Milton in the Puritan Revolution;* Christopher Hill, *Milton and the English Revolution;* and Austin Woolrych, "Political Theory and Political Practice," in C. A. Patrides and Raymond B. Waddington, eds., *The Age of Milton: Backgrounds to Seventeenth-Century Literature,* p. 51, for discussion of these ideas.

30. Milton's *Commonplace Book,* Yale 1:424. Compare the Leveller protest that "its a Badg of our Slavery to a Norman Conqueror, to have our Laws in the French Tongue," in *A Declaration of Some Proceedings* (1648) in William Haller and Godfrey Davies, eds., *The Leveller Tracts, 1647–1653,* p. 109, and Lilburne's premises in *A Remonstrance of Many Thousand Citizens* (1646) in Don M. Wolfe, ed., *Leveller Manifestoes of the Puritan Revolution.*

31. *History of Britain,* Yale 5, pt. 1:291, 392.

32. Sir Thomas Herbert, *Memoirs of the Two Last Years of the Reign of King Charles I,* in Gertrude Scott Stevenson, ed., *Charles I in Captivity,* p. 175.

33. Junius Brutus, *A Defence of Liberty Against Tyrants: A Translation of the "Vindiciae Contra Tyrannos" by Junius Brutus,* pp. 153–54.

34. *The Readie and Easie Way,* Yale 7:463.

35. *A Letter from General Monck to King Charles,* printed in 1660, *SCT,* 6:559.

36. Thomas Shipman, "The Restauration and Welcome: 1660," secs. 4, 6, in *Carolina, or, Loyal Poems;* The English Channel is the Red Sea.

37. Abraham Cowley, "Ode Upon His Majesties Restoration and Return," st. 8, *Poems.*

38. Paulus Orosius, *Seven Books of History Against the Pagans: The Apology of Paulus Orosius,* 7:363.

39. See John Calvin, *Commentaries on the Epistle of Paul the Apostle to the Romans,* pp. 477–91. The Prince is "an executioner of God's wrath" (p. 481). See also Ronald Stuart Wallace's useful account of Calvin's disapproval of armed resistance to tyranny in *Calvin's Doctrine of the Christian Life,* pp. 166–69. Michael Fixler is especially helpful on the eschatological implications of *Paradise Lost,* 9 and 10, in *Milton and the Kingdoms of God,* pp. 226–33.

40. Named as Busiris in 1.307.

Notes to Chapter 2

Sultan and Barbarian

1. *A True Relation of the taking of Cirencester* (1642), *SCT,* 4:512.

2. *King Charles His Case, SCT,* 5:218.

3. *The True Portraiture of the Kings of England, SCT,* 6:88.

4. *An Appeale from the degenerate Representative Body of the Commons of England,* in Don M. Wolfe, *Leveller Manifestoes of the Puritan Revolution,* p. 165.

5. "A Speech against Peace at the Close Committee" (1643), in Theodore Howard Banks, ed., *The Poetical Works of Sir John Denham* (London and New Haven: Yale University Press, 1928.

6. "The Cities Welcome to Colonel Rich and Colonel Baxter," st. 1, in W. W. Wilkins, ed., *Political Ballads of the Seventeenth and Eighteenth Centuries,* vol. 1.

7. "A true and impartial Narrative," *SCT,* 6:480.

8. "Twenty-seven Queries," *SCT,* 6:511.

9. John Harrington, *The Common-wealth of Oceana,* in *The Oceana of John Harrington, Esq; and His Other Works,* p. 62. Junius Brutus, in the wider Protestant debate about sovereignty, also argues from the Turkish example (*A Defence of Libery Against Tyrants: A Translation of the "Vindiciae Contra Tyrannos" by Junius Brutus,* pp. 115, 130, 161).

10. See Samuel Claggett Chew, *The Crescent and the Rose: Islam and England during the Renaissance,* p. 141.

11. See J. B. Broadbent, *Some Graver Subject: An Essay on "Paradise Lost,"* pp. 100 ff.; John Peter, *A Critique of "Paradise Lost,"* p. 42.

12. Balachandra Rajan, *"Paradise Lost" and the Seventeenth Century Reader,* p. 95.

13. See Edward Arthur Thompson, *A History of Attila and the Huns,* p. 88.

220, *Images of Kingship*

14. Fynes Moryson, *Shakespeare's Europe: The Fourth Part of Fynes Moryson's Itinerary*, pp. 3, 13.

15. See *The Journals of Sir Simonds D'Ewes*, p. 305, where he reports Pym as comparing Strafford's criminality with "the Minister of the Great Turke or some other Muhametan Prince, then of a Christian Monarke and a Gratious King."

16. See John M. Steadman, *Nature into Myth: Medieval and Renaissance Moral Symbols* (Pittsburgh: Duquesne University Press, 1979), p. 294, n. 50.

17. Richard Knolles, *The Generall Historie of the Turkes, from the First Beginning of the Nation to the Rising of the Othoman Famillie*, p. 209.

18. Ibid., pp. 2–3.

19. See Milton's *Animadversions*, Yale 1:698, where he looks forward to the reduction of the episcopacy "to the ancient, end equall house of Libra," and the use of Libra/*libra*/scales images throughout *Paradise Lost* as a symbol of God's ultimate justice.

20. Christopher Grose, *Milton's Epic Process: "Paradise Lost," and Its Miltonic Background*, p. 168.

21. See Chapter 3.

22. They are reported by Christopher Ricks in *Milton's Grand Style*, p. 51.

23. *Milton's "Paradise Lost": A New Edition* (London, 1732). See Ants Oras, *Milton's Editors and Annotators from Patrick Hume to Henry John Todd (1695–1801)* (London: Oxford University Press, 1931), pp. 50–74, for a just account of Bentley's editorial principles, based on a "true sense."

24. Milton, *Poetical Works*, 1:351 n.; Grose, *Milton's Epic Process*, p. 170.

25. See, for instance, E. D. Phillips, *The Royal Hordes: Nomad Peoples of the Steppes*, pp. 108–9; Harold Lamb, *The March of the Barbarians*, pp. 3–20. On Renaissance cartography, see Robert Rawson Cawley, *Unpathed Waters: Studies in the Influence of the Voyagers on Elizabethan Literature* (London: Cass, 1967); George Wesley Whiting, *Milton's Literary Milieu*, pp. 94–127.

26. See Christopher Hill, *Milton and the English Revolution*, pp. 371–72. Sylvester's Du Bartas notes the commonplace association of the north with prodigious fertility, explaining it "scientifically" by suggesting that in the north it is too cold to enjoy copulation: semen is saved for making children. He lists the northern barbarian tribes who "Have swarmed (like Locusts) round about this Ball" in *The Divine Weeks and Works of Guillaume de Saluste du Bartas*, trans. Joshua Sylvester, ed. Susan Snyder (Oxford: Clarendon Press, 1979), 1:457.

27. See Tacitus, *Germania*, 43, 44, 45, in *"The Agricola" and "The Germania."*

28. Ammianus Marcellinus, *History*, 1. 31. 2. 1.

29. *The Gothic War*, in *Works*, 2:331–33. Isabel Gamble MacCaffrey's suggestion that the flood of barbarians is analogous to the biblical Deluge (*"Paradise Lost" as "Myth,"* pp. 128–29) is very apt.

30. *State Papers, Literas Majestatis*, Cromwell to the King of Denmark, 1565, Yale 5, pt. 2:778 (see also *Quoties Communion*, 1658); *Ostendit Nobis*, Cromwell to the Duke of Tuscany, 1657, ibid., 134; *Instructions for the Agent to Russia*, 1657, ibid., 786.

31. In Aeschylus, *"Prometheus Bound" and Other Plays*, trans. and ed. Philip Vellacott (Harmondsworth: Penguin, 1961). Line references are hereafter given parenthetically in the text.

32. Jerome, *Select Letters*, pp. 330–31.

33. Herodian of Antioch, *History of the Roman Empire from the Death of Marcus Aurelius to the Accession of Gordian III.*

34. Samuel Purchas, *Hakluytus Posthumus, or, Purchase His Pilgrimes* (Glasgow: James Maclehose and Sons, 1905), 1:93, 3:38.

35. Chew, *The Crescent and the Rose*, p. 219.

36. Robert R. Cawley, *Milton and the Literature of Travel*, pp. 78–79.

37. St. 68 in *Poems and Dramas of Fulke Greville, First Lord Brooke*, vol. 1.

38. See, for instance, his *History of Britain*, Yale 5, pt. 1:258 ff. This is a republican commonplace, expressed, for instance, in John Hall's satiric *Paradoxes*, p. 6, where he ironically explains that desire for autocratic monarchy cannot "proceed from *cowardize*: for we see the old and modern *Persians*, the stoutest *Septentrionall Nations*, the *Turks, Scithians*, and *Muscovites* at this day, pride themselves so much in that Government, this they adore their Emperors as gods."

39. "To My Noble and Judicious Friend Mr. Henry Blount upon his Voyage," ll. 38–40, in Bishop Henry King, *The Poems*.

40. In *The Works of John Milton*, 10:332. (It is not yet available in the Yale ed.) Page references are hereafter given parenthetically in the text.

41. This abortiveness is recognized, for instance, in Fulke Greville's dramas, *Mustapha* and *Alaham*, and in poetic compendia like Sir William Alexander's *Doomes-Day*.

42. See Richard Hakluyt, *Voyages*, 2. 1. 305; Knolles, *The Generall Historie*, p. 252.

43. Hakluyt, *Voyages*, 2. 1. 305.

44. Cawley, *Milton and the Literature of Travel*, pp. 53–54.

45. In 1674, years after the publication of *Paradise Lost*, Milton translated the *Letters Patent* of King John III of Poland and was able to record the triumph of Western military power over the Turkish formation, which "might be repressed by a Standing Fight . . . broken and routed at one stroke" and could conclude (what *Paradise Lost* had suggested) that barbarian invasions had as their purpose to bring "to the most serene Elect, matter of Glory, Victory" (*The Works of John Milton*, 6:277).

Notes to Chapter 3

Imperial Caesar

1. See Jan Kott, *The Eating of the Gods: An Interpretation of Greek Tragedy*, pp. 117–19.

2. Seneca, *Octavia*, pp. 630–33, in *Four Tragedies and Octavia*, trans. E. F. Watling (Harmondsworth: Penguin, 1966).

3. This is a commonplace of Renaissance historial theory, reflecting the Stoic view of Providence as set forth in Seneca's *De Clementia*, and followed by Raleigh, Barckley, and Munday in their histories.

4. See *Paradise Lost*, 6. 746–59 n. and 761 n., for triumphal structure and symbolism, also Alastair Fowler's *Triumphal Forms: Structural Patterns in Elizabethan Poetry*, and Gunnar Qvarnström's *The Enchanted Palace: Some Structural Aspects of "Paradise Lost."*

5. On Milton's use of classical epic, see John M. Steadman, *Milton's Epic Characters: Image and Idol*, *Milton and the Renaissance Hero*, and *Epic and Tragic Structure in "Paradise Lost"*; Francis C. Blessington, *"Paradise Lost" and the Classical Epic*; and Joan M. Webber, *Milton and His Epic Tradition*.

6. See, for instance, Eutropius's account of Nero's luxuries in his *Roman History*, 7, in *Justin, Cornelius Nepos and Eutropius*, trans. John Selby Watson (London: George Bell and Sons, 1875), p. 502.

7. See Donald McFayden, *The History of the Title Imperator under the Roman Empire*.

8. Historically, this might be paralleled with the acclamation by the troops as *Imperator*, which by Claudius's time gave the victor imperial powers, the army being the real force in government. See Suetonius, *The Lives of the Caesars*, 5. 10.

9. Tacitus, *The Annals*, 1. 7, in *The Annals and the Histories*, trans. Alfred John Church and William Jackson Brodribb, ed. Hugh Lloyd-Jones (Chalfont St. Giles: Sadler and Brown, 1966), pp. 7, 9.

10. *Shakespeare's Plutarch*, 1:92.

11. Tacitus, *The Annals*, 1. 13.

12. See Titus Livy, *The History of Rome*, 22. 8–11, on this institution.

13. See Ernst Hartwig Kantorowicz, *The King's Two Bodies: A Study in Medieval Political Theology*, on this important concept.

14. *The Annals*, 1. 4. 5; 7. 7.

15. See Niccolò Machiavelli, *The Prince*, trans. G. Bull, pp. 25, 130–33; *Discourses on the First Decade of Titus Livy*, 3. 31. 442–46; Christopher Marlowe, *Tamburlaine the Great*, 1. 4. 4.

16. See Milton's *History of Britain*, Yale 5:66–67, recording Claudius's manifold triumphal acclamations in his war against the Britons.

17. See David Moore Bergeron, *English Civic Pageantry, 1558–1642*, pp. 9–121; John G. Demaray, *Milton and the Masque Tradition*; John Nichols, ed., *The Progresses and Public Processions of Queen Elizabeth*.

18. See list in M. Lefkowitz, ed., *Trois Masques a la Cour de Charles Ier d'Angleterre*, p. 10.

19. *The Triumph of Peace*, ibid., p. 65.

20. John G. Demaray, *Milton's Theatrical Epic: The Invention and Design of "Paradise Lost,"* pp. 71–72.

21. Appianus in *The Punic Wars*, 9. 66, shows Scipio Africanus's triumphal procession with Scipio arriving last with his army (in *Appian's Roman History*). Aemilius appears on the last of his three days of triumph in Plutarch's *Lives* (*Life of Aemilius Paullus*, 6.32–35.441–49).

22. See Fowler, *Triumphal Forms*, pp. 27–28.

23. Tertullian, *Apologeticus*, 33.4, in *Apology, De Spectaculis, and Minucius Felix*, p. 157.

24. Ibid., 33.2, p. 157.

25. Ibid., p. 223.

26. Suetonius, *The Lives of the Caesars*, 1.37.51.

27. Tacitus, *Agricola*, 39.44. Likewise Caligula in *Germania*, 37.87.

28. Plutarch, *Shakespeare's Plutarch*, 1.85.

29. *Res gestae*, 4, in Donald R. Dudley, *Urbs Roma: A Source Book of Classical Texts on the City and Its Monuments*, p. 63.

30. See *Of Reformation in England*, Yale, 1:554–57, for a characteristic attack on the giver of the supposed "Donation" to Pope Sylvester, who was thus held responsible for the Roman Church's worldly power.

31. Its inscription is reproduced and its iconography accounted for in Dudley, *Urbs Roma*, p. 138.

32. See John Ferguson, *Utopias of the Classical World*, p. 180.

33. See Fowler, *Triumphal Forms*, pp. 29–33.

34. For formulation of this pattern of violated central structure, see Douglas Brooks, *Number and Pattern in the Eighteenth-Century Novel: Defoe, Fielding, Smollett and Sterne*, pp. 138–41.

35. See Charlton T. Lewis and Charles Short, *A Latin Dictionary* (Oxford: Clarendon Press, 1966), s.v. "fulgeo," and so on.

36. S. K. Heninger, *A Handbook of Renaissance Meteorology with Particular Reference to Elizabethan and Jacobean Literature*, pp. 87–101, notes that comets, meteors, and lightning were regarded as being less bright than the sun. W. B. Hunter, "Satan as Comet: *Paradise Lost*, II. 708–711," interestingly but inconclusively interprets Satan's return to Hell as resembling a supernova.

Notes to Chapter 4

Feudal Lord

1. See *The Readie and Easie Way,* Yale 7:426.
2. Malcolm MacKenzie Ross, *Milton's Royalism: A Study of the Conflict of Symbols and Idea in the Poems,* p. 99. See also G. Wilson Knight, *Chariot of Wrath: The Message of John Milton to Democracy at War.*
3. William Empson, *Milton's God.*
4. Leland Ryken, *The Apocalyptic Vision in "Paradise Lost,"* pp. 18–19 and n. 17. See also p. 71 for his use of a "contextual qualification" to distinguish "kingship in an apocalyptic state and in a demonic state." Another contextual approach is Lawrence W. Hyman, *The Quarrel Within: Art and Morality in Milton's Poetry.*
5. Defined by Dionysius the Areopagite (Pseudo-Dionysius) in *The Mystical Theology and the Celestial Hierarchies.*
6. Empson, *Milton's God,* pp. 79–80, 103.
7. Marc Bloch, *Feudal Society,* pp. 145–46.
8. Ibid., pp. 115–16.
9. Ibid., p. 162.
10. Ibid., p. 164.
11. François Hotman, *Francogallia,* ch. 19 and p. 296.
12. Junius Brutus, *A Defence of Liberty Against Tyrants: A Translation of the "Vindiciae Contra Tyrannos" by Junius Brutus,* p. 78.
13. On this theme, see Joan Webber, "Milton's God." God's sternness is that of "a revolutionary leader who is in the process of bringing freedom out of chaos" (p. 522). Webber does not, however, perceive the feudal content of the idea.
14. See Barbara W. Tuchman, *A Distant Mirror: The Calamitous 14th Century,* p. xv.
15. Boyd M. Berry, in "Puritan Soldiers in *Paradise Lost,*" p. 380, explains the problem of the military order of Heaven as a representation of the Puritan notion of the beauty of order.
16. C. S. Lewis, *A Preface to "Paradise Lost,"* pp. 72–80.
17. Empson, *Milton's God,* p. 103.
18. Percy Ernst Schramm, *A History of the English Coronation,* p. 96.
19. Christopher Wordsworth, ed., *The Manner of the Coronation of King Charles the First of England,* p. 12.
20. See Chapter 6, below, for analysis of the relationship between "ornament" and "essence" in terms of Milton's representation of heavenly majesty.
21. Schramm, *History of English Coronation,* p. 69.
22. J. N. Figgis, *The Divine Right of Kings,* p. 32; Schramm, *History of English Coronation,* p. 21.
23. On Milton's extensive knowledge of heraldry, see Theodore Howard Banks, *Milton's Imagery.*
24. W. B. Hunter, "The War in Heaven: The Exaltation of the Son," in *Bright Essence: Studies in Milton's Theology,* pp. 115–30.
25. *A New-Yeers Gift Sent to the Parliament and Armie,* 1650, in Gerrard Winstanley, *The Works of Gerrard Winstanley,* pp. 353, 355.
26. See Keith R. Crim, *The Royal Psalms,* p. 72; Moses Buttenweiser, *The Psalms, Chronologically Treated With a New Translation* (New York: Ktav, 1969), p. 793; William Theophilus Davison, *The Praises of Israel: An Introduction to the Study of the Psalms,* pp. 219, 222.
27. See, for example, John Peter, *A Critique of "Paradise Lost,"* pp. 66–81.

28. Empson, *Milton's God*, p. 77.

29. Bloch, in *Feudal Society*, p. 270, defines niefs as slaves, as opposed to serfs, under English feudalism.

30. This image of civil war within the fallen soul is a commonplace of humanistic thought. See Giovanni Pico della Mirandola's analysis of "grievous internal wars, wars more than civil" in his *Oration: On the Dignity of Man*, 1486, in Stevie Davies, *Renaissance Views of Man*, p. 73.

31. Bloch, *Feudal Society*, p. 292. For the medieval equation of *miles* with *vassus* and *nobilis*, see Fredric Lawrence Cheyette, ed., *Lordship and Community in Medieval Europe: Selected Readings*, pp. 137–39.

32. See Northrop Frye's penetrating speculations on the medieval concept of the king as "merely *primus inter pares*," with reference to Malory, Spenser, and Milton, in *Five Essays on Milton's Epics*, pp. 110–11.

33. See, for example, Desmond M. Hamlet, *One Greater Man: Justice and Damnation in "Paradise Lost"* (Lewisburg and London: Bucknell University Press, 1976), p. 116.

34. See Frederic Austin Ogg, ed., *A Sourcebook of Medieval History*, for instance of legal "forfeiture."

35. Authorities are George Newton Conklin, *Biblical Criticism and Heresy in Milton*; Harris Francis Fletcher, *Milton's Semitic Studies and Some Manifestations of them in his Poetry*; Kitty Cohen, *The Throne and the Chariot: Studies in Milton's Hebraism*.

36. J. Douglas Canfield's idea that the Platonic Year may be the literal birthday of the Son is very pleasing ("The Birthday of the Son in *Paradise Lost*," pp. 113–15).

37. Robert Graves and Joshua Podro, *The Nazarene Gospel Restored*, 8. a. 106–7; 7. d. 97. See also Artur Weiser, *The Psalms: A Commentary*, p. 113.

38. See Figgis, *Divine Right of Kings*, p. 7; Schramm, *History of English Coronation*, p. 7.

39. *The New Law of Righteousness*, 1649, in Winstanley, *Works*, p. 166.

40. Junius Brutus, *A Defence of Liberty*, p. 178.

41. Ibid., pp. 178–80.

42. Don Cameron Allen has a most beautiful description of the angels' unity in throwing down their crowns in *The Harmonious Vision: Studies in Milton's Poetry*, pp. 99–100.

43. Rosemond Tuve, in *Images and Themes in Five Poems by Milton* (Cambridge, Mass.: Harvard University Press, 1967), gave valuable clues to this silent poetry; the numerologists—Gunnar Qvarnström and Alastair Fowler—gave others; typological readings, such as William G. Madsen's *From Shadowy Types to Truths: Studies in Milton's Symbolism* and Barbara Lewalski's *Milton's Brief Epic: The Genre, Meaning, and Art of 'Paradise Regained,"* yield still others.

44. See Graves and Podro, *Nazarene Gospel*, 8. j. 111–12.

45. See 2 Chron. 18:23; 1 Kings 22:24 (the smiting of Micaiah).

46. Empson, *Milton's God*, pp. 108–9. See also A. J. A. Waldock, *"Paradise Lost" and Its Critics*, p. 108. A defense may be found in Frank Kermode's "Adam Unparadised," *The Living Milton*, pp. 104–5.

47. See *Paradise Lost*, 5.636–40 n.

48. Schramm, *History of English Coronation*, pp. 61–67.

49. Geoffrey of Monmouth, *The History of the Kings of Britain*, pp. 228–29.

50. Schramm, *History of English Coronation*, pp. 64–67.

51. Ibid., p. 87.

Notes to Chapter 5

The Father-King

1. See Judge Jenkins, *Lex Terrae; or Law of the Land, SCT,* 5:108.

2. John Locke, *Two Treatises on Civil Government by John Locke, Preceded by Sir Robert Filmer's "Patriarcha,"* p. 21.

3. Aristotle, *Politics,* 1252B, 1259B, in *The Politics of Aristotle.*

4. Cicero, *De Re Publica,* 1. 61. 64, in *De Re Publica; De Legibus.*

5. See Chapter 3 above. For the iconography of this concept, Roman coinage is useful: Michael Hewson Crawford, *Roman Republican Coinage,* pp. 485–93; Michael Grant, *From "Imperium" to "Auctoritas,"* pp. 3–79; Harold Mattingley, ed., *Coins of the Roman Empire in the British Museum,* 1:lxiv–lxxx.

6. Judge Jenkins, *A Plea, delivered in to the Earl of Manchester and the Speaker of the House of Commons, sitting in the Chancery,* 1647, *SCT,* 5:93.

7. Thomas Fuller, "Panegyrick on His Majesty's Happy Return," st. 35, in *The Poems and Translations in Verse.*

8. Kenneth Meyer Setton, *Christian Attitude towards the Emperor in the Fourth Century Especially As Shown in Addresses to the Emperor,* p. 115.

9. Henry King, "A Deep Groane, fetch'd," line 170, in *The Poems of Henry King.*

10. Abraham Cowley, "Ode Upon his Majesties Restoration and Return," st. 8, in *Poems.*

11. Thomas Shipman, "The Royal Martyr," lines 23–38, in *Carolina: or, Loyal Poems,* 1683. See also "Chronosticon," "An Elegie Upon King Charles the First," and "An Elegie on The best of Men, and Meekest of Martyrs, Charles I" in John Cleveland, *Poems, 1653.* In John Collop's "To the Son of the Late King," line 37, *The Poems of John Collop,* the crown of thorns is passed down from father to son. Thomas Stanley's psalm sequence, *Psalterium Carolinum, 1657,* in *The Poems and Translations of Thomas Stanley,* is of interest, since its structure is clearly based on that of *Eikon Basiliké.*

12. Charles I, *Eikon Basiliké: The Portraiture of His Majesty Charles I,* p. 62.

13. John Dryden, "Astraea Redux: A Poem on the Restoration of Charles the Second," lines 79, 276, in *Poems, 1647–1680, The Works of John Dryden,* vol. 1.

14. See Plato, *Parmenides;* Plotinus, *Enneads,* 6.9.6: "The nature of the one is such, that it is the fountain of the most excellent things and a power generating beings" (*Select Works,* p. 309).

15. See "Milton's Outlines for Tragedies," in *The Works of John Milton,* 18:229.

16. C. A. Patrides, ed., *The Cambridge Platonists* (London: Edward Arnold, 1969), p. 105. See also Irene Samuel, *Plato and Milton,* on Milton's Platonism.

17. *The Cry of the King's Blood,* Yale 4, pt. 2:1049.

18. Aeschylus, *Prometheus Bound,* line 610, in *"Prometheus Bound" and Other Plays,* trans. and ed. Philip Vellacott (Harmondsworth: Penguin, 1961).

19. Aristotle, *The Nicomachean Ethics,* 569B.

20. Roland M. Frye's comments on this subject in *God, Man, and Satan: Patterns of Christian Thought and Life in "Paradise Lost," "Pilgrim's Progress," and the Great Theologians* are, as always, perceptive. Creation "is the basis for dependence, whereas autogeny is the basis for autonomy"; Satan repudiates "an objective basis for truth" (p. 28).

21. G. Wilson Knight, *Chariot of Wrath: The Message of John Milton to Democracy at War;* Malcolm MacKenzie Ross, *Milton's Royalism: A Study of the Conflict of Symbol and Idea in the Poems.*

22. Ross, *Milton's Royalism*, p. 99.

23. Henry King, "A Deep Groane, fetch'd," in *The Poems of Henry King*.

24. Gunnar Qvarnström, *The Enchanted Palace: Some Structural Aspects of "Paradise Lost*," pp. 58–60, on Ezekiel's chariot, the *Merkabah*, and its relation to cabalistic tradition. On the symbolism of the triumphal chariot in general, see Samuel Claggett Chew, "The Allegorical Chariot in English Literature of the Renaissance," pp. 37–54.

25. See Pietro Bongo, *Numerorum Mysteria*, pp. 197, 573.

26. Christopher Hill, *Milton and the English Revolution*, p. 372.

27. See, for example, William Empson, *Milton's God*, p. 108; John Peter, *A Critique of "Paradise Lost*," pp. 63–65; A. J. A. Waldock, *"Paradise Lost" and Its Critics*, pp. 97–118.

28. Boyd M. Berry, "Puritan Soldiers in *Paradise Lost*."

29. For the controversy over which person(s) of the Trinity issues forth in Book 7, see Kester Svendsen, "Epic Address and Reference and the Principle of Decorum in *Paradise Lost*," *Philological Quarterly* 28 (1949): 199 (the Son); C. A. Patrides, "The Godhead in *Paradise Lost*: Dogma or Drama?" *Journal of English and Germanic Philology* 64 (1965): 33 (the Trinity itself); Leland Ryken, *The Apocalyptic Vision in "Paradise Lost*," p. 169 (a "fusion of identities").

30. The limiting hinges and compass stand symbolically beside the "numberless" angels (7.197), the "Myriads" (201), and the "immeasurable abyss" (211). See Joseph H. Summers, *"Paradise Lost*: The Pattern at the Centre," in *The Muse's Method: An Introduction to "Paradise Lost*," pp. 112–46, for exquisite treatment of these themes, and George Wesley Whiting, *Milton and This Pendant World*, pp. 88–121, on iconography.

31. Andrew Tooke, *The Pantheon, representing the fabulous histories of the heathen gods and most illustrious heroes*, p. 55.

32. See, for example, Diodorus Siculus, *The Library of History*, 2. 38. 5, in *Diodorus of Sicily*, 2:15; Edmund Spenser, *The Faerie Queene*, 5. 1. 2, for a Renaissance usage.

33. Tooke, *The Pantheon*, pp. 67–68.

34. See Marsilio Ficino, "Letter to Martinus Uranius," 1492, in *Opera omnia*, p. 933, and *Orphei carmina*, in *Opera omnia*, p. 934. See also D. P. Walker, *The Ancient Theology: Studies in Christian Platonism from the Fifteenth to the Eighteenth Century*, pp. 22–41.

35. In *Christian Doctrine*, line 5, Milton shows that "to Adam, formed out of the dust, God was creator rather than Father; but he was in a real sense Father of the Son" (Yale 6:209). It follows that the Son "fathers" man by himself becoming human. The opinion expressed in *Christian Doctrine* that the Son is God's glorious secondary reflection, rather than an "equal God," brings him much closer to the society of men.

Notes to Chapter 6

Naked Majesty

1. For an account of this motif, see Joan Webber, *Milton and His Epic Tradition*, pp. 67–84. Francis C. Blessington, in *"Paradise Lost" and the Classical Epic*, proposes with great insight that Milton elevates the traditional "beloved companion" of classical epic (Patroklos, Achates) into a joint heroism composed of male and female. For Milton's interpretation of Eve's role in the original myth, see John M. Evans, *"Paradise Lost" and the Genesis Tradition* (London: Oxford University Press, 1968).

2. Compare Edward Le Comte's conclusions in *Milton and Sex* (London and Basingstoke: Macmillan, 1978).

3. See John H. S. Armstrong, *The Paradise Myth* (London, New York, and Toronto: Oxford University Press, 1969), p. 21.

4. Compare the "image-doting rabble" of *Eikonoklastes,* Yale 3:601.

5. This is a disputed point, of course. See Arnold Stein in *The Art of Presence: The Poet and "Paradise Lost,"* pp. 119–20, and Louis L. Martz, *Poet of Exile: A Study of Milton's Poetry,* p. 134, for views analogous to my own.

6. See Johannis Wycliffe, *Tractatus de Civili Dominio,* book 1, lines 18. 41C, 21. 49C.

7. *Animadversions Upon the Remonstrants Defence Against Smectymnuus,* 1641, Yale, vol. 1. See *Defence of the People of England,* Yale 4, pt. 1: e.g. 395, 403.

8. Christopher Ricks, *Milton's Grand Style,* pp. 135–38.

Bibliography

Primary Sources

1. *Milton*

Complete Prose Works of John Milton. Edited by Don M. Wolfe. 7 out of 8 vols. New Haven: Yale University Press, 1953–.

The Poems of John Milton. Edited by John Carey and Alastair Fowler. London: Longman, 1968.

The Poetical Works of John Milton. Edited by Douglas Bush. London and Oxford: Oxford University Press, 1969.

The Works of John Milton. Edited by Frank Allen Patterson. 18 vols. New York: Columbia University Press, 1931–1938.

2. *Others*

Alexander, Sir William (Earl of Stirling). *The Poetical Works.* Edited by L. E. Kastner and H. B. Charlton. 2 vols. Manchester: Manchester University Press, 1921, 1929.

Ammianus Marcellinus. *History.* Translated by J. C. Rolfe. 3 vols. London and Cambridge, Mass.: Heinemann, 1935–1939.

Appianus. *Appian's Roman History.* Translated by H. White. 4 vols. London and New York: Heinemann, 1912.

Aristotle. *The Nicomachean Ethics.* Translated by H. Rackham. London and New York: Heinemann, 1926.

———. *The Politics of Aristotle.* Translated by E. Barker. Oxford: Oxford University Press, 1946.

Arrianus, Flavius. *The Life of Alexander the Great.* Translated by A. de Sélincourt. London: Folio Society, 1970.

Bible, The. *The Geneva Bible.* A facsimile of the 1560 ed. Introduction by Lloyd E. Berry. Madison, Milwaukee, and London: University of Wisconsin Press, 1969.

Bongo, Pietro. *Numerorum Mysteria.* Bergamo, 1599.

Brutus, Junius. *A Defence of Liberty Against Tyrants: A Translation of the "Vindiciae Contra Tyrannos" by Junius Brutus.* Introduction by H. J. Laski. London: G. Bell, 1924.

Caesar, Julius. *The Gallic War.* Translated by H. J. Edwards. London and New York: Heinemann, 1933.

Calvin, John. *Calvin's Commentary on Seneca's "De Clementia."* Translated by F. W. Battles and A. M. Hugo. Leiden: Brill for the Renaissance Society of America, 1969.

————. *Commentaries on the Epistle of Paul the Apostle to the Romans.* Translated by J. Owen. Edinburgh: Calvin Translation Society, 1849.

Charles I. *Eikon Basiliké: The Portraiture of His Majesty Charles I.* Edited by Catherine Mary Phillimore. Oxford and London: James Parker and Co., 1879.

Cicero, Marcus Tullius. *De Natura Deorum.* Translated by H. Rackham. London: Heinemann, 1951.

————. *De Re Publica; De Legibus.* Translated by Clinton Walker Keyes. London: Heinemann, 1928.

Clarendon, Earl of (Edward Hyde). *The History of the Rebellion and Civil Wars in England.* Edited by W. D. Macray. 6 vols. Oxford: Oxford University Press, 1888.

Claudian. *Works.* Translated by Maurice Platnauer. 2 vols. New York and London: Heinemann, 1922.

Cleveland, John. *Poems, 1653.* Menston: Scolar Press, 1971.

————. *The Poems.* Edited by Brian Morris and Eleanor Withington. Oxford: Clarendon Press, 1967.

Collop, John. *The Poems.* Edited by Conrad Hilberry. Madison: University of Wisconsin Press, 1962.

Corbett, Richard. *The Poems.* Edited by J. A. W. Bennett and H. R. Trevor-Roper. Oxford: Clarendon Press, 1955.

Cowley, Abraham. *Poems.* Edited by A. R. Waller. Cambridge: Cambridge University Press, 1905.

————. *Prose Works.* Edited by T. Sprat. London: William Pickering, 1826.

Davies, Stevie, ed. *Renaissance Views of Man.* Manchester: Manchester University Press, 1978.

D'Ewes, Sir Simonds. *The Journal of Sir Simonds D'Ewes.* Edited by Wallace Notestein. New Haven: Yale University Press, 1923.

Diodorus Siculus. *Works.* Translated by C. H. Oldfather. 10 vols. London and Cambridge, Mass.: Heinemann, 1935.

Dionysius the Areopagite. *The Mystical Theology and the Celestial Hierarchies.* Editor unnamed. Godalming: Shrine of Wisdom, 1965.

Dryden, John. *The Works.* Edited by Edward Niles Hooker and H. T. Swedenberg, Jr. 18 vols. Berkeley and Los Angeles: University of California Press, 1956–1976.

Fanshawe, Sir Richard. *Shorter Poems and Translations.* Edited by N. W. Bawcutt. Liverpool: Liverpool University Press, 1964.

Ficino, Marsilio. *Opera omnia.* Introduction by P. O. Kristeller. 2 vols. 1576. Reprint. Torino: Bottega d'Erasmo, 1962.

Filmer, Sir Robert. *Patriarcha; or, the Natural Power of Kings.* See under Locke, John.

Fletcher, Giles and Phineas. *Poetical Works.* Edited by F. S. Boas. 2 vols. Cambridge: Cambridge University Press, 1908.

Fuller, Thomas. *The Poems and Translations in Verse.* Edited by Alexander B. Grosart. Edinburgh: Crawford and M'Cabe, 1868.

Geoffrey of Monmouth. *The History of the Kings of Britain.* Translated by Lewis Thorpe. Harmondsworth: Penguin, 1966.

Giovius, Paulus. *Opera.* Edited by R. Meregazzi et al. 8 vols. Rome: Societa Storica Comense, 1956–1972.

Greville, Fulke (First Lord Brooke). *Poems and Dramas.* Edited by Geoffrey Bullough. 2 vols. Edinburgh and London: Oliver and Boyd, 1938.
————. *The remains: being poems of monarchy and religion.* Edited by G. A. Wilkes. Oxford: Oxford University Press, 1965.

Hall, John. *Paradoxes* (1650). Introduction by Don Cameron Allen. Delmar, N.Y.: Scolar Press, 1977.

Haller, William, and Davies, Godfrey, eds. *The Leveller Tracts, 1647–1653.* New York: Columbia University Press, 1944.

Harrington, John. *The Oceana of John Harrington, Esq; and His Other Works.* Dublin, 1737.

Herodian of Antioch. *History of the Roman Empire from the Death of Marcus Aurelius to the Accession of Gordian III.* Translated by Edward Echols. Berkeley and Los Angeles: University of California Press, 1961.

Herodotus. *History.* Translated by A. D. Godley. 4 vols. London and New York: Heinemann, 1928.

Hobbes, Thomas. *Leviathan, or the Matter, Forme and Power of a Commonwealth Ecclesiastical and Civil.* 1651.

Hotman, François. *Francogallia.* Edited by R. E. Giesey. Translated by J. H. M. Salmon. Cambridge: Cambridge University Press, 1972.

James I. *The Political Works.* Introduction by Charles Howard McIlwain. 1616. Reprint. Cambridge, Mass.: Harvard University Press, 1918.

Jerome. *Select Letters.* Translated by F. A. Wright. London and New York: Heinemann and Putnam, 1933.

Josephus. *Works.* Translated by H. St. J. Thackeray. 11 vols. London and New York: Heinemann and Putnam, 1930.

King, Bishop Henry. *The Poems.* Edited by Margaret Crum. Oxford: Clarendon Press, 1965.

Knolles, Richard. *The Generall Historie of the Turkes, from the First Beginning of the Nation to the Rising of the Othoman Famillie.* 1603. London, 1631.

Lactantius. *The Works.* Translated by W. Fletcher. 2 vols. Edinburgh: Clark, 1871.

Laud, Archbishop William. *Works.* Edited by W. Scott. 9 vols. Oxford, 1847–1860.

Lefkowitz, Murray, ed. *Trois Masques à la Cour de Charles 1er d'Angleterre.* Paris: Centre National de la Recherche Scientifique, 1970.

Legg, J. Wickham, ed. *Three Coronation Orders*. London: Publications of the Henry Bradshaw Society, 1900.

Legg, L. G. Wickham, ed. *English Coronation Records*. London: Constable, 1901.

Livy, Titus. *The History of Rome*. Translated by W. M. Roberts. 3 vols. London and New York: Dent, 1912.

Locke, John. *Two Treatises of Government, preceded by Sir Robert Filmer's "Patriarcha,"* London, 1884.

Machiavelli, Niccolò. *Discourses on the First Decade of Titus Livius*. Translated by Ninian Hill Thomson. London: Routledge and Kegan Paul, 1883.

————. *The Prince*. Translated by G. Bull. Harmondsworth: Penguin, 1961.

Marlowe, Christopher. *Tamburlaine the Great*. Edited by U. M. Ellis-Fermor. London: Methuen, 1930.

May, Thomas. *The History of the Parliament of England, which began November 3, 1640, with a Short and Necessary View of Some Precedent Years*. Edited by F. Maseres. Oxford: Oxford University Press, 1854.

Moryson, Fynes. *Shakespeare's Europe: The Fourth Part of Fynes Moryson's Itinerary*. Introduction by Charles Hughes. Manchester: Manchester University Press, 1902.

Nedham, Marchamont. *The Case of the Commonwealth of England, Stated*. Edited by P. A. Knachel. Charlottesville, Va.: University of Virginia Press, 1969.

Nichols, John, ed. *The Progresses and Public Processions of Queen Elizabeth*. 3 vols. London, 1823.

Ogg, Frederic Austin. *A Sourcebook of Medieval History*. New York: Cooper Square Publishers, 1972.

Orosius, Paulus. *Seven Books of History Against the Pagans: The Apology of Paulus Orosius*. Morningside Heights, N.Y.: Columbia University Press, 1936.

Paris, Matthew. *English History*. Translated by J. A. Giles. 2 vols. London: Bohn, 1852.

Patrides, C. A., ed. *The Cambridge Platonists*. London: Edward Arnold, 1969.

Petrarca, Francesco. *Trionfi: Lord Morley's "Tryumphes of Fraunces Petrarcha."* Edited by D. D. Carnicelli. Cambridge, Mass.: Harvard University Press, 1971.

Philo Judaeus. *Works*. Translated by F. H. Colson and G. H. Whitaker. 11 vols. London and Cambridge, Mass.: Heinemann, 1949.

Pico della Mirandola (Count Giovanni). *Opera omnia*. Introduction by E. Garin. 2 vols. Torino: Bottega d'Erasmo, 1971.

Plato. *The Republic*. Translated by P. Shorey. 2 vols. London and Cambridge, Mass.: Heinemann, 1946.

Plato. *The Timaeus.* Translated by R. G. Bury. London and Cambridge, Mass.: Heinemann, 1942.

Plotinus. *Select Works.* Translated by Thomas Taylor. Edited by G. R. S. Mead. London: G. Bell, 1929.

Plutarch. *Lives.* Translated by B. Perrin. 11 vols. Reprint. London and New York: Heinemann and Harvard University Press, 1959–1971.

———. *Shakespeare's Plutarch.* Translated by Sir Thomas North. Edited by C. F. Tucker-Brooke. 2 vols. London: Chatto and Windus, 1909.

Rugg, Thomas. *The Diurnal of Thomas Rugg, 1659–1661.* Edited by W. L. Sachse. London: Royal Historical Society Camden Publications, 1961.

Scott, Sir Walter, ed. *A Collection of Scarce and Valuable Tracts.* Collected by Lord Somers. Vols. 4, 5, 6. London, 1811.

Seneca. *Moral Essays.* Translated by John W. Basore. 3 vols. London and New York: Heinemann and Putnam, 1928–1935.

Shakespeare, William. *Complete Works.* Edited by W. J. Craig. London, New York, and Toronto: Oxford University Press, 1905.

Shipman, Thomas. *Carolina, or, Loyal Poems.* 1683. Facsimile reprint. Farnborough: Gregg, 1971.

Sidonius. *Poems and Letters.* Translated by W. B. Anderson. 2 vols. London and Cambridge, Mass.: Heinemann and Harvard University Press, 1936.

Spenser, Edmund. *Poetical Works.* Edited by J. C. Smith and E. de Selincourt. London: Oxford University Press, 1909–1912.

Stanley, Thomas. *The Poems and Translations.* Edited by Galbraith Miller Crump. Oxford: Clarendon Press, 1962.

Suetonius. *The Lives of the Caesars.* Translated by J. C. Rolfe. 2 vols. London and New York: Heinemann, 1914.

Tacitus. *"The Agricola" and "The Germania."* Translated by R. B. Townshend. London: Methuen, 1899.

———. *The Annals and the Histories.* Translated by Alfred John Church and William Jackson Bredribb. Edited by Hugh Lloyd-Jones. London: Sadler and Brown, 1966.

Tertullian. *Apology, De Spectaculis, and Minucius Felix.* Translated by T. R. Glover and H. Rendall from W. C. A. Kerr. London and Cambridge, Mass.: Heinemann, 1931.

Vaughan, Henry. *The Works.* Edited by L. C. Martin. Oxford: Clarendon Press, 1957.

Waller, Edmund. *The Poems.* Edited by G. Thorn Drury. London and New York: Lawrence and Bullen, 1893.

Whitelock, Bulstrode. *Memorials of the English Affairs from the Beginning of the Reign of Charles the First to the Happy Restoration of King Charles the Second.* 6 vols. Oxford, 1853.

Wilkins, W. W., ed. *Political Ballads of the Seventeenth and Eighteenth Centuries.* 2 vols. London: Longman, 1860.

Winstanley, Gerrard. *The Works.* Edited by G. H. Sabine. New York: Russell and Russell, 1965.

Wolfe, Don M. ed. *Leveller Manifestoes of the Puritan Revolution.* New York: Humanities Press, 1967.

Woodhouse, A. S. P. *Puritanism and Liberty: Being the Army Debates, 1647 – 9. . . .* London: Dent, 1938.

Wordsworth, Christopher, ed. *The Manner of the Coronation of King Charles the First of England, at Westminster, 2 Feb., 1626.* London: Bradshaw Society Publications, 1892.

Wycliffe, Johannis. *Tractatus de Civili Dominio.* Edited by R. L. Poole. London: Wyclif Society, 1885.

Secondary Sources

1. *Milton (books)*

Allen, Don Cameron. *The Harmonious Vision: Studies in Milton's Poetry.* Baltimore and London: Johns Hopkins University Press, 1954.

Banks, Theodore Howard. *Milton's Imagery.* New York: Columbia University Press, 1950.

Barker, Arthur E. *Milton and the Puritan Dilemma, 1641–1660.* Toronto: University of Toronto Press, 1942.

Berry, Boyd M. *Puritan Religious Writing and "Paradise Lost."* Baltimore and London: Johns Hopkins University Press, 1976.

Blessington, Francis C. *"Paradise Lost" and the Classical Epic.* Boston, London, and Henley: Routledge and Kegan Paul, 1979.

Bouchard, Donald F. *Milton: A Structural Reading.* London: Edward Arnold, 1974.

Broadbent, J. B. *Some Graver Subject: An Essay on "Paradise Lost."* London: Chatto and Windus, 1960.

Burden, Dennis H. *The Logical Epic: A Study of the Argument of "Paradise Lost."* London: Routledge and Kegan Paul, 1967.

Cawley, Robert R. *Milton and the Literature of Travel.* Princeton, N.J.: Princeton University Press, 1951.

Cohen, Kitty. *The Throne and the Chariot: Studies in Milton's Hebraism.* The Hague and Paris: Mouton, 1975.

Conklin, George Newton. *Biblical Criticism and Heresy in Milton.* New York: King's Crown Press, Columbia University, 1949.

Cope, Jackson I. *The Metaphoric Structure of "Paradise Lost."* Baltimore: Johns Hopkins University Press, 1962.

Crump, Galbraith Miller. *The Mystical Design of "Paradise Lost."* Lewisburg and London: Bucknell University Press and Associated University Presses, 1975.

Daiches, David. *Milton.* London: Hutchinson, 1959.

Darbishire, Helen, ed. *Early Lives of John Milton.* London: Constable, 1932.

Demaray, John G. *Milton and the Masque Tradition.* Cambridge, Mass.: Harvard University Press, 1968.

————. *Milton's Theatrical Epic: The Invention and Design of "Paradise Lost."* Cambridge, Mass., and London: Harvard University Press, 1980.

Diekhoff, John S. *Milton's "Paradise Lost": A Commentary on the Argument.* London: Routledge and Kegan Paul, 1946.

Empson, William. *Milton's God.* London: Chatto and Windus, 1965.

Ferry, Anne Davidson. *Milton's Epic Voice: The Narrator in "Paradise Lost."* Cambridge, Mass.: Harvard University Press, 1963.

Fish, Stanley E. *Surprised by Sin: The Reader in "Paradise Lost."* London, Melbourne, Toronto and New York: Macmillan and St. Martin's Press, 1967.

Fixler, Michael. *Milton and the Kingdoms of God.* London: Faber and Faber, 1964.

Fletcher, Harris Francis. *Milton's Semitic Studies and Some Manifestations of Them in his Poetry.* New York: Gordian Press, 1966.

Fogle, French R., and Trevor-Roper, H. R. *Milton and Clarendon: Two Papers on Seventeenth Century English Historiography.* Los Angeles: University of California Press, 1965.

French, J. Milton, ed. *The Life Records of John Milton.* 5 vols. New York: Gordian Press, 1966.

Frye, Northrop. *Five Essays on Milton's Epics.* London: Routledge and Kegan Paul, 1966.

Frye, Roland Mushat. *God, Man, and Satan: Patterns of Christian Thought and Life in "Paradise Lost," "Pilgrim's Progress," and the Great Theologians.* Princeton, N.J.: Princeton University Press, 1960.

Gardner, Helen. *A Reading of "Paradise Lost."* Oxford: Clarendon Press, 1967.

Grierson, Sir Herbert J. C. *Milton and Wordsworth: Poets and Prophets.* London: Chatto and Windus, 1950.

Grose, Christopher. *Milton's Epic Process: "Paradise Lost" and Its Miltonic Background.* New Haven and London: Yale University Press, 1973.

Hartwell, Kathleen Ellen. *Lactantius and Milton.* Cambridge, Mass.: Radcliffe Collection Publications, 1929.

Hill, Christopher. *Milton and the English Revolution.* London: Faber and Faber, 1977.

Hughes, Merritt Y. "Satan and the 'Myth' of the Tyrant." See under MacLure, Millar.

Hunter, W. B., Patrides, C. A., and Adamson, J. H. *Bright Essence: Studies in Milton's Theology.* Salt Lake City: University of Utah Press, 1971.

Hyman, Lawrence W. *The Quarrel Within: Art and Morality in Milton's Poetry.* Port Washington, N.Y., and London: Kennikat Press, 1972.

Kelley, Maurice. *This Great Argument: A Study of Milton's "De Doctrina Christiana" as a Gloss upon "Paradise Lost."* Gloucester, Mass.: Peter Smith, 1962.

Kermode, Frank, ed. *The Living Milton: Essays by Various Hands.* London: Routledge and Kegan Paul, 1960.

Kerrigan, William. *The Prophetic Milton.* Charlottesville, Va.: University Press of Virginia, 1974.

Knight, G. Wilson. *Chariot of Wrath: The Message of John Milton to Democracy at War.* London: Faber and Faber, 1942.

Lewalski, Barbara Kiefer. *Milton's Brief Epic: The Genre, Meaning, and Art of "Paradise Regained."* Providence and London: Brown University and Methuen, 1966.

Lewis, C. S. *A Preface to "Paradise Lost."* London, New York, and Toronto: Oxford University Press, 1967.

Lieb, Michael. *The Dialectics of Creation: Patterns of Birth and Regeneration in "Paradise Lost."* Cambridge, Mass.: University of Massachusetts Press, 1970.

MacCaffrey, Isabel Gamble. *"Paradise Lost" as "Myth."* Cambridge, Mass.: Harvard University Press, 1959.

McColley, Grant. *"Paradise Lost": An Account of Its Growth and Major Origins, with a Discussion of Milton's Use of Sources and Literary Patterns.* New York: Russell and Russell, 1963.

MacLure, Millar, and Watt, F. W. *Essays in English Literature from the Renaissance to the Victorian Age, Presented to A. S. P. Woodhouse.* Toronto: Toronto University Press, 1964.

Madsen, William G. *From Shadowy Types to Truth: Studies in Milton's Symbolism.* New Haven and London: Yale University Press, 1968.

Malekin, Peter. *Liberty and Love: English Literature and Society, 1640–88.* London and Melbourne: Hutchinson, 1981.

Martz, Louis L. *Poet of Exile: A Study of Milton's Poetry.* New Haven and London: Yale University Press, 1980.

Mohl, Ruth. *Studies in Spenser, Milton and the Theory of Monarchy.* New York: King's Crown Press, Columbia University, 1949.

Parker, William Riley. *Milton: A Biography.* 2 vols. Oxford: Clarendon Press, 1968.

Patrides, C. A. *Milton and the Christian Tradition.* Oxford: Clarendon Press, 1966.

Patrides, C. A., and Waddington, Raymond B. *The Age of Milton: Backgrounds to Seventeenth Century Literature.* Manchester: Manchester University Press, 1980.

Peter, John. *A Critique Of "Paradise Lost."* New York: Archon Books, 1970.

Qvarnström, Gunnar. *The Enchanted Palace: Some Structural Aspects of "Paradise Lost."* Stockholm: Almqvist and Viksell, 1967.

Rajan, Balachandra. *"Paradise Lost" and the Seventeenth Century Reader.* London: Chatto and Windus, 1966.

Raleigh, Walter. *Milton.* London: Edward Arnold, 1909.

Reesing, John. *Milton's Poetic Art: "A Mask," "Lycidas" and "Paradise Lost."* Cambridge, Mass.: Harvard University Press, 1968.

Richmond, Hugh Macrae. *The Christian Revolutionary: John Milton.* Berkeley, Los Angeles, and London: University of California Press, 1974.

Ricks, Christopher. *Milton's Grand Style.* Oxford: Clarendon Press, 1963.

Riggs, William G. *The Christian Poet in "Paradise Lost."* Berkeley, Los Angeles, and London: University of California Press, 1972.

Ross, Malcolm Mackenzie. *Milton's Royalism: A Study of the Conflict of Symbol and Idea in the Poems.* Ithaca, N.Y.: Cornell University Press, 1943.

Rowse, A. L. *Milton the Puritan: Portrait of a Mind.* London and Basingstoke: Macmillan, 1977.

Ryken, Leland. *The Apocalyptic Vision in "Paradise Lost."* Ithaca, New York, and London: Cornell University Press, 1970.

Samuel, Irene. *Dante and Milton: The "Commedia" and "Paradise Lost."* Ithaca and New York: Cornell University Press, 1966.

———. *Plato and Milton.* Ithaca, New York, and London: Cornell University Press, 1947.

Saurat, Denis. *Milton, Man and Thinker.* London: Dent, 1944.

Staveley, Keith W. *The Politics of Milton's Prose Style.* New Haven and London: Yale University Press, 1975.

Steadman, John M. *Milton's Epic Characters: Image and Idol.* Chapel Hill: University of North Carolina Press, 1959.

———. *Milton and the Renaissance Hero.* Oxford: Clarendon Press, 1967.

———. *Epic and Tragic Structure in "Paradise Lost."* Chicago and London: University of Chicago Press, 1977.

Stein, Arnold. *Answerable Style: Essays on "Paradise Lost."* Minneapolis: University of Minnesota Press, 1953.

———. *The Art of Presence: The Poet and "Paradise Lost."* Berkeley, Los Angeles, and London: University of California Press, 1977.

Summers, Joseph H. *The Muse's Method: An Introduction to "Paradise Lost."* London: Chatto and Windus, 1962.

Tillyard, E. M. W. *Milton.* London: Chatto and Windus, 1930.

Waldock, A. J. A. *"Paradise Lost" and Its Critics.* Cambridge: Cambridge University Press, 1966.

Webber, Joan. *Milton and His Epic Tradition.* Seattle and London: University of Washington Press, 1979.

West, Robert Hunter. *Milton and the Angels.* Athens: University of Georgia Press, 1955.

Whiting, George Wesley. *Milton and This Pendant World.* Austin: Octagon Books, 1958.

———. *Milton's Literary Milieu.* New York: Russell and Russell, 1964.

Wolfe, Don M. *Milton in the Puritan Revolution.* New York: Humanities Press, 1963.

Woodhouse, A. S. P. *The Heavenly Muse: A Preface to Milton.* Edited by Hugh MacCallum. Toronto: University of Toronto Press, 1972.

2. *Milton (Articles)*

Bennett, Joan S. "God, Satan, and King Charles: Milton's Royal Portraits." *PMLA* 92 (1977): 441–57.

Berry, Boyd M. "Puritan Soldiers in *Paradise Lost.*" *Modern Language Quarterly* 35 (1974): 376–402.

Bowers, Anthony Robin. "Milton and Salmasius: The Rhetorical Imperatives." *Philological Quarterly* 52 (1973): 55–68.

Canfield, J. Douglas. "The Birthday of the Son in *Paradise Lost.*" *English Language Notes* 13 (1975–1976): 113–15.

Davies, Stevie. "John Milton on Liberty." *Memoirs and Proceedings of the Manchester Literary and Philosophical Society* 117 (1974–75): 37–51.

Demaray, John G. "The Thrones of Satan and God: Backgrounds to Divine Opposition in *Paradise Lost.*" *The Huntington Library Quarterly* 31 (1967–1968): 21–33.

Egan, James. "Public Truth and Personal Witness in Milton's Last Tracts." *ELH* 40 (1973): 231–48.

———. "Milton and the Marprelate Tradition." *Milton Studies* 8 (1975): 103–21.

Goldman, Jack. "Insight into Milton's Abdiel." *Philological Quarterly* 49 (1970): 249–54.

Hodge, Robert. "Satan and the Revolution of the Saints." *Literature and History* (1978): 20–33.

Hunter, W. B. "Satan as Comet: *Paradise Lost,* II. 708–711." *English Language Notes* 5 (1967–1968): 17–21.

———. "Milton on the Exaltation of the Son: The War in Heaven in *Paradise Lost.*" *ELH* 36 (1969): 215–31.

———. "The Centre of *Paradise Lost.*" *English Language Notes* 7 (1969–1970): 32–34.

Patterson, Annabel. "The Civic Hero in Milton's Prose." *Milton Studies* 8 (1975): 71–101.

Revard, Stella Purce. "Milton's Critique of Heroic Warfare in *Paradise Lost* V and VI." *Studies in English Literature, 1500 –1900* 7 (1967): 119 –39.

———. "The Dramatic Function of the Son in *Paradise Lost*: A Commentary on Milton's 'Trinitarianism.'" *Journal of English and Germanic Philology* 66 (1967): 45 –58.

———. "Satan's Envy of the Kingship of God: A Reconsideration of *Paradise Lost*, Book 5, and Its Theological Background." *Modern Philology* 70 (1972 –1973): 190 –98.

———. "The Warring Saints and the Dragon: A Commentary upon Revelation 12:7 –9 and Milton's War in Heaven." *Philological Quarterly* 53 (1974): 181 –98.

Webber, Joan. "The Son of God and Power of Life in Three Poems by Milton." *ELH* 37 (1970): 175 –94.

———. "Milton's God." *ELH* 40 (1973): 514 –31.

3. *Others*

Battenhouse, Roy Wesley. *Marlowe's "Tamburlaine": A Study in Renaissance Moral Philosophy*. Nashville: Vanderbilt University Press, 1964.

Bergeron, David Moore. *English Civic Pageantry, 1558 –1642*. London: Edward Arnold, 1971.

Bianchi Bandinelli, Ranuccio. *Rome, the Centre of Power: Roman Art to A.D. 200*. Translated by Peter Green. London: Thames and Hudson, 1970.

Blake, William. *Poetry and Prose*. Edited by Geoffrey Keynes. London: Nonesuch Press, 1961.

Bloch, Marc. *Feudal Society*. Translated by L. A. Manyon. Introduction by M. M. Postan. Frome and London: Routledge and Kegan Paul, 1961.

Bowle, John Edward. *Western Political Thought: An Historical Introduction from the Origins to Rousseau*. London: Cape, 1947.

Brilliant, Richard. *Roman Art from the Republic to Constantine*. London: Phaidon, 1974.

Brooks, Douglas. *Number and Pattern in the Eighteenth-Century Novel: Defoe, Fielding, Smollett and Sterne*. London and Boston: Routledge and Kegan Paul, 1973.

Brooks-Davies, Douglas. *Spenser's "Faerie Queene": A Critical Commentary on Books I and II*. Manchester: Manchester University Press, 1977.

Cary, George. *The Medieval Alexander: A Study of the Posthumous European Reputation of Alexander the Great to the Renaissance*. Edited by D. J. A. Ross. Cambridge: Cambridge University Press, 1956.

Chew, Samuel Claggett. *The Crescent and the Rose: Islam and England during the Renaissance*. New York: Oxford University Press, 1937.

———. "The Allegorical Chariot in English Literature of the Renaissance." See under Meiss, Maynard.

Cheyette, Fredric Lawrence, ed. *Lordship and Community in Medieval Europe: Selected Readings.* New York, London: Holt, Rinehart and Winston, 1969.

Cohn, Norman. *The Pursuit of the Millennium.* London: Secker and Warburg, 1957.

Crawford, Michael Hewson. *Roman Republican Coinage.* 2 vols. London: Cambridge University Press, 1974.

Crim, Keith R. *The Royal Psalms.* Richmond, Va.: John Knox Press, 1962.

Davison, William Theophilus. *The Praises of Israel: An Introduction to the Study of the Psalms.* London: Charles H. Kelley, 1893.

Dudley, Donald R., ed. *Urbs Roma: A Source Book of Classical Texts on the City and Its Monuments.* London: Phaidon, 1967.

Ferguson, George Wells. *Signs and Symbols in Christian Art.* London, Oxford, and New York: Oxford University Press, 1973.

Ferguson, John. *Utopias of the Classical World.* London: Thames and Hudson, 1975.

Figgis, J. N. *The Divine Right of Kings.* Cambridge: Cambridge University Press, 1922.

Fowler, A. D. S. *Triumphal Forms: Structural Patterns in Elizabethan Poetry.* Cambridge: Cambridge University Press, 1970.

Gardiner, Samuel Rawson. *History of the Great Civil War, 1642–1649.* 4 vols. New York: Longman, 1965.

Graves, Robert R., and Podro, Joshua. *The Nazarene Gospel Restored.* London: Cassell, 1953.

Hadas, Moses. *Hellenistic Culture: Fusion and Rediffusion.* New York and London: Columbia University Press and Oxford University Press, 1959.

Heninger, S. K. *A Handbook of Renaissance Meteorology with Particular Reference to Elizabethan and Jacobean Literature.* Durham, N.C.: Duke University Press, 1960.

Hill, Christopher. *Puritanism and Revolution: Studies in Interpretation of the English Revolution of the Seventeenth Century.* London: Martin, Secker and Warburg, 1958.

———. *The Century of Revolution, 1603–1714.* Edinburgh: Thomas Nelson, 1961.

———. *Society and Puritanism in Pre-Revolutionary England.* London: Martin, Secker and Warburg, 1964.

———. *Intellectual Origins of the English Revolution.* Oxford: Clarendon Press, 1965.

———. *God's Englishman: Oliver Cromwell and the English Revolution.* London: Weidenfeld and Nicolson, 1970.

———. *The World Turned Upside Down: Radical Ideas during the English Revolution.* London: Maurice Temple Smith, 1972.

Hill, Sir George Francis. *Medals of the Renaissance*. Oxford: Clarendon Press, 1920.

Johnson, Samuel. *The Lives of the English Poets; and a Criticism on Their Works*. Dublin, 1779.

Kantorowicz, Ernst Hartwig. *The King's Two Bodies: A Study in Medieval Political Theology*. Princeton: Princeton University Press, 1957.

Korshin, Paul J., ed. *Studies in Change and Revolution: Aspects of English Intellectual History, 1640–1800*. Menston: Scolar Press, 1972.

Kott, Jan. *The Eating of the Gods: An Interpretation of Greek Tragedy*. Translated by B. Taborski and E. J. Czerninski. London: Eyre Methuen, 1974.

Lamb, Harold. *The March of the Barbarians*. New York; Literary Guild of America, 1940.

Lamont, William, and Oldfield, Sybil. *Politics, Religion and Literature in the Seventeenth Century*. London: Dent, 1975.

Lewis, Ewart. *Medieval Political Ideas*. London: Routledge and Kegan Paul, 1954.

Lovejoy, Arthur Oncken. *The Great Chain of Being: A Study of the History of an Idea*. New York: Harper and Row, 1960.

McFayden, Donald. *The History of the Title Imperator under the Roman Empire*. Chicago: University of Chicago Press, 1920.

McGee, J. Sears. *The Godly Man in Stuart England: Anglicans, Puritans, and the Two Tables, 1620–1670*. New Haven and London: Yale University Press, 1976.

Madan, Francis Falconer. *A New Bibliography of the "Eikon Basiliké" of King Charles the First*. London: Oxford Bibliographical Society Publications, 1950.

Manning, Brian. *The English People and the English Revolution*. London: Heinemann, 1976.

Mattingley, Harold, ed. *Coins of the Roman Empire in the British Museum*. London: Trustees of the British Museum, 1923.

Meiss, Maynard, ed. *De Artibus Opuscula XL: Essays in Honour of Erwin Panofsky*. 2 vols. New York: New York University Press, 1961.

Panofsky, Erwin. *Studies in Iconology: Humanistic Themes in the Art of the Renaissance*. New York and Evanston: Harper and Row, 1962.

Patrides, C. A. *The Grand Design of God: The Literary Form of the Christian View of History*. London: Routledge and Kegan Paul, 1972.

Phillips, E. D. *The Royal Hordes: Nomad Peoples of the Steppes*. London: Thames and Hudson, 1965.

Porter, H. C. *Puritanism in Tudor England*. London and Basingstoke: Macmillan. 1970.

Robertson, Anne Strachan. *Roman Imperial Coins in the Hunter Coin Cabinet*. London, Glasgow, and New York: University of Glasgow Press, 1962.

Rogers, Philip George. *The Fifth Monarchy Men.* London, New York, and Toronto: Oxford University Press, 1966.

Saunders, John Joseph. *The History of the Mongol Conquests.* London: Routledge and Kegan Paul, 1971.

Schramm, Percy Ernst. *A History of the English Coronation.* Translated by L. G. Wickham-Legg. Oxford: Oxford University Press, 1937.

Setton, Kenneth Meyer. *Christian Attitude towards the Emperor in the Fourth Century Especially As Shown in Addresses to the Emperor.* New York: Columbia University Press, 1941.

Stevenson, Gertrude Scott, ed. *Charles I in Captivity.* London: Arrowsmith, 1927.

Thompson, Edward Arthur. *A History of Attila and the Huns.* Oxford: Clarendon Press, 1948.

Tooke, Andrew. *The Pantheon, representing the fabulous histories of the heathen gods and most illustrious heroes.* London, 1824.

Tuchman, Barbara W. *A Distant Mirror: The Calamitous 14th Century.* Beccles and London: Macmillan, 1979.

Underdown, David. *Pride's Purge: Politics in the Puritan Revolution.* Oxford: Clarendon Press, 1970.

Vale, Marcia. *The Gentleman's Recreations: Accomplishments and Pastimes of the English Gentleman, 1580–1630.* Cambridge and Totowa: Brewer, 1977.

Waith, Eugene M. *The Herculean Hero in Marlowe, Chapman, Shakespeare and Dryden.* London: Chatto and Windus, 1962.

Walker, D. P. *The Ancient Theology: Studies in Christian Platonism from the Fifteenth to the Eighteenth Century.* London: Duckworth, 1972.

Wallace, John Malcolm. *Destiny His Choice: The Loyalism of Andrew Marvell.* Cambridge: Cambridge University Press, 1968.

Wallace, Ronald Stuart. *Calvin's Doctrine of the Christian Life.* Edinburgh and London: Oliver and Boyd, 1959.

Watson, D. R. *The Life and Times of Charles I.* London: Weidenfeld and Nicolson, 1972.

Wedgwood, C. V. *The Trial of Charles I.* London: Collins, 1964.

Weiser, Artur. *The Psalms: A Commentary.* London: SCM, 1959.

Wind, Edgar. *Pagan Mysteries of the Renaissance.* Harmondsworth: Penguin, 1967.

Yates, Frances A. *Astraea: The Imperial Theme in the Sixteenth Century.* London and Boston: Routledge and Kegan Paul, 1975.

Yule, George. *The Independents in the Civil War.* Cambridge: Cambridge University Press, 1958.

Zagorin, Perez. *A History of Political Thought in the English Revolution.* London: Routledge and Kegan Paul, 1954.

Index

Abdiel, 9, 91, 140; as triumphator, 120; as king's champion, 129, 161–68; as authority on god's paternity, 172–76, 184

Abraham, as type of Christ, 39

Accommodation, theory of, 128–29

Adam: as king of Eden, 8, 195–216; as Solomon, 8, 27, 212–16; as royal namer of animals, 23–24 187, 209; as feudal lord, 24, 208–9; fall to matriarchal principle of, 29; sexual love of, 37; true dream of, 38–39; vision of, 46–47, 86–88; "native honour" of, 90, 195–96, 207–8; contrition of, 115, 119, 124; redemption of, 154, 161; "feudal" banquet of, 159; as Icarus, 181; fall from vision of Heavenly Crown of, 192; uncoercive rule over Eve of, 197–211; as head of commonwealth, 201–5

Aeschylus: *The Persians*, 70–71, 80–81; *Prometheus Bound*, 174

Ahab, King of Israel, as type of evil king, 30

Ahaz, King of Israel, as type of evil king, 29

Alaric, 66

Alcairo, 56, 68; as *Babylon Aegypti*, 62

Alfred the Great, King of England: as law-giver, 40; as type of just ruler, 121

Algiers, 54

Ammianus Marcellinus, 65–66

Amurat III, sultan, 82

Androgyny, as emblem of commonwealth, 201

Anglo-Saxons, as founders of English law, 40–41

Antichrist: Charles I as, 43–44, 54; Satan as, 47; Turkish Sultan as, 73

Antonines, the, Roman Emperors, 97

Aristocracy: of Hell, 106–7, 148; of heaven, 130–31, 135–39. *See also* Feudalism

Aristotle: *Politics*, 37, 164, 205; *Nicomachean Ethics*, 175

Army: of Satan, 13, 36, 100–101, 146–48; of Charles I, 36, 51, 65; in antipathy to own leader, 82–85; of

Caesars, as foundation of autocracy, 83, 100–106; of Turks, 82; of Christ, 122–24, 137–38. *See also* New Model Army

Arthur, King of England: coronation ritual of, 160; as ideal ruler, 176

Astarte (Astoreth): as female lunar deity, 26, 29, 201; connection with Turkish crescent, 74–75. *See also* Moon

A True Relation of the taking of Cirencester, 51

Attila: as fratricide, 59, as northern barbarian, 66

Augustine, Saint, view of history of, 47

Augustus, Emperor of Rome: deification of, 95; as patron of arts, 96; dictatorship of, 100; militaristic tyranny of (as Octavian), 102–3; betrayal of republic, 107; triumph of, 116

Baal-peor (Chemos), 5; as idol of Anglican Church, 24; as king-god, 26–28

Babel, Tower of: as image of satanic pride, 14; as image of monarchial confusion, 32–33, 54, 215; as source of Divine mirth, 38; as image of English Commonwealth, 45–46; splendor of, 68; fall of, 73, 123; Chaos as, 93. *See also* Baghdad

Babylon: as metaphor for Christian's providential suffering, 48; as tyrannous state, 54–55; God's judgment against, 62–63. *See also* Scourge of God

Bacchus (Dionysus): as emblem of Stuart license, 32–33; as emblem of Restoration court in relation to Orphic poet, 190–92

Baghdad, as "new Babylon," 62

Baldac, Caliph of, as image of providential self-punishment, 73–74

Barbarians: Royalists as, 51; Puritans as, 51, 52; Huns as, 51, 63, 65, 69, 86; Turks, as, 51–99 passim; as scourge, 53–54, 64; lawlessness of, 54; Moors as, 54; Scythians as, 57, 69; Massagetae as, 59, 86; Vandals as, 63; Goths as, 63, 65; mutual hatred of, 64, 83–86; images of, 65–68, 78–79; love of gold of, 67–70; Persians as, 67–71, 78–79, 83–88; disunity of, 77, 83–86; Tartars as, 84; inhabitants of Hell as, 85–86; roman conquests of, 116; Rebel angels as, 182; British subjection to queens as, 202; Adam as innocent barbarian, 211

Beelzebub: as vizier, 59–60, 83; as Strafford, 60–61; as Satan's instrument of propaganda, 101, 103–5, 108; 188–89

Belial: loss of original name of, 23; as Dionysian principle, 31–33, 188–89

Benjamin, son of Jacob, 170

Bible: as legal precedent, 30; Geneva version, 218n; conflation with feudalism, 132–33; translations of "coronation psalm" in, 141–43, 155

Bleda, 59

Boadicea, Queen of Britain, 202

Body politic: Satan's attitude to, 122; theory of, 164

Bridge, made by Sin and Death, 77–82, 94–96, 110–12. *See also* Triumphal arch

Brutus, Junius (pseud.), *Vindiciae Contra Tyrannos*, 44, 132–33, 154

Buckingham, George Villiers, Duke of, 92

Busiris, Pharaoh, 44, 55, 219n

Caesar, Julius: as destroyer of Senate, 99; as aspirant to crown, 106; in *Paradise Regained*, 109; sham triumph of, 115, 117

Caligula, 89, 97, 99; incest of, 107

Calvin, John, *Commentaries*, 48

Caracalla, Antoninus, Emperor of Rome, 107

Cartimandua, Queen of Britain, 202

Cathay, as goal of human endeavor, 78–79, 81, 84

Catholicism: European Protestant dissension with, 67–68; worldliness of, 121

Cavalier, 32; antiregicide arguments of, 164–65, 166–68

Chain of Being: Satan's travesty of, 49; as *scala humilitatis*, 143

Chaos, 94–96, 133–44

Chariot. *See* Triumph

Charles I, King of England: as warlord, 10, 34; as usurper, 10, 40–41; as image of Satan, 11; throne of, 11–12; as sun-king, 15–18; as Nimrod, 33–39, 41, 50; as fratricide, 48; as Sultan, 54, 76; as Pharaoh, 76; as Nero, 91–92; as Caesar, 103, 112; coronation of, 137; as false god, 109, 183; as father-king, 164–67, 175–78; as type of Christ, 166–67, 173, 177; prerogative of, 198. *See also* Antichrist; Triumph

Charles II, King of England, 32, 191; as Moses, 47; as David, 168; as Astraea, 168. *See also* Bacchus; Belial

Charles IX, King of France, 60

Chiron, Christ as, 174

Chosen People, the English as, 47–48, 140–41

Christ: as *sol iustitiae*, 14–18, 98, 122, 124, 158, 178–79; as King, 109, 139–43, 150–60, 171–72, 175–76; as mediator, 119, 141, 148, 152, 161–62, 181; as heir, 123–24; as Messiah, 133, 139–40, 141–42, 145, 186, 187; exaltation of, 139–40; baptism of, 155; as Creator and Giver, 160–61, 162–63, 169, 185–87; as Light, 171, 172; birthday of, 185–86

Christendom, disunity of, 70–73

Cicero: *Republic*, 164; as *pater patriae*, 177

Civil War, the English, 25, 33–34, 36, 51, 71, 112, 190; fratricide of, 182–83; War in Heaven as, 183

Claudius, Emperor of Rome, 97

Cleveland, John, 225n

Collop, John, 225n

Commonwealth, Eden as, 199, 203–5

Commonwealth, the English, 45–47; rigged Parliaments of, 99; as image of Heaven, 183

Constantine, Emperor of Rome, 121–22

Cook, John, 34, 51, 165–66

Coronation. *See* Kingship, ritual of

Council of State, 83

Cowley, Abraham, 47, 167

Christina, Queen of Sweden, as Athene, 202–3

Cromwell, Oliver: Satan as, 4; as Pharaoh, 47; as Mogul, 51; as

scourge of God, 52; foreign policy of, 52–53, 68, 71; claim to kingship of, 166, 176–77; as *pater patriae*, 176–77
Cronos, 174
Crown, pastoral, 212. *See also* Kingship, ritual of
Crusades, the, 72–73
Cudworth, Ralph, 171

Dagon, 39
Danaë (and Zeus), 68; as mother of Perseus, 80
Dante Alighieri, 138
Danube, River, 65; as boundary of Europe, 67
Darius, King of Persia, 80–81
Davenant, Sir William, 111–12
David, King of Israel, 26, 27, 168
Death: as king, 9, 36, 49; as member of satanic royal family, 41; as predator, 43–44; as link between north and south, 78, 80–81; as architect, 94–96, 111–12; as viceroy, 106; as barbarian, 121
Diana (Artemis), 202
Diodorus Siculus, 37, 226n
Divine right of kings, Stuart claim to, 14, 61, 164–65
Doge (of Venice), 52
Domitian, Emperor of Rome, 89; faked triumph of, 115
Dryden, John, 168
Du Moulin, Pierre, 166–67, 173

Eden, 148, 152; displacement of, 87–88; as kingdom of Adam, 195–98, 206. *See also* Commonwealth
Edgar, King of England, 160
Edgehill, Battle of, as analogy to War in Heaven, 2, 183
Edward the Confessor, King of England: as law-giver, 40; as good king, 121
Egypt: gods of, 29; Israel's escape from, 47; as image of England's captivity, 47–49; destruction of, 73, 214
Eikon Alethine, 165
Eikon Basiliké (attrib. Charles I), 17, 44, 49, 165, 167
Elizabeth I, Queen of England: as exceptionally good ruler, 121, 202; manner of choosing heir of, 149

Emperor. *See* Caesar; Rome
Empire. *See* Rome; Turks
Empress. *See* Eve
England's Petition to their King, 36, 165
Errour (in Spenser's *Faerie Queene*), 44
Eve: lunar associations of, 16–17, 29, 74–75; as empress, 29, 39, 211; sexual bond with Adam as source of patriarchy, 37–38; dream of, 38–39, 74, 125; as Ceres, 75; contrition of, 115, 119; acceptance of parent of, 175; as mother, 189; subjection of, 198–201; freedom of, 200; as queen, 201–3, 205, 211; as Venus, 205–6; as Sheba, 214–15

Fall of society: as providential, 48–49; to barbarism, 72; in Rome, 92–93, 96–97; in Britain, 96–97; in Eden, 211–16
Fealty: of animals to Adam, 23–24, 129–30, 181, 208–9; as sworn by king, 154; breaking in Heaven of, 181. *See also* Feudalism
Feudalism: as type of Divine, liberty-guaranteeing rule, 6, 132; vassal and lord in, 23–24, 130–32, 137, 142, 143, 154, 160; serfs in, 130, 145; regnal year in, 134–35; as image of order, 133, 136–38; heraldic emblems of, 136–37, 138, 146–47, 182, 197; *promissio regis* in, 137; feud in, 144, 148; Satan's militarized travesty of, 144–48; circle of nobility in, 150–51; Round Table in, 160
Filmer, Sir Robert, 164
Fletcher, Giles, 170, 203
Fletcher, Phineas, 84
Fuller, Thomas, 165

Gauden, Dr. John, 218n. *See also Eikon Basiliké*
Gaunt, John of (in *Richard II*), 42–43
Geoffrey of Monmouth, 160
Greece: as civilized power, 69, 80–82; as fallen power, 76
Greville, Fulke (Lord Brooke), 72, 221n
Gunpowder, invention of, 39

Harrington, John, 52
Harrison, Thomas, 43
Henrietta Maria, Queen of England, 29

Hercules, in Seneca's *Hercules Furens*, 90–91
Heredity. *See* Law
Herodian of Antioch, 69, 114
Herodotus, 59, 86
History, cyclical theory of, 37, 47–48, 49, 89, 96–97
Hobbes, Thomas, 107, 163, 204
Hotman, François, 131–32
Huguenots, radical view of feudalism of, 131–33, 154

Idol: King Charles I as, 10, 49; English royalists as worshipers of, 12–13; fallen angels as, 24–29, 31–32; Roman emperors as, 166; Satan as, 180–81, 183; rebel angels as worshipers of, 183. *See also* Solomon
India: inhabitants as king-worshipers, 13; as source of wealth, 68, 70; inhabitants as pitiable, 248
Interregnum, the, 32, 51, 52, 177, 202

James I, King of England: as hunter, 36; alleged murder of, 92, 165
Jenkins, Judge, 164
Jeroboam, King of Israel, as rebel, 30–31
Jerome, Saint, on barbarians, 69
Jews, the, as types of the English people, 25–28, 34–35, 46–50, 54–55
John the Baptist, 155
John III, King of Poland, 221n
Josiah, King of Israel, as *Eikonoklastes*, 28–29, 49
Julia, Empress of Rome, 107
Justice: Sword of, 22, 97, rod of, 54; Moses' rod as sign of, 62–63; Libra as sign of, 62–63, 75, 83; hall of, 83; embodied as person, 95, 154; as reflex of Mercy, 170–71, 178
Justinian, Emperor of Rome, 93–94, 96

King, Bishop Henry, 76, 167, 177
King (earthly): as sun, 10, 14–19, 111, 126, 127–28; as rebel, 10, 39–40; popular adoration of 12–13; luxuries of, 12–13; accountability of, 26, 39–40; as warrior, 34–35; hereditary power of, 37, 41, 149; as *medicus regni* and *sponsus regni*, 164; as *pater patriae*, 164–67; as *filius patriae*, 168. *See also* Idol; Nimrod
Kingship (ritual of): anointing in, 8, 129, 139, 142, 153–54, 157–58, 163, 179; coronation in 8, 114, 129, 135–40; investiture, 127, 137; coronation as charter of rights in, 154; enthronement in, 154–55; banquet in, 159–61; king's champion in, 161–63
Knolles, Richard, 62, 86

Lactantius, 47
Last Judgment, 19, 47–48, 92; parody of, 58; as exaltation of Christ, 155
Law: of conquest, 39–41; of Anglo-Saxon England, 39–41, 136; of nature, 39, 49, 167; of reason, 96; of heredity, 104, 148, 152, 170; of God, 108, 109, 156, 163; of *seisin*, 131, 132, 144, 149; of Aragon, 154
Lawlessness, winds as image of, 67, 78
Levelers, the, 1, 51
Liberty: king as threat to, 10; of Anglo-Saxons, 40; of Europe, 52–54; under Islam, 54; of Jews under Moses, 63–64; of Greeks, 76, 80; of Rome, 89, 90; of ancient Britons, 97; under Long Parliament, 97; of individual spirit, 120, 163; under legitimate (Divine) monarchy, 135–36, 140–41, 163; of will, 184; of unfallen man, 209
Lilburne, John, 3, 219n
Livy, Titus, 102, 222n

Machiavelli, Niccolò, 110
Magna Carta, 144
Mammon, 23; barbarous gold-lust of, 68–70, 106, 189
Marcus Aurelius, Emperor of Rome, 97
Marlowe, Christopher, 53, 110
Mary Stuart, Queen of Scots: sexual license attributed to, 10, 213; Elizabeth I's tactics toward, 149
May, Thomas, 218n
Memphis, opulent evil of, 56, 68, 73
Mercury (Hermes): Raphael as, 206; as phoenix, 206; as king, 206–7
Meritocracy: Satan's version of, 103–4, 111; God's version of, 152, 190, 194
Michael, 33, 35, 47, 48, 86, 87, 156
Millenarianism, 19–20, 43–44; dissolution of Milton's, 192

Milton, John: *Animadversions*, 220n, 227n; *Areopagitica*, 135; *Commonplace Book*, 40, 73–74, 107, 131–32, 136, 149, 202; *Defence of the English People*(first *Defence*), 12–13, 22, 26, 30, 37, 56, 89–92, 96–97, 99, 102–3, 105, 107, 135–36, 140, 141, 163, 167–68, 171–72, 198, 212–13; *Doctrine and Discipline of Divorce*, 37, 199, 210; *Eikonoklastes*, 10, 12, 15, 17–18, 19, 21, 28, 34, 36, 43, 45, 49, 54, 61, 72, 76, 97, 109, 136, 165, 171, 178, 198, 203; *History of Britain*, 40, 66–67, 76, 96, 97, 196, 201; *Letters Patent*, 82; *Lycidas*, 97, 191; *Mansus*, 65; *Moscovia*, 79–80, 84; *Observations on the Articles of Peace*, 60, 61; *Of Christian Doctrine*, 141, 148, 226n; *Of Education*, 96; *Of Reformation in England*, 24, 153, 222n; *Paradise Regained*, 109; *The Readie and Easie Way*, 45–46, 168, 183, 191, 223n; *Reason of Church Government*, 65; *Second Defence*, 13, 21, 131–32, 163, 166, 173, 176–77, 198, 202–3, 204, 218; *State Papers*, 52, 53, 68, 220n; *Tenure of Kings and Magistrates*, 30, 33–34, 37, 54, 76–77, 97, 198, 218n; *Tetrachordon*, 199

Moloch: as king-god, 5, 9, 10, 25–26; destruction of, 27–28; as type of Charles II, 32–33; 36, 39, 41, 49, 106, 212; temple of, 213–14

Monck, Gen. George, 47

Moon: eclipsing royal sun, 15–17; as female principle, 29, 236–37; as crescent Turkish symbol, 74–75, 88. *See also* Astarte; Diana; Eve

Moryson, Fynes, 59

Moses, 46; as royalist emblem of Charles's Restoration, 47; as deliverer, 48; as God's just scourge, 62–63; as type of Christ, 63

Nebuchadnezzar, King of Assyria, 53

Nero, Emperor of Rome, 89; as actor, 91; as type of Charles I, butchering own people, 91–92; as scourge, 97

New Model Army: Christ's soldiers as, 4; God's angels as, 135; Son as, 183

Nimrod, the first king: as warrior and builder of Babel, 9, 10, 25, 32,

49–50, 195, 212; as satanic embodiment, 24, 121; as emblem of Stuart kingship, 33–38, 39–40; as rebel, 39–40; etymological relation to Charles I's title, 40–41; Cromwell as, 47; associated with Bacchus, 191

Normans: conquest as source of Stuart title, 10, 40–41; coronation ceremonial of, 130–31, 135–36, 160, 161, 162

North: as source of evil, 65–66, 66–67, 78; as landscape of Hell, 66; of England as royalist base, 65; as source of rebellion in Heaven, 108

Orcan, Sultan, 81–82

Ormus, as source of wealth, 13, 68, 70

Orosius, Paulus, 47–48

Orpheus, as poet under Restoration tyranny, 190–91

Overton, Richard, 51

Pandemonium, 11, 106; oriental splendor of, 68–69; as Sultan's court, 72; as Persian high palace, 80; as oriental hall of justice, 83; construction of, 96, 98; as place of triumph, 113; as Stuart court, 146

Parliament, 51, 76, 83, 97, 99, 164; Roman Senate as, 89

Patriarchy, as basis of civil law, 37, 196–97

Persia: defeat by Greeks of, 79–82; Perseus as founder of, 80; as scourge of Turks, 83–85; Sophy of, 85; Gulf of, 88

Pharaoh: as type of tyrant, 5, 47, 48, 53, 54–55, 63, 64, 66, 121, 129; Charles I as, 59

Philotime (in *Faerie Queene*), 195

Plato: *Republic*, 14, 173; *Timaeus*, 134, 149; *Parmenides*, 225n

Platonism, in *Paradise Lost*, 128, 146, 170–71

Plutarch, 99, 117

Pompey, sons of, 115–16

Prince, connotations of, 23, 61; as *princeps*, 100–101, 103

Pseudo-Dionysius, 138, 145–46

Purchas, Samuel, 69

Puritanism: as revolutionary, 16, 51, 52, 183; anointing in, 153–54; community of saints in, 184; dislike of ornament in, 207–8

Pym, John, 60

Queen: Milton's disapproval of, 202–3; Truth as, 203. *See also* Eve; Moon

Raphael. *See* Mercury

Rebellion: subjects' duty of, 89; of Satan, 133, 143–48

Red Sea: English Channel as, 47, 219n; regicide as crossing of, 48

Regicide: Milton the poet as a, 13, 60; Christ's purge of Heaven as paralleled by, 28; justification of, 33–34, 90, 203; crucifixion as image of, 165; as deicide and parricide, 173

Rehoboam, King of Israel, 30

Republicanism, fall from, 36, 97; Roman abandonment of, 92–93; as ideal, 168, 201; ants as emblem of, 204–5

Richard II, King of England: in Shakespeare, 42–43; coronation ceremony of, 161

Richard III, as tyrant, 36

Rizzio, David, 213

Roman Emperor: death of, 92; as false god, 95, 108–9; as scourge, 97; rise of, 97–98, 98–107; Christ as, 98–99; as *imperator,* 99–104, 115, 129; as enemy of liberty, 104; incestuous habits of, 107; as type of Stuart rule, 111–12; hatred of subjects to, 120–21; as father of Rome, 164, 166. *See also* Caesar

Rome: as civilizer and embodiment of reason, 5–6, 93–94; Commonwealth as, 45; Empire (*Imperium*) of, 67, 115, 122; Praetorian guard in, 82, 93; technological materialism of, 96; as birthplace of liberty, 97; army of, 101, 138, 182. *See also* Senate

Salmasius (Claude de Saumaise), 12, 26, 30, 89, 91–92, 99, 102, 132, 166, 187, 198

Satan. *See* Antichrist; Army; Charles I; Feudalism; Idol; Meritocracy; Nimrod; Roman Emperor; Scourge of God; Sultan; Turks

Scipio Africanus, triumph of, 222

Scourge of God: Satan as, 17, 73; scourge of, 44–45, 52–53, 74–75, 81, 85; Sultan and Turks as, 51, 62–64, 73; Babylon as, 53; Roman Emperors as, 97; of kings, 132–33

Senate (Roman), 89, 95, 99, 104, 164; decline of, 107

Seneca, 91. *See also* Hercules

Sheba, Queen of, Eve as, 214, 215

Shipman, Thomas, 36, 167

Sin: as predator, 35–36, 81, 86, 121; as emblem of vicious sensuality, 36; as member of satanic royal family, 41, 107; as Whore of Babylon, 43; as architect, 77, 78, 94–95; as scourge, 86; as viceroy, 106

Sobietski, Jan, 82

Solomon, King of Israel. *See* Adam

Spenser, Edmund, 44, 84, 195, 203

Stanley, Thomas, 225n

Strafford, Sir Thomas Wentworth, Earl of: as associated by Charles I with sun, 18; as vizier, 60, 61

Suetonius (Gaius Suetonius Tranquillus), 91, 99, 221n, 222n

Sultan, 7, 55, 121, 129; as incarnate Devil, 53; as autocrat, 54, 56, 73; as Grand Seigneur, 54, 56, 64, 72, 212; as murderer, 57; Satan as, 58–64, 72–73, 75, 158–59; as enemy of own kin, 59; vizier of, 59, 83; as scourged, 63–64, 75, 158–59; as imperialist, 76

Tacitus, Cornelius, 65, 99, 101–2, 107, 115, 220n

Tamburlaine (Timur), popularity of as scourge of Turks, 53, 73, 82, 110

Tertullian, 47; on triumph, 114, 115, 121

Throne: of Satan, 11–12, 70, 103–4, 104–5, 106, 113, 115, 125; of Chaos, 134; of Christ i God, 139

Tiberius, Emperor of Rome, 97; rise of, 99, 101–2, 106, 107; in *Paradise Regained,* 109–10

Triumph: of Satan, 42, 80, 106, 111–12; of humility, 98, 114, 115; of Satan as anti-triumph, 112–13, 115, 117, 118–19, 124–26; of Abdiel, 120; of Christ, 122–24; chariot in, 178–80; of Resurrection, 193

Triumphal arch: bridge built by Sin and Death as, 8, 42–43, 94–96; as structure of *Paradise Lost* and emblem of Divine authority, 8, 122, 178–79; of Emperor Constantine, 121; Renaissance revival of, 121–22

Turks, the: as term of political abuse, 51–52; Protectorate attitude to, 52–54, 60; militarism and unity of, 53, 67–68, 71–74, 75, 82, 93; as despotic, 54–55, 117; in relation to Satan, 84–85, 109. *See also* Sultan; Moon

Tyrant: agony of, 20, 22, 175; frivolity of, 35–36; anonymity of, 39–40; as scourge of own nation, 46–49, 76; suicidal tendencies of, 54–55, 82; nation's hatred of, 58–60, 83, 85–87, 118; attitude to law of, 102–3; duty of revolt against, 132; as parricide, 173–75

Uriel, as God's spy, 183–84

Vasiliwich, Juan, 84
Vespasian, Emperor of Rome, 100
Virgil, 96

William the Conqueror, King of England, 40–41
Winstanley, Gerrard, 140–41, 154
Wycliffe, John, 211

Xerxes, 80–81, 95

Zeus: eagle as, 98; as usurper, 174